MW01194819

James Buchanan and the Coming of the Civil War

UNIVERSITY PRESS OF FLORIDA

Florida A&M University, Tallahassee
Florida Atlantic University, Boca Raton
Florida Gulf Coast University, Ft. Myers
Florida International University, Miami
Florida State University, Tallahassee
New College of Florida, Sarasota
University of Central Florida, Orlando
University of Florida, Gainesville
University of North Florida, Jacksonville
University of South Florida, Tampa
University of West Florida, Pensacola

James Buchanan's inauguration, March 4, 1857. Photograph by John Wood. Montgomery C. Meigs Papers, Library of Congress.

James Buchanan and the Coming of the Civil War

Edited by John W. Quist and Michael J. Birkner

University Press of Florida

Gainesville · Tallahassee · Tampa · Boca Raton

Pensacola · Orlando · Miami · Jacksonville · Ft. Myers · Sarasota

This book may be available in an electronic edition.

First cloth printing, 2013
First paperback printing, 2014

Library of Congress Cataloging-in-Publication Data
James Buchanan and the coming of the Civil War / edited by John W. Quist and Michael J.
Birkner.
p. cm.
Includes bibliographical references and index.
ISBN 978-0-8130-4426-2 (cloth: alk. paper)
ISBN 978-0-8130-6099-6 (pbk.)
1. Buchanan, James, 1791–1868. 2. United States—History—Civil War, 1861–1865. 3. United
States—Politics and government—1857–1861. I. Quist, John W. II. Birkner, Michael J., 1950–
E436.J36 2012
973.6'8—dc23   2012031869

The University Press of Florida is the scholarly publishing agency for the State University
System of Florida, comprising Florida A&M University, Florida Atlantic University, Florida
Gulf Coast University, Florida International University, Florida State University, New College
of Florida, University of Central Florida, University of Florida, University of North Florida,
University of South Florida, and University of West Florida.

University Press of Florida
15 Northwest 15th Street
Gainesville, FL 32611-2079
http://www.upf.com

Contents

Figures

Acknowledgments

This book owes its gestation to the vision of individuals associated with James Buchanan's home, Wheatland, now incorporated into a campus of history at Lancasterhistory.org. Thomas R. Ryan, executive director of Lancasterhistory.org, and Patrick Clarke, director of James Buchanan's home, Wheatland, believe strongly in scholarly outreach to a larger public audience. That impulse lay behind their desire to host a symposium that would bring together leading scholars to share recent findings and fresh interpretations of Buchanan's presidency. The conference that met in September 2008 was the first such conference since 1991.

In shaping the conference program and choosing speakers, Ryan, Clarke, and the editors of this volume were joined by David Schuyler, Shadek Professor of Humanities at Franklin & Marshall College, and Adam B. Lawrence, associate professor of government at Millersville University. We are grateful to them for their good spirit and helpful insights in advancing this enterprise. We also thank Maury Klein, Randall M. Miller, and Matthew Pinsker for helping make the symposium a success.

The conference that served as this book's foundation could not have taken place without the generous financial support of the Richard C. Von Hess Foundation, Rodgers & Associates, and the Lancaster County Community Foundation. Franklin & Marshall College provided the venue for most of the sessions, which kicked off on the campus of history at Lancasterhistory.org with a well-attended reception and lively plenary session featuring professors Michael F. Holt and William W. Freehling.

Because of the consistently high quality of both the papers at the Buchanan conference and the conversations they provoked, the editors of this volume encouraged the symposium presenters to revise their essays for this book. Completion of this project would not have been possible had our contributors not been willing to revise and, in certain instances, rethink their arguments regarding one of the least respected chief executives in American history. For their patience with our many requests and for their confidence in entrusting their work to us, we thank them.

We are grateful to the editorial staff of the University Press of Florida for their professionalism in moving a large manuscript into print. Press director, Meredith Morris-Babb, and project editor Jesse Arost merit particular appreciation, as does our copy editor, Jonathan Lawrence. The manuscript's anonymous readers offered numerous useful suggestions that improved the individual essays while helping those essays cohere into a book. We also gladly thank James Gerencser, Dickinson College archivist, for valuable suggestions regarding illustrations, Marianne S. Heckles, co-ordinator of photograph collections at Lancasterhistory.org, for tracking down photographs, and Robert E. Coley for transcribing the conversation with William W. Freehling and Michael F. Holt.

Michael Birkner wishes to acknowledge support from the faculty de-velopment fund at Gettysburg College, which made possible research conducted in the James Buchanan Papers at the Historical Society of Pennsylvania and the archives of Lancasterhistory.org. He also expresses appreciation to Lancasterhistory.org archivist Heather Tennies for her as-sistance in navigating the Buchanan Wheatland Papers, an essential source for the epilogue.

John Quist wishes to thank the numerous individuals who, over the past few years, have inquired about the book's progress and have discussed with him James Buchanan, the Buchanan administration, and nineteenth-century American politics.

Introduction

Bum Rap or Bad Leadership?

The nation's fifteenth president—voted into office as the candidate most likely to keep the nation prosperous and peaceful—departed the White House in March 1861 with a broken union and the nation on the brink of civil war. Not good for one's reputation.

With a few notable exceptions, among them biographers George Ticknor Curtis and Philip S. Klein, scholars have been critical of Buchanan, consistently consigning him to the basement in virtually every presidential performance poll.[1] In the view of many historians, among them Henry Steele Commager and James McPherson, Buchanan was the nation's worst president, and not simply because he failed to stifle secessionist movements in the winter of 1860–61.[2] Buchanan's cabinet appointments (particularly the Southern ones who aligned with the Confederacy before his term's expiration), his self-defeating patronage policies, his ethically dubious intervention in the shaping of the *Dred Scott* decision, his stubborn and politically disastrous Kansas policy that exacerbated sectional tensions, his rants against abolitionists—all these defects, considered alongside his response to secession, have imprinted Buchanan in common memory as a loser in the White House.

Buchanan, of course, did not see things that way. Like two twentieth-century presidents whom historians have found wanting, Herbert Hoover and Jimmy Carter, Buchanan made no apologies about his presidential performance. In his correspondence with associates and then in a memoir published after the Civil War, Buchanan pronounced himself well satisfied with the state of the country during his presidency, save for the final days when Southern fire-eaters refused to listen to reason.[3] In Buchanan's telling, he had done what he set out to accomplish. Although he failed to prevent seven states from seceding, a matter of deep regret, he had handed over the keys to the White House to Abraham Lincoln with the nation still at peace. Aside from casting blame on others, Buchanan, to his death in 1868, remained supremely unreflective about the ways that his turbulent presidency had gone wrong.

Buchanan's positive assessment of his presidency has not weathered well. This volume does not aim to transform him into an underappreciated hero. Yet anyone seriously studying a period as complex as the four years preceding the Civil War will recognize that contending interpretations of characters and events often prove to be the rule. History is not about simplicity, but rather, as Laurel Thatcher Ulrich once observed, about "depth and complexity."[4] Certainly the years of Buchanan's presidency exemplify that dictum, in the range of leading political figures in Washington and the respective states, the fluidity of political alignments, and the impact of unanticipated events, among them the John Brown raid. Few Americans in 1857 could envision a bloody civil war. But the sectional tensions already rife when Buchanan took office became, over time, unmanageable, in part because of the fifteenth president's policymaking.

In terms of political and governmental experience, Buchanan came into office better prepared, on paper, than any chief executive since John Quincy Adams.[5] A state legislator, congressman, senator, diplomat, secretary of state, a perennial candidate for president who also declined a U.S. Supreme Court appointment, and a master of Pennsylvania's labyrinthine politics, Buchanan served presidents from Jackson through Pierce with shrewdness and competence, if not brilliance. His political nickname, "The Old Public Functionary," suggested his durability as a public figure as well as the contempt that some people held for him and his lack of imagination.[6] Recognized as a conservative within his party, in 1856 Buchanan became the Democratic Party's most available man, largely because he had been serving abroad as minister to England while other Democrats' entanglement with the explosive Kansas-Nebraska legislation diminished their national appeal. Running against Republican John Charles Frémont and the American Party's Millard Fillmore, Buchanan became the nation's best hope for sustaining prosperity while keeping a lid on sectional animosity. With a national government dominated by his party, Buchanan launched his presidency with these objectives seemingly within reach.

Figure I.1. *A Serviceable Garment—or Reverie of a Bachelor*. New York: N. Currier, 1856. Lithograph. The cartoon depicts James Buchanan as a calculating aspirant for the presidency—one willing to embrace positions that will benefit him politically. The quotation reads: "My Old coat was a very fashionable Federal coat when it was new, but by patching and turning I have made it quite a Democratic Garment. That Cuba patch to be sure is rather unsightly but it suits Southern fashions at this season, and then. (If I am elected,) let me see, $25,000 pr. annum, and no rent to pay, and no Women and Babies about, I guess I can afford a new outfit."

It was not to be. Despite his valuable experience and lengthy record as a capable politician, Buchanan was not up to the task. His insensitivity to political corruption, his determination to punish Senator Stephen Douglas for slights known only to himself, his insistence on pressing for Kansas's admission to the union as a slave state in the face of ample evidence that most Kansans had no desire for such a result, and his misfortune to be president during the economic contraction that ensued from the Panic of 1857—all these things dissipated the goodwill Buchanan enjoyed as he entered the White House.[7]

Buchanan's contradictions create challenges to understanding his presidency. A strict constructionist, Buchanan served mostly as a negative force on economic matters, rejecting federal intervention in a hurting economy in 1857 and vetoing Republican-sponsored legislation to prop up the economy through infrastructure programs. But Buchanan's laissez-faire economic policies stood in striking contrast to his activism on other fronts. His determination to demonstrate federal authority in Utah, partly based on a misreading of the situation there, nearly led to a different civil war. In foreign policy, Buchanan sought opportunities to expand the nation's borders by purchasing Cuba, to put down filibusters in Latin America, and to negotiate constructively with Great Britain, a nation many Americans still viewed as an adversary. Buchanan's response to secession underwent several iterations before he resolved, by early January 1861, to retain the remaining federal forts within the already-seceded states.

Most historians find much to criticize in Buchanan's stewardship during the secession crisis. Others maintain that, given his lame-duck status, Buchanan confronted secession as well as he could, and that his policies and actions during his presidency's final two months fit into the mainstream of Northern opinion. These interpretive differences merit assessment in conjunction with a broader examination of Buchanan's leadership. Buchanan's course in response to the secession movement was, from his perspective, preeminently practical. He claimed to recognize the situation's gravity and pursued what he perceived as a middle-of-the-road position. His annual message to Congress blamed the secession crisis on abolitionist agitation, denounced secession as illegal, and denied that the federal government could coerce secessionists. Even with his country falling apart, Buchanan's response seemed reasonable to him—and, he insisted, consistent with his constitutional powers. By this time, though, Buchanan could no longer satisfy secession-friendly Southerners or determined Northern Unionists. That Buchanan had lost respect, that his power was dwindling, and that he feared alienating old Southern friends did not help. In the end, Buchanan blamed the failure to compromise on Republicans. By 1861 his marginalized position had reduced him to carrying out the explicit functions of his office and working to prevent war from breaking out before his presidency's expiration.

*　*　*

This volume originated from a September 2008 conference in Lancaster, Pennsylvania, that aimed to revisit familiar narratives in search of fresh insight while simultaneously expanding the range of Buchanan scholarship and pointing it in new directions.[8] It also plays homage to the most detailed study of the Buchanan years, *The Disruption of American Democracy*, published more than six decades ago by the University of Pennsylvania's Roy Franklin Nichols.[9] Nichols influenced scholarly understanding of the breakdown of the regnant Democratic Party—a prelude to the breakup of the Union—in various ways, most especially in his emphasis on politicians' poor management of complex regional and cultural forces during Buchanan's presidency. Nichols illustrated the contexts in which politicians of the late 1850s operated, including an unstable party system, pervasive government corruption, economic dislocations, an electoral system that stoked emotionalism, and an every-man-for-himself mentality in Washington. *The Disruption of American Democracy* offered zesty anecdotes and keen insights wrapped inside a complex narrative. Recipient of the Pulitzer Prize for history in 1949, Nichols's master work has had staying power as an anatomy of national politics during the Buchanan administration.[10] The book's major protagonist was American's only bachelor president, who frittered away his substantial political capital through personality quirks and by political errors of his own making.[11]

Nichols may have been gentler on Buchanan than some historians, but not by much. In Nichols's telling, Buchanan overestimated his own sagacity in dealing with difficult issues, made no effort to reach out to those who did not share his outlook or priorities, and rarely solicited political advice beyond the Southern and doughface counselors in his cabinet. He was a politician past his prime who lacked the creativity and vision that his office demanded. Nichols's depiction of the fifteenth president stands as part of a lengthy historiographic tradition that has judged Buchanan unfavorably.[12]

On the issue of slavery, however, *Disruption* stands less compelling in light of subsequent scholarship. Historians today place slavery at the center of the political crisis of the 1850s.[13] By contrast, Nichols intended to show that the Civil War was "not so much [about] slavery as the personal ambitions and fears" of politicians.[14] Some historians immediately challenged this approach, and it has since lost its interpretive appeal.[15] Once widely viewed as a book that helped explain the coming of the Civil War, today *Disruption*'s enduring value stems from its in-depth narrative of the Buchanan years, particularly given historians' neglect of the Buchanan administration over the past half-century.[16] Considering this lengthy quiescence, the Civil War's sesquicentennial is an opportune moment to give Buchanan and his administration another look.

Besides revisiting some of the themes raised by Nichols, this volume's essayists also blaze some fresh interpretive trails. Some reinterpret Buchanan's leadership style as impetuously forceful particularly with respect to developments in Kansas and Utah, the *Dred Scott* case, and federal patronage. On a different track, several contributors suggest that some elements of the fifteenth president's statecraft merit more respect than previously accorded it, particularly as relating to Buchanan's conduct of foreign affairs and his managing of the secession crisis. Readers seeking a definitive take on Buchanan's role in the crisis, however, will get no satisfaction in this volume. Since secession remains the most contested aspect of Buchanan's presidency, it should come as no surprise that the interpretations of this volume's contributors regarding secession differ also.

Over the years historians have adopted several divergent positions regarding Buchanan and secession. One view, reflected in the work of Philip G. Auchampaugh, Frank W. Klingberg, and Philip S. Klein, embraced Buchanan's version of events and argued that the president heroically tried to steer the ship of state between Northern and Southern extremism.[17] Other historians, such as Allan Nevins and French Ensor Chadwick, have insisted—as did many contemporary Republicans and Northern Democrats—that Buchanan should have threatened secessionists with resolute action, just as Andrew Jackson did during South Carolina's nullification crisis almost three decades earlier. Such action, they presume, would have nipped secession in the bud.[18] James Ford Rhodes and John William Burgess argued that Buchanan's policies effectively aided the inchoate Confederacy while unnecessarily delaying the Union's preparation for war against secessionists.[19]

By contrast, Kenneth Stampp and David Potter argued that by the end of Buchanan's presidency this "old friend of slaveholding politicians" had transformed his cabinet and administration into a "northern sectional administration" that stood accused of hostility toward the South.[20] And Roy Franklin Nichols held to the view that Buchanan's indecisiveness, hesitation, and quasi-hysteria shaped the secession crisis. Some historians, such as Samuel Eliot Morison, maintain that Buchanan's irresolution stemmed from the president's emotional instability, while others, such as Samuel Wylie Crawford (a historian, Civil War general, and the army surgeon during Fort Sumter's bombardment), propose that Buchanan's "timidity . . . 'wholly incapacitated him for action.'"[21] A few of these perspectives overlap, and some historians have created arguments that encompass more than one of these positions.

This interpretive diversity finds expression in the best recent scholarship. Russell McClintock, for example, sees Buchanan as understanding the complexities arising from secession better than most Northerners and as seeking "an increasingly elusive balance between remaining within his limited constitutional authority and rescuing his imperiled country from both dissolution and war." While not viewing Buchanan as the peacemaker that Buchanan imagined himself to be, McClintock's view of Buchanan stands as a modified version of Philip S. Klein's position. Shearer Davis Bowman acknowledges that Buchanan may have been sensitive to "complexity and ambiguity" but argues that this sensitivity effectively paralyzed the president from acting decisively—an echo of Samuel Eliot Morison's argument. Ernest B. Furgurson follows Morison more closely by describing Buchanan as "weak and miserable," weeping often, as "the ultimate lame duck, unsure of his duty, [and] hoping to hold the Union together for another few weeks, long enough to let Lincoln decide what to do."[22]

In *Days of Defiance*, Maury Klein depicts Buchanan as a man out of his element: "All his life he had been less a statesman than a lawyer; now he found himself in a world ruled by madmen where the lawyer's logic was scorned." Buchanan's lawyerly approach to secession was "utterly inadequate to the gravity of the crisis," as the country needed "not a brief or a sermon but a course of action"—a restatement of the argument made by Allan Nevins and others.[23] James McPherson and Doris Kearns Goodwin portray Buchanan the politician as a tool of Southern interests; Buchanan "dithered" during the secession crisis and only had his backbone "stiffened" against secessionists after his cabinet reshuffle. Their positions are softer renditions of the Rhodes-Burgess argument of Buchanan as an abettor of secessionists and of Crawford's view that Buchanan did nothing useful during the crisis. Harold Holzer adopts the Rhodes-Burgess argument, while Jean Baker presses the point further; she titles her chapter on Buchanan's approach to the secession crisis "Appeasing the South."[24]

While differing regarding Buchanan's role during the secession crisis, other leading historians have likewise adopted or modified preexisting arguments. Eric Foner follows Kenneth Stampp in declaring that "Buchanan ended his presidency presiding over a northern, Unionist administration," as does Brian Holden Reid, who notes that "Buchanan struggled obstinately, though unheroically, not to make Lincoln's intractable difficulties even worse than they already were."[25] William Freehling weaves together several of these interpretive frameworks. While agreeing with Stampp that Buchanan alienated his slaveholding friends during the secession crisis, Freehling adds that Buchanan's policies, particularly his decision to send the *Star of the West* to Charleston, accelerated secession throughout the Lower South. This action, Freehling argues, accorded with Buchanan's long-standing pattern of "errant decisiveness" and of his "deploy[ing] power imprudently." Freehling implicitly accepts the premise Buchanan expressed in his presidential memoirs: that Northern patience and a measured federal response might have slowed the secession train. Yet Freehling criticizes Buchanan, asserting that the president's after-the-fact apologia did not match his actions.[26]

These interpretive differences underline the inadequacy of simply declaring that Buchanan stands among America's worst presidents. After all, historians who emphasize Buchanan's failure during the secession crisis do not agree on the reasons for his failure, as they either stress his emotional instability, his Southern sympathies, his inability to make decisions, or his impulsiveness. Historians less critical of Buchanan see him as either that rare Northerner who understood the Union's fragility in late 1860 and labored to mend a broken political system, or as a president who went from being dominated by Southern slave owners to one who worked closely with Lincoln's future advisers to sustain federal authority.

This volume's essays will not settle historians' long-standing differences, but collectively they provide a more nuanced interpretation of the nation's fifteenth president. While they differ regarding Buchanan's presidential effectiveness, most depict him as more decisive and less capricious than some previous scholars have portrayed him. They offer room for debate about a presidency often characterized by a dismissive word or phrase. And they remind us that Buchanan's leadership during his single term of office was more wide-ranging and more interesting than conventional wisdom allows. Consequently it opens new pathways for the ambitious scholar. Always enigmatic, James Buchanan emerges in this volume in fuller dimension—albeit, in key respects, still an exasperating and elusive persona.

*   *   *

When historians have portrayed Buchanan's presidential leadership in negative terms, they have usually cited Buchanan's inability to respond constructively to the Panic of 1857 and subsequent economic stagnation, his demand for the rendition of fugitive slaves, and his failure to deal effectively with the secessionists who threatened his beloved Union. Some of Buchanan's reticence to act stemmed from his ideological commitment to a federal government with limited powers.[27]

But from the outset of his presidency Buchanan could be both forceful and manipulative when it suited his purposes. As Paul Finkelman reminds readers in this volume's first essay, Buchanan played an activist role in the U.S. Supreme Court's most infamous decision, *Dred Scott v. Sandford*. In his March 4, 1857, inaugural address, Buchanan urged Americans to accept the Court's forthcoming decision regarding Congress's power to exclude slavery from the federal territories. After examining the background of the *Dred Scott* case, Finkelman shows that Buchanan's foreknowledge of how the Court would rule led to his disingenuous endorsement of the decision, two days before the Court read it from the bench. While rejecting contemporary Republican claims of Buchanan's joining a conspiracy to nationalize slavery, Finkelman argues that Buchanan engaged in grossly unethical behavior seeking to influence the outcome of *Dred Scott*. Using his inaugural address to buttress the Court's impending decision served

Figure I.2. James Buchanan delivering his inaugural address on March 4, 1857. *Harper's Weekly*, March 14, 1857.

as the unfortunate opening act of a failed presidency, not least because of Buchanan's unwarranted expectation that one court decision could stifle an impending crisis over the slavery question.

Because political historians of the 1850s have continued to focus on events connected with the coming of the Civil War, they have often ig-nored those aspects of Buchanan's presidency apart from slavery and the secession crisis. Yet by looking at other challenges Buchanan faced we can interpret the decisions he made during his final crisis through a new lens. William P. MacKinnon, for example, shows that Buchanan had good reason to believe that the Mormons in Utah Territory were in rebellion against the federal government. In 1857, Buchanan acted with boldness. He consulted neither Congress nor General Winfield Scott, the nation's chief military officer, when he ordered U.S. troops to Utah. Buchanan's actions nearly resulted in significant bloodshed to no good purpose. He clearly had little understanding of the campaign he had launched. MacKinnon praises Buchanan for restoring federal authority in Utah yet blames him for the Utah Expedition's numerous failures. He also suggests that Buchanan's chastening experience in Utah discouraged him from acting forcefully during the secession crisis, with or without congressional approval.

Nicole Etcheson summarizes the complicated series of events marking Kansans' attempt to secure statehood in 1857 and 1858. Despite the obvious predominance of free-state sentiment there, Buchanan had hoped to resolve the Kansas problem by pushing for statehood under the pro-slavery Lecompton Constitution. Free-state settlers inevitably formed a rival state government and called upon Congress to reject Kansas's statehood application. Etcheson accounts for the failure of Buchanan's Kansas policy by citing his excessive closeness to Southern politicians, his moral tone deafness regarding slavery, his blame-abolitionists-first outlook while ignoring white Southerners' role in the ongoing skirmishing between sides, and his inability to resolve his differences with Northern Democrats—Stephen A. Douglas in particular. Americans of the 1850s, Etcheson says, longed for a leader reminiscent of Andrew Jackson. Buchanan, unfortunately, came up short when compared to the Old Hero.

Much as William MacKinnon portrays Buchanan as willing to act boldly in a sphere where he was confident of his authority, so John Belohlavek argues that Buchanan's direction of foreign affairs was sensible and productive. With his deep foreign-policy experience, Buchanan intended to act as his own secretary of state and hoped to focus national attention on foreign affairs, in some measure to deflect attention from sectional problems. Belohlavek reexamines several episodes of Buchanan's diplomacy, particularly his determination to suppress the slave trade, the Paraguayan expedition of 1858, the British presence in Central America, and the dispute with Great Britain in the Puget Sound known as the "Pig War." Conceding the deficiencies of Buchanan's domestic policies, Belohlavek judges his foreign policy to have been largely successful.

Michael A. Morrison examines Buchanan's presidency through the lens of Democratic Party factionalism and growing sectional hostility. In 1856, Southern rights advocates viewed Buchanan the candidate with disfavor; as president, his unwise Kansas policy earned him mistrust and enmity from Democrats in both sections and exacerbated tensions within the party, particularly in the administration's efforts to proscribe Stephen Douglas and his followers. Buchanan's failure on the domestic front, Morrison avers, included issues not directly related to slavery. Corruption in his administration discredited the Buchanan presidency and gave Republicans another campaign issue, while patronage battles made intraparty divisions irreconcilable. Facing a serious economic downturn early in his presidency, Buchanan retreated to Jacksonian-Democrat dogma, arguing that the federal government could do nothing to alleviate human suffering. In the end, Buchanan damaged his standing and hurt his party through his insensitivity to corruption, economic depression, and the machinations of the slave power. Buchanan also failed to see how slavery's expansion had become an issue freighted with the intensity—and more—of the 1830s' Bank War.

Criticism of Buchanan's response to the secession crisis began in the early the 1860s, particularly by Republican politicians and newspapers. Elements of that stinging assessment emerge in Jean Baker's essay for this volume. Buchanan, in Baker's telling, consistently sided with Southern interests throughout his presidency. His unwillingness to assert federal authority during the secession crisis angered both Republicans and many Northern Democrats, who saw him pursuing an "activist prosouthern antiunion agenda." Baker notes that Buchanan never objected when secessionists seized federal property in the South, nor did he act forcefully in reinforcing Fort Sumter. His administration organ in the nation's capital, the *Washington Constitution*, printed editorials supporting secession. Baker refers to Buchanan's final months in office as "collaboration with the South," observing that his favoritism toward the South "bordered on disloyalty."

William G. Shade and Daniel Crofts offer a different take on Buchanan's response to the secession crisis. Shade sees Buchanan as being in step with much of Northern political opinion, particularly the sentiment of the lower North. All Republicans and most Northern Democrats, for example, agreed on the perpetuity of the Union and on secession's illegitimacy—which they deemed as revolution. In this way Buchanan and his archrival Thaddeus Stevens—ironically Buchanan's own representative in Congress—were not so much antipodes as overlapping in their approach to secession. Although historians commonly criticize Buchanan for failing to respond forcefully to secession, Shade reminds us that neither Lincoln nor Douglas favored the use of force, as both believed compromise remained possible throughout the secession winter. And while Stevens, the quintessential radical, deemed compromise during the secession crisis futile, he eschewed military coercion and only favored retaliation through

a naval blockade, cutting off mail to the Confederacy, and punishing secessionists—not the mass of white Southerners—for treason.

Acknowledging Buchanan's shortcomings, Daniel Crofts reexamines
secession through the experiences of Joseph Holt, Buchanan's postmaster
general and in the final months of his presidency, secretary of war. A Kentucky native and member of Buchanan's cabinet, Holt opposed secession
but did not initially know how to challenge it. The course of events in
late 1860, however, pushed Holt's unconditional Unionism to the fore, and
Holt joined the Northern members of Buchanan's cabinet in demanding
that the president firmly resist secessionists. During the Civil War Holt
became Lincoln's confidante while serving as the army's judge advocate
general, a post he held until 1875. Despite a lengthy tenure working with
Republican presidents, Holt never embraced that party's pervasive derision
of Buchanan and, decades afterwards, continued to defend Buchanan's decisions during the secession crisis. Crofts's account of Holt's career offers a
fresh angle on Buchanan's conduct in the closing months of his presidency.
In Crofts's analysis, Buchanan made the best he could of an impossible
situation. By refusing to abandon Fort Sumter—and at the same time refusing to provoke the fire-eaters in South Carolina—Buchanan handed an
intact Union to Lincoln. When he assumed the presidency in March 1861,
Lincoln shared Buchanan's outlook toward the newly established Confederacy and slaveholding border states. Buchanan's refusal to take dramatic
action at Sumter, or even to reprovision it (given Major Robert Anderson's
insistence he could get by with the supplies he had), enabled Lincoln to
play his best hand. In the end, Southerners fired the first shot, giving Lincoln the leverage he needed to suppress an overt rebellion.

In the opening session at the 2008 Buchanan symposium in Lancaster,
Michael F. Holt and William W. Freehling discussed sectionalism, the
coming of the Civil War, historical contingency, shifts in the historical
profession, and their own views of antebellum American political culture.
Like other contributors to this collection, Holt and Freehling view Buchanan as a strong-willed president whose missteps exacerbated sectionalism. Yet neither argues that had Buchanan raised his voice and called out
the troops secession would have withered on the vine. Freehling argues, to
the contrary, that Buchanan's hasty decision to send the *Star of the West*
to resupply Fort Sumter in January 1861 stoked the secessionist impulse
across the Deep South. And both historians argue that Lincoln should

have offered the South explicit reassurances regarding slavery during the seventeen weeks that separated the 1860 election from his March 4, 1861, inauguration.

This volume includes an edited transcript of Holt and Freehling's lively conversation about the political crisis of the 1850s. While neither historian has hewed to one fixed argument regarding the Civil War's coming, both continue to hold fast to positions they advanced in their most widely read books, Holt's *Political Crisis of the 1850s* and Freehling's two-volume *Road to Disunion*. While discussing Buchanan's politics and statecraft, as well as broader issues concerning the Civil War era, Freehling and Holt responded to audience questions with keen wit and thoughtful analysis. We believe readers will find their remarks valuable and provocative.

Michael Birkner's epilogue examines Buchanan's post-presidency and emphasizes the former president's sympathies for Abraham Lincoln and support for the Union cause. All the while, Buchanan retained his old-school Democratic loyalties and, long into the conflict, expressed the hope that the "Union as it was" might be reconstituted. In effect, Buchanan hoped for the continuation of the slaveholders' republic even as the Civil War forever destroyed it.

*   *   *

In this volume we are less concerned with Buchanan's standing in the presidential ratings than in underlining the complexity of the Buchanan years and in showing how historians continue to disagree in how they assess Buchanan and his administration. Much of his presidency remains in the shadows, most notably with respect to the behind-the scenes maneuvers in the executive mansion during the secession crisis.

For some historians, Buchanan was pathetically weak when strength was most needed. Yet Buchanan was more forceful in responding to issues than the traditional image of a "weak" or "timid" president would suggest— even during secession. "Errant decisiveness," in William Freehling's phrase, is of course no more creditable to a president's reputation than being overly timid in responding to challenges, but it does alter one's angle of vision on this particular president. For the purposes of understanding Buchanan's America, and some of the key elements of his presidency, we present these essays in the hope that readers will find material that enriches our understanding Buchanan's statecraft and points the way to fresh investigation.

Notes

1. George Ticknor Curtis, *Life of James Buchanan: Fifteenth President of the United States*, 2 vols. (New York: Harper and Brothers, 1883); Philip S. Klein, *President James Buchanan* (University Park: Pennsylvania State University Press, 1962); John Updike, *Buchanan Dying: A Play* (New York: Knopf, 1974) and *Memories of the Ford Administration: A Novel* (New York: Knopf, 1992). Updike acknowledged Klein's influence in his fictional portrait of Buchanan. See *Buchanan Dying*, 183–85, 189, 191–95; *Memories of the Ford Administration*, 25–27 (and numerous other references to Klein throughout the book); and Michael J. Birkner, "A Conversation with Philip S. Klein," *Pennsylvania History* 56 (October 1989): 244–45. For recent presidential performance rankings see Arthur M. Schlesinger Jr., "Rating the Presidents: Washington to Clinton," *Political Science Quarterly* 11 (Summer 1997): 179–90; Nathan Miller, *Star-Spangled Men: America's Ten Worst Presidents* (New York: Simon and Schuster, 1998); William J. Ridings and Stuart B. McIver, *Rating the Presidents: A Ranking of U.S. Leaders, from the Great and Honorable to the Dishonest and Incompetent* (New York: Kensington Books, 2000); *Wilmington (N.C.) Morning Star*, August 21, 2002, A2; James Taranto and Leonard Leo, eds., *Presidential Leadership: Rating the Best and the Worst in the White House* (New York: Free Press, 2004); *Troy Record* (New York), July 2, 2010.

2. Henry Steele Commager, "What Are We Waiting For?" *New Republic*, July 6, 1968, 18 (see also Updike, *Buchanan Dying*, 202, regarding Commager's assessment); McPherson quoted in *USA Today*, February 21, 2005.

3. James Buchanan, *Mr. Buchanan's Administration on the Eve of the Rebellion* (New York: D. Appleton, 1866).

4. Ulrich quoted in Suzanne Gordon, "Herstory in the Making," *Boston Globe Sunday Magazine*, January 31, 1993, 39.

5. For a brief description of Buchanan's career, see Michael J. Birkner "Getting to Know James Buchanan, Again," in *James Buchanan and the Political Crisis of the 1850s*, ed. Birkner (Selinsgrove, Pa.: Susquehanna University Press, 1996), 17–36. P. S. Klein, *President James Buchanan*, remains the standard biography. For a pungent, unsympathetic account of Buchanan, see Jean H. Baker, *James Buchanan* (New York: Times Books, 2004).

6. Regarding the contrasting views that historians and contemporaries have held regarding James Buchanan, see Birkner, "Getting to Know James Buchanan, Again," 17–19.

7. On the corruption issue, see especially Mark W. Summers, *The Plundering Generation: Corruption and the Crisis of the Union, 1849–1861* (New York: Oxford University Press, 1987); and Michael F. Holt, *The Political Crisis of the 1850s* (New York: Wiley, 1978).

8. A similar conference in 1991 yielded Birkner, *James Buchanan and the Political Crisis of the 1850s*.

9. Roy Franklin Nichols, *The Disruption of American Democracy* (1948; paperback edition, New York: Collier Books, 1962; all citations in this essay to *Disruption* come from the 1962 paperback printing). For further information on Nichols, see his autobiography, *A Historian's Progress* (New York: Knopf, 1968), and *Pennsylvania History* 38 (January 1971), edited by William G. Shade, which contains several essays examining Nichols's life and scholarship.

10. David Potter—whose *Impending Crisis, 1848–1861* (New York: Harper and Row, 1976) may be the most influential account of the Civil War's coming written during the late twentieth century—wrote in 1971 that there were few scholars, if any, "whose account of the road to war can compare with that of Nichols," and praised Nichols for having contributed significantly to the "rehabilitation of American political history." Michael Holt called *Disruption* "the best history of a political party ever written" and the "classic account of the Buchanan administration . . . which contains the best single analysis of how the fight over the Lecompton constitution and subsequent events ruptured the Democratic party." William Freehling calls *Disruption* "the finest monograph on Buchanan's election and administration." Potter, "Roy F. Nichols and the Rehabilitation of American Political History," *Pennsylvania History* 38 (January 1971): 8, 20; Michael F. Holt, "Rethinking Nineteenth-Century American Political History," *Congress and the Presidency: A Journal of Capital Studies* 19 (Autumn 1992): 97–111; Holt, *Political Crisis of the 1850s*, 277; William W. Freehling, *The Road to Disunion*, vol. 2, *Secessionists Triumphant, 1854–1861* (New York: Oxford University Press, 2007), 548.

11. See, for example, Nichols, *Disruption*, 74–78.

12. James Ford Rhodes, *History of the United States from the Compromise of 1850 to the Final Restoration of Home Rule at the South in 1877*, 7 vols. (New York: MacMillan, 1906), 2:244–45, 248, 280, 290, 292; 3:127–38, 143–44, 181, 191, 227–31, 286, 634; Theodore Clarke Smith, *Parties and Slavery, 1850–59* (New York: Harper and Brothers, 1906), 216–26, 235, 237, 240, 254; French Ensor Chadwick, *Causes of the Civil War* (New York: Harper and Brothers, 1906), 151, 158–64, 203, 217, 263; Woodrow Wilson, *Division and Reunion, 1829–1889* (New York: Longman, Green, 1906), 214; John William Burgess, *The Civil War and the Constitution*, vol. 1 (New York: Scribner, 1910), 84–87. For Nichols's most unflattering comments regarding Buchanan, see *Disruption*, 26, 163, 421, 424, 425; and "James Buchanan: Lessons in Leadership in Trying Times," in *Bulwark of Liberty: Early Years at Dickinson. The Boyd Lee Spahr Lectures in American History* (New York: Fleming H. Revell, 1950), 174. On historians' views of Buchanan since World War II, see Birkner, "Getting to Know James Buchanan, Again," 17–19. Recent works that view Buchanan unfavorably include Baker, *James Buchanan*; Harold Holzer, *Lincoln President-Elect: Abraham Lincoln and the Great Secession Winter, 1860–1861* (New York: Simon and Schuster, 2008), 3, 127–32, 158, 161, 212, 275; Maury Klein, *Days of Defiance: Sumter, Secession, and the Coming of the Civil War* (New York: Knopf, 1997), 111, 126, 135, 171, 173, 151, 208, 282, 312; Shearer Davis

Bowman, *At the Precipice: Americans North and South during the Secession Crisis* (Chapel Hill: University of North Carolina Press, 2010), 262, 266; James M. McPherson, *Battle Cry of Freedom: The Civil War Era* (New York: Oxford University Press, 1988), 118, 156, 167, 194, 223, 248, 265–66; Eric H. Walther, *The Shattering of the Union: America in the 1850s* (Wilmington, Del.: Scholarly Resources, 2004), 163–64; Doris Kearns Goodwin, *Team of Rivals: The Political Genius of Abraham Lincoln* (New York: Simon and Schuster, 2005), 297, 319, 675; Freehling, *The Road to Disunion*, 2:119, 136–37, 159, 488–89, 497; Douglas R. Egerton, *Year of Meteors: Stephen Douglas, Abraham Lincoln, and the Election that Brought on the Civil War* (New York: Bloomsbury Press, 2010), 154–55, 196, 224, 226, 286, 324.

13. Some of Nichols's other assessments of the 1850s have not weathered well. These include Nichols's framing national political disintegration around "hyperemotionalism," his ignoring of ideology, and his defining of politicians in terms of their greed and relentless pursuit of power (*Disruption*, 8, 104, 502, 504). Michael F. Holt qualified his admiration for *Disruption* by remarking that Nichols ignores or minimizes voters, policymaking, and state parties' impact on the actions of national politicians ("Rethinking Nineteenth-Century American Political History"). Regarding Nichols's historiographic context, see Frank Towers, "Partisans, New History, and Modernization: The Historiography of the Civil War's Causes, 1861–2011," *Journal of the Civil War Era* 1 (June 2011): 245.

14. Nichols, *Historian's Progress*, 36.

15. Arthur M. Schlesinger Jr., for example, in an otherwise favorable review of *Disruption*, criticized Nichols for minimizing slavery's role in the politics of the 1850s and the coming of the Civil War—a position that Nichols continued to maintain two decades later, even as historians placed greater emphasis on slavery. See "The Great Internal American War," *The New Leader*, May 22, 1948, 10. In Nichols's *Stakes of Power, 1845–1877* (New York: Hill and Wang, 1961), slavery occupies a larger role in the coming of the Civil War than Nichols had accorded it in 1948. Yet in his "A Hundred Years Later: Perspectives on the Civil War," *Journal of Southern History* 33 (May 1967): 153–62, Nichols felt that contemporary "racial strife" made it easier to understand the "hyperemotion" of the Civil War era (153). And in his autobiography, published a year later, Nichols discussed his current thinking on the Civil War's coming, conduct, and consequences and barely mentioned slavery. *Historian's Progress*, 205–24.

Some of the many books that center Civil War causation on slavery include Potter, *Impending Crisis*; Eugene D. Genovese, *The Political Economy of Slavery* (New York: Pantheon, 1965); Eric Foner, *Free Soil, Free Men, Free Labor: The Ideology of the Republican Party before the Civil War* (New York: Oxford University Press, 1970); McPherson, *Battle Cry of Freedom*; Bruce Levine, *Half Slave and Half Free: The Roots of the Civil War* (New York: Hill and Wang, 1992); Egerton, *Year of Meteors*.

16. Important words on Buchanan since 1962 include Lawson Alan Pendleton, "James Buchanan's Attitudes toward Slavery" (Ph.D. diss., University of North

Carolina, 1964); David E. Meerse, "James Buchanan, the Patronage, and the Northern Democratic Party, 1857–1858" (Ph.D. diss., University of Illinois, 1969); Frederick Moore Binder, *James Buchanan and the American Empire* (Selinsgrove, Pa.: Susquehanna University Press, 1994); Elbert B. Smith, *The Presidency of James Buchanan* (Lawrence: University Press of Kansas, 1975); Baker, *James Buchanan*; Birkner, *James Buchanan and the Political Crisis of the 1850s*; Updike, *Buchanan Dying*; and Updike, *Memories of the Ford Administration*. Of these works, only Pendleton, Meerse, and Binder make extensive use of the voluminous Buchanan manuscripts. Meerse also published several articles that develop topics he addressed in his dissertation, including "Buchanan's Patronage Policy: An Attempt to Achieve Political Strength," *Pennsylvania History* 40 (January 1973): 37–52; "Origins of the Buchanan-Douglas Feud Reconsidered," *Journal of the Illinois State Historical Society*, 67 (April 1974): 154–74; "Presidential Leadership, Suffrage Qualifications, and Kansas: 1857," *Civil War History* 24 (December 1978): 293–313; and "Buchanan, the Patronage, and the Lecompton Constitution: A Case Study," *Civil War History*, 41 (December 1995): 291–312.

17. Philip G. Auchampaugh, *James Buchanan and His Cabinet on the Eve of Secession* (Lancaster, Pa.: Lancaster Press, 1926); Frank Wysor Klingberg, "James Buchanan and the Crisis of the Union," *Journal of Southern History* 9 (November 1943): 455–74; P. S. Klein, *President James Buchanan*; Buchanan, *Mr. Buchanan's Administration*. Klein wanted to title his biography "Cursed Are the Peacemakers," but his publisher insisted upon a declarative title. Birkner, "Conversation with Philip S. Klein," 265. And although he does not address Buchanan's role in the secession crisis, the scholarship of David E. Meerse (cited in note 16 above), views Buchanan more favorably than do most historians.

18. Chadwick, *Causes of the Civil War*, 161; Allan Nevins, "The Needless Conflict: If Buchanan Had Met the Kansas Problem Firmly He Might Have Avoided Civil War," *American Heritage* 7 (August 1955): 4–9, 88–90. Regarding contemporary Northerners' lament that Buchanan failed to act as Jackson did during the Nullification Crisis, see David M. Potter, *Lincoln and His Party in the Secession Crisis* (New Haven: Yale University Press, 1942), 274; Kenneth M. Stampp, *And the War Came: The North and the Secession Crisis, 1860–1861* (Baton Rouge: Louisiana State University Press, 1950), 11, 50, 61, 95, 97–98, 209–10.

19. Rhodes, *History of the United States*, 3:127–38, 143; Burgess, *The Civil War and the Constitution*, 1:84–87.

20. Stampp, *And the War Came*, 57, 82; Michael J. Birkner, Don Fehrenbacher, Kenneth M. Stampp, Robert Johannsen, and Elbert Smith (discussants), "The Presidency of James Buchanan: A Reassessment," in Birkner, *James Buchanan and the Political Crisis of the 1850s*, 195–97; Potter, *Impending Crisis*, 521, 542. See also Richard N. Current, *Lincoln and the First Shot* (Philadelphia: J. B. Lippincott, 1963), 24–25; Potter, *Lincoln and His Party*, 319, 324, 329.

21. Nichols, *Disruption*, 421, 424, 425; Nichols, "James Buchanan: Lessons in

Leadership in Trying Times," 174; Samuel Eliot Morison, *The Oxford History of the American People* (New York: Oxford University Press, 1965), 593, 608; Samuel Wylie Crawford, *The Genesis of the Civil War: The Story of Sumter, 1860–1861* (New York: Charles L. Webster, 1887), 285–87. Elbert B. Smith, however, questions Buchanan's purported emotional instability by noting that Buchanan's cabinet members, with whom he met "daily in long, often agonizing sessions," and who often disagreed with his decisions, depicted Buchanan as "firm and energetic" even if he "occasionally vacillated." Smith, *Presidency of James Buchanan*, 144. For contemporary references and reminiscences critical of Buchanan's frame of mind, see William Salter, *The Life of James W. Grimes, Governor of Iowa, 1854–1858; a Senator of the United States, 1859–1869* (New York: D. Appleton, 1876), 132; Mrs. Roger A. Pryor (Sara Agnes Rice Pryor), *Reminiscences of Peace and War* (New York: Macmillan, 1904), 110); William Gillette, *Jersey Blue: Civil War Politics in New Jersey, 1854–1865* (New Brunswick, N.J.: Rutgers University Press, 1995), 114.

22. Russell McClintock, *Lincoln and the Decision for War* (Chapel Hill: University of North Carolina Press, 2008), 61–62, 66–69, 85, 253; Bowman, *At the Precipice*, 266; Ernest B. Furgurson, *Freedom Rising: Washington in the Civil War* (New York: Knopf, 2004), 24–25, 28. For the most generous recent assessment of Buchanan's actions during the secession crisis see David Detzer, *Allegiance: Fort Sumter, Charleston, and the Beginning of the Civil War* (New York: Harcourt, 2001), 66–69, 75, 77–79, 88–90, 97, 139–44, 169.

23. M. Klein, *Days of Defiance*, 126, 151.

24. McPherson, *Battle Cry of Freedom*, 118, 156, 167, 194, 223, 265–66; Goodwin, *Team of Rivals*, 297, 319, 675; Holzer, *Lincoln President-Elect*, 130; Baker, *James Buchanan*, 107–43.

25. Eric Foner, *The Fiery Trial: Abraham Lincoln and American Slavery* (New York: Norton, 2010), 147; Brian Holden Reid, *The Origins of the American Civil War* (London: Addison Wesley Longman, 1996), 312–18, 336–39.

26. Freehling, *Road to Disunion*, 2:488–89; Buchanan, *Mr. Buchanan's Administration*, 141–52, 164–65, 170, 175.

27. Buchanan, *Mr. Buchanan's Administration*, 116.

I

James Buchanan, Dred Scott, and the Whisper of Conspiracy

PAUL FINKELMAN

The president-elect stood up to give his inaugural address. As he walked to the podium, the sixty-five-year-old Buchanan stopped to chat briefly with Roger B. Taney, the nearly eighty-year-old chief justice. The two men had much in common. They had grown up in adjoining states—Maryland and Pennsylvania—and come of age in the wake of the American Revolution. Both were graduates of Dickinson College, Taney in 1795 and Buchanan in 1809. They both practiced law and then entered politics. They had both begun their careers as Federalists, but by 1828 both had become fervent supporters of Andrew Jackson. Old Hickory had appointed Buchanan as the American ambassador to Russia while eventually placing Taney on the Supreme Court. Now, after a lifetime in politics, the last Jacksonian president would be sworn in by the long-lasting Jacksonian chief justice. Surely they had much to say, and certainly Taney wanted to say a private word to his old friend and ally, before Buchanan gave his address.

We do not know what they talked about—old friends, family, the historic event they now shared, their shared alma mater, or nothing important at all. But for a few moments they stood there, two old political leaders, relics of the age of Jackson, the embodiment of proslavery Democratic politics, whispering in front of the nation. The conversation over, Buchanan went to the podium to give his speech and then be sworn in by Taney. The next day Americans read in their newspapers about the inaugural address and the president's conversation with the chief justice.

The first part of Buchanan's speech focused on the central question of the day: the problem of slavery in the territories. Buchanan heartily

Figure 1.1. James Buchanan's inauguration, March 4, 1857. From left: Chief Justice Roger Taney, incoming vice-president John C. Breckinridge, outgoing president Franklin Pierce, and Buchanan. *Frank Leslie's Illustrated Newspaper* March 14, 1857.

endorsed the Kansas-Nebraska Act and the concept of popular sovereignty. The new president declared:

> What a happy conception, then, was it for Congress to apply this simple rule, that the will of the majority shall govern, to the settlement of the question of domestic slavery in the Territories! Congress is neither "to legislate slavery into any Territory or State nor to exclude it therefrom, but to leave the people thereof perfectly free to form and regulate their domestic institutions in their own way, subject only to the Constitution of the United States."[1]

The new president ignored the ongoing violence and bloodshed in Kansas—the sacking of Lawrence, the massive voter fraud in the territory, the deaths of some fifty people, the pitched battles. Buchanan seemed unaware (although he surely was not) that his "contemporaries called the summer of 1856 . . . Bleeding Kansas." He did not acknowledge that this bloodshed had been going on for two years.[2] Ostrich-like, the new chief executive reduced the issue of Bleeding Kansas to a narrowly legalistic one. He noted that under the concept of popular sovereignty, as set out in the Kansas-Nebraska Act, Congress had decided that when Kansas became a state it would "be received into the Union with or without slavery, as their constitution may prescribe at the time of their admission." The only issue in controversy, the president declared, was "A difference of opinion . . . in regard to the point of time when the people of a Territory shall decide this question for themselves."[3]

While men were dying over precisely this issue, Buchanan asserted that it was "happily, a matter of but little practical importance."[4] It is hard to imagine why he thought this was not an important issue and a deeply practical one, given the level of violence in the territory and the high-stakes debate over slavery there. His Southern allies insisted that there had to be a slave code in Kansas to protect their slave property during the territorial period, so that the territory could then evolve into a slave state. Since Buchanan had been elected by carrying fourteen of fifteen slave states but only a handful of Northern states, he surely understood that whether or not slavery could be prohibited before statehood was of central importance to Southerners.[5] On the other hand, Northerners were arguing that the voters of the territory should be able to ban slavery well before statehood, thus guaranteeing a free Kansas. The issue of when or if a territory could ban slavery—or if a territory could protect slavery—had enormous practical consequences. But it was an issue Buchanan hoped to avoid in his administration.

Buchanan acknowledged within the nation "a difference of opinion . . . in regard to the point of time when the people of a Territory shall decide this question" whether slavery would be allowed or banned in the territory. But, he said, he did not really have to worry about this question. The status of slavery in the territories, the new president explained, was

> a judicial question, which legitimately belongs to the Supreme Court of the United States, before whom it is now pending, and will, it is understood, be speedily and finally settled. To their decision, in common with all good citizens, I shall cheerfully submit, whatever this

may be, though it has ever been my individual opinion that under the Nebraska-Kansas act the appropriate period will be when the number of actual residents in the Territory shall justify the formation of a constitution with a view to its admission as a State into the Union.[6]

The case "now pending" before the Court was *Dred Scott v. Sandford*, which had been before the Court for nearly two years.[7] The Court had heard arguments in the case in 1856, before the presidential election, but had declined to decide the case in March 1856, at the end of the 1855 term. Instead, the Court held the case over, to be reargued when the December 1856 term began—which was *after* the upcoming presidential election. The Court heard arguments again in December 1856, after Buchanan was elected, but once again it did not decide the case immediately. The case was still undecided when Taney swore Buchanan in as president.

Buchanan's inaugural address was both revolutionary in its implications and unique in the arguments it offered. To understand the importance—and the truly radical nature of Buchanan's position—it is necessary to briefly examine the history of congressional regulation of the territories, and of slavery in the territories.

In 1787, while the Articles of Confederation were still in effect, Congress passed the Northwest Ordinance, which provided a comprehensive plan for regulating and governing the federal land north of the Ohio River—the present-day states of Ohio, Indiana, Illinois, Michigan, and Wisconsin. In Article 6 of the ordinance the Congress banned all slavery in the territories north and west of the Ohio River.[8] In 1789 the Congress, operating under the recently adopted United States Constitution, reenacted this law.[9] The reenactment of the Northwest Ordinance illustrates that no one in the first Congress, dominated by the men who had written and ratified the Constitution, doubted the power of Congress to regulate slavery in the territories. Underscoring this point is the fact that this was the eighth act passed by the new government. Before the new Congress created the federal courts or even the Treasury Department, it regulated the territories and banned slavery in some of them. A year later Congress organized the southwestern territories with no ban on slavery.[10] Thus from its inception Congress clearly assumed that it had the power to regulate the territories and prohibit or allow slavery in them.

The subsequent history of congressional regulation of slavery in the territories was well known to Buchanan and his generation. After reenacting the Northwest Ordinance, the Congress passed the Southwest Ordinance, which allowed slavery in what would become Mississippi and Alabama. In 1820 Congress passed the Missouri Compromise, which admitted Missouri as a slave state but banned slavery north of the southern boundary of that state along the 36°30' parallel in the territory acquired from France through the Louisiana Purchase. Using the Missouri Compromise line as its guide, Congress continued to allow or ban slavery as it organized territories west of the Mississippi. In 1836 Congress passed the "Wisconsin Enabling Act," which banned slavery in what is today Wisconsin, Minnesota, and Iowa.[11] In 1845 Congress annexed Texas and admitted it as a slave state. Texas's admission was also consistent with the Missouri Compromise line.

The acquisition of vast lands from Mexico reopened the issue of slavery in the territories, leading to a prolonged debate in Congress. Most Northerners wanted to ban slavery in all the new territories of the Mexican Cession, and thus the House of Representatives, with its large Northern majority, repeatedly passed the Wilmot Proviso, in one form or another. Introduced in August 1846 by Congressman David Wilmot of Pennsylvania, a first-term Democrat, the Wilmot Proviso declared that "as an express and fundamental condition to the acquisition of any territory from the Republic of Mexico by the United States, by virtue of any treaty which may be negotiated between them, and to the use by the Executive of the moneys herein appropriated, neither slavery nor involuntary servitude shall ever exist in any part of said territory, except for crime, whereof the party shall first be duly convicted."[12] The Senate, where Southerners were in the majority until the admission of Wisconsin in 1848, easily defeated the Wilmot Proviso. Even after 1848 there were always a few Northern senators who would join a unanimous South to defeat the proviso.

Instead of an absolute ban on slavery in all the new territories, some Northerners, and many Southerners, wanted to apply the Missouri Compromise line to the territories, which would have opened present-day New Mexico, Arizona, southern California, and west Texas to slavery but prohibited the institution in the rest of the Mexican Cession, which included all of present-day Utah, Nevada, and northern California, and portions of Wyoming, Colorado, and Kansas. More aggressive Southerners wanted all of the newly acquired territory open to slavery.

In a series of laws passed in 1850—known as the Compromise of 1850—Congress dealt extensively with slavery in the territories recently acquired from Mexico. Congress admitted California to the Union as a free state, which complied with the wishes of the people living there. By the time of statehood California had about 100,000 people and almost no slaves. But the Congress refused to admit New Mexico as a free state, despite the desires of the majority of the inhabitants who opposed slavery. Indeed, before the Congress acted, residents in New Mexico wrote and ratified a constitution that banned slavery. President Millard Fillmore—the first of three proslavery Northerners to inhabit the White House in the 1850s—refused to submit the New Mexico constitution to Congress and bring New Mexico into the Union as a free state.[13] Instead, Fillmore pushed for, and Congress passed, legislation allowing slavery in the two newly created territories: New Mexico (which included most of present-day New Mexico and Arizona) and Utah (which included present-day Utah, Nevada, and parts of Colorado, Wyoming, and Kansas). Thus, while California entered the Union as free state, the rest of the Mexican Cession was set aside for slavery.

The Compromise of 1850 eviscerated the principle of the Missouri Compromise line by allowing slavery in the Utah Territory, which was entirely north of the Missouri Compromise line.[14] At this point in American history every territory that had been organized without a ban on slavery had become a slave state. There was no reason to doubt the same dynamic would happen for the 380,000 square miles that encompassed the New Mexico and Utah Territories.[15] This land included more than 180,000 square miles that were north of the 36°30' parallel.

This abrogation of the Missouri Compromise line was not technically an abandonment of the Compromise itself, because the line still applied to the unorganized territory that remained from the Louisiana Purchase. However, most Americans—in the North and the South—understood that this "compromise" was really a huge victory for slavery. By rejecting a compromise that followed the principle of the Missouri Compromise, Congress and President Fillmore signaled a fundamental shift in the politics of territorial expansion. Instead of attempting to hem in slavery, or at least balance the expansion of freedom and slavery, the new policy would now allow slavery to spread everywhere in the West.

Whatever the politics of this outcome were, no one in Congress seemed to think there were any constitutional problems with this law. Nor did President Fillmore, a conservative Northern doughface. Nor did any national leaders in this debate doubt that Congress had the constitutional power to allow slavery in these new territories. The debates of 1850 were over whether Congress *should* ban slavery or allow it in the new territories, not whether Congress *could* ban slavery or allow it.[16] In the Kansas-Nebraska Act, passed in 1854, Congress, dominated by Buchanan's fellow Democrats, finally destroyed what was left of the Missouri Compromise, voting to allow slavery in the newly created Nebraska Territory, which included the present-day states of Kansas, Nebraska, South Dakota, North Dakota, Montana, and parts of Colorado and Wyoming.

The bottom line in all of this was that Congress had always had the power to regulate slavery in the territories. With the exception of a few extreme proslavery Southern nationalists, no one in Congress had ever doubted the power of the national legislature to regulate slavery in the federal territories.

Thus, Buchanan's position—that this was "a judicial question, which legitimately belongs to the Supreme Court of the United States"—ran counter to the entire political history of the United States up to that point.[17] Furthermore, it ran counter to the entire judicial history of the United States. In *Marbury v. Madison* (1803) the Supreme Court had struck down a tiny portion—literally a few words—of the Judiciary Act of 1789.[18] There the Court held that Congress lacked the power to expand the original jurisdiction of the Supreme Court. *Marbury* is correctly considered a landmark decision because it established the power of the Court to exercise judicial review over federal statutes. But, importantly, at the time of Buchanan's inauguration, the Court had never struck down a federal law since *Marbury*.[19] The Court had, however, ruled that Congress had the power to both acquire territory and govern it. In *American Insurance Company v. Canter*, Chief Justice Marshall had emphatically asserted that "The Constitution confers absolutely on the government of the Union, the powers of making war, and of making treaties; consequently, that government possesses the power of acquiring territory, either by conquest or by treaty," and that Congress had full power to govern the territory "by virtue of that clause in the Constitution, which empowers Congress 'to make all needful rules and regulations, respecting the territory, or other property belonging to the United States.'"[20]

Thus it is extremely odd that an incoming president would have begun his administration by saying that Congress and the executive branch should cede power and authority to the judiciary to solve a major political issue. No president, before or after Buchanan, ever voluntarily and openly ceded such power to the Supreme Court. Until Buchanan's inaugural address, no one had imagined that the issue of slavery in the territories was "a judicial question, which legitimately belongs to the Supreme Court of the United States." On the contrary, it had always been a *political* question for the Congress and the president to solve. Moreover, under the decision in *American Insurance Company v. Canter*, regulating and governing a territory had always been the responsibility of Congress.

Even more odd, perhaps, was Buchanan's assertion that "in common with all good citizens" he would "cheerfully submit," to the decision, "whatever this may be."[21] No other president, in advance of a Supreme Court decision, has so unequivocally endorsed the result. Nor had any other president discussed (much less endorsed) an unannounced Supreme Court opinion in his inaugural address. Buchanan's announcement during his inaugural was truly unprecedented in American politics.

Buchanan's supine deference to the Court on an issue that had been so deeply a political question also contrasted dramatically with the political hero of Buchanan and Chief Justice Taney: Andrew Jackson. In his famous veto of the rechartering of the Second Bank of the United States,[22] which Roger B. Taney as attorney general had drafted, President Jackson bluntly asserted that as president he was not bound to follow the logic of the Supreme Court's decision in *McCulloch v. Maryland*.[23] In that case, Chief Justice John Marshall had upheld the constitutionality of the Bank of the United States. However, Jackson argued that he could determine for himself if the bank was constitutional, and since he believed the bank was unconstitutional, he could exercise his own constitutional judgment in vetoing the recharter bill.[24] In fact, Jackson seemed generally to be hostile to the idea that the Court should determine national policy. This hostility to the Court had been a main tenet of the Democratic Party since Thomas Jefferson's presidency. Suddenly, this hostility to the Court disappeared as Buchanan, the heir to the mantle of both Jefferson and Jackson, took office.

In an unprecedented move, Buchanan publicly ceded power to the Court to legislate, in effect, for the nation on the most important political issue of the age.

The Articulation of the Judicial Question

Two days after Buchanan took office, the Supreme Court announced its decision in *Dred Scott*. The case was remarkable. Each of the nine justices wrote an opinion in the case. This was only the second time before the Civil War that this development occurred.[25] The opinions range in size from Justice Robert C. Grier's half-page concurrence to Justice Benjamin R. Curtis's seventy-page dissent. Chief Justice Taney's "Opinion of the Court" is fifty-four pages long. The nine opinions, along with a handful of pages summarizing the lawyers' arguments, consume 260 pages of *United States Reports*.

In *Dred Scott*, Chief Justice Taney declared unconstitutional the portion of the Missouri Compromise that prohibited slavery in all of the federal territories north and west of the state of Missouri. As already noted, this case was only the second Supreme Court decision to strike down a federal law. Moreover, it was the first case in which the Supreme Court held unconstitutional a major federal statute. The contrast with *Marbury v. Madison* is important. *Marbury* held unconstitutional a minor portion of the Judiciary Act of 1789—a provision of the 1789 act that had never been used before and which had only been on the books for a very short time. *Dred Scott* struck down a law that had been on the books for thirty-seven years—more than half of the entire history of the nation since the Constitution was adopted—and been the basis of most subsequent legislation covering territorial expansion. The decision was truly a revolution in American jurisprudence.

Dred Scott had been the slave of a U.S. Army surgeon, Captain John Emerson, who took Scott to military posts at Fort Armstrong in Illinois and later at Fort Snelling in modern-day Minnesota. After Emerson died, Scott sued Emerson's widow, Irene Sanford Emerson, for freedom, arguing that he had become free while living in Illinois and in the federal territory north of Missouri, which had been made free by the Missouri Compromise. Following more than a quarter of a century of Missouri precedents, in 1850 a jury in St. Louis declared that Scott, his wife, and their two

Figure 1.2. Dred Scott, 1857. *Century Magazine*, June 1887, 208; adapted from illustration in *Frank Leslie's Illustrated Newspaper* June 27, 1857.

children were all free based on their residence in free jurisdictions. Emerson's widow, however, appealed this result to a newly constituted Missouri Supreme Court.[26]

In 1852, in *Scott v. Emerson*, the Missouri Supreme Court reversed the lower court and declared that Scott was still a slave. The decision was frankly political. It was made, not on the basis of legal precedent, but because of popular prejudice. Chief Justice William Scott stated:

> Times are not now as they were when the former decisions on this subject were made. Since then, not only individuals but States have been possessed with a dark and fell spirit in relation to slavery, whose gratification is sought in the pursuit of measures, whose inevitable consequence must be the overthrow and destruction of our Government. Under such circumstances, it does not behoove the State of Missouri to show the least countenance to any measure which might gratify this spirit. She is willing to assume her full responsibility for the existence of slavery within her limits, nor does she seek to share or divide it with others.[27]

At this point the case ought to have ended. However, by the time the Missouri Supreme Court had decided the case, Irene Emerson had moved to Massachusetts and remarried. In conjunction with her move she transferred ownership of Dred Scott and his family to her brother John F. A. Sanford,[28] a New Yorker with numerous business and family connections in St. Louis. In 1854 a new attorney for Scott, Roswell Field, initiated a new freedom suit in federal court, based on "diversity jurisdiction."[29] Under diversity jurisdiction, a citizen of one state may sue a citizen of another state in federal court. Thus, Scott claimed he was a citizen of Missouri who had been harmed and falsely deprived of his liberty by Sanford, a citizen of New York.

Sanford responded by denying that the Court had jurisdiction over the parties. He did not deny that he was a citizen of New York, or that Scott resided in Missouri, but Sanford did deny that Scott was a "citizen" of Missouri. Sanford's response was in the form of a plea in abatement, which effectively asked the Court to stop—or "abate"—the case immediately and throw Scott's suit out of court on the grounds that the Court had no jurisdiction to hear the case. Sanford argued that "Dred Scott, is not a citizen of the State of Missouri, as alleged in his declaration, because he is a negro of African descent; his ancestors were of pure African blood, and were brought into this country and sold as negro slaves."[30] In essence, Sanford argued that no black person could be a citizen of Missouri, and thus even if Dred Scott was free, the federal court did not have jurisdiction to hear the case.

United States District Judge Robert W. Wells rejected Sanford's plea. A slaveowner originally from Virginia, Wells was neither an advocate of black equality nor opposed to slavery. But he did believe that free blacks were entitled to minimal legal rights, including the right to sue in a federal court. Scott, in other words, would have a right to sue in federal court, to determine if Sanford was wrongly holding him as a slave. In reaching this conclusion Wells did not declare that Scott, or any free black, was entitled to full legal, social, or political equality in Missouri or anywhere else in the country. Wells merely held that right to sue as a "citizen" in Article III of the Constitution was the equivalent to being a free—non-slave—full-time resident or inhabitant of a state. If Dred Scott was in fact not a slave, then he met this minimal criterion and was a "citizen" solely for the purpose of suing in federal court.[31]

After hearing the case, however, Judge Wells concluded that Scott was still a slave, because the federal courts were obligated to follow state precedents when interpreting state law. Wells also believed that Dred Scott's status—as a slave or a free person—should be determined entirely by Missouri law and based this conclusion on the U.S. Supreme Court's decision in *Strader v. Graham* (1851).[32] In that case the Court had held that, except as limited by the Constitution, every state had complete authority to decide for itself the status of all people within its borders. Thus, the Northern states could free visiting slaves, like Dred Scott, but not free fugitive slaves, because the Constitution protected the right of a master to recover fugitive slaves. Similarly, the Southern states had complete discretion to decide for themselves if a slave who had lived in the North had become free.

Judge Wells's ruling made sense for Dred Scott's claim to freedom based on his Illinois residence. That is, Missouri was free to enforce or ignore the Illinois Constitution, and once the Missouri court decided this issue the federal courts in Missouri were obligated to follow the Missouri rule. But because of his residence at Fort Snelling, Scott also claimed his freedom under the Missouri Compromise and other federal laws organizing the territories north of Missouri. Under the Supremacy Clause of the U.S. Constitution, the states were obligated to uphold all federal laws. Thus, Judge Wells might have concluded that Scott should be free because the Missouri Supreme Court had misconstrued federal law. Wells could have determined that under the Missouri Compromise and other federal laws, Dred Scott was free and the state courts had to respect his change of status because it had occurred under federal law. But Wells did not follow this route, and Scott remained a slave.

Scott appealed the outcome of his case to the U.S. Supreme Court, arguing that under the Missouri Compromise and other federal laws he was entitled to his freedom. Sanford had lost on the plea in abatement, but he did not appeal Judge Wells's ruling on this point, because he had won the entire case and thus had no reason to appeal anything. The Supreme Court heard arguments in the case in February 1856, but that spring—the spring before the presidential election—the Court did not rule on the case. Instead, the Court held the case over for reargument the following December—after the presidential election. The case had not been decided when Buchanan gave his inaugural address. Thus, in his inaugural, Buchanan asserted that when the Court announced its judgment, he, "in common with all good citizens," would "cheerfully submit, whatever this may be." The incoming president then added that it had always been his "individual opinion that under the Nebraska-Kansas act the appropriate period will be when the number of actual residents in the Territory shall justify the formation of a constitution with a view to its admission as a State into the Union."[33]

In other words, Buchanan claimed to have held that under the Kansas-Nebraska Act a territory could not ban slavery until its citizens wrote a pre-statehood constitution, followed by that document's going into effect. Yet this position made his inaugural internally contradictory. On one hand he argued that the status of slavery in the territories was a "judicial question, which legitimately belongs to the Supreme Court of the United States." But then he asserted his belief that the issue had in fact been settled by Congress because "under the Nebraska-Kansas act the appropriate period will be when the number of actual residents in the Territory shall justify the formation of a constitution with a view to its admission as a State into the Union."[34]

If this latter position were correct, then the issue was certainly not a constitutional matter. Nor was it even a judicial question. At most it was an issue of statutory interpretation. The distinction here is technical but critical. Buchanan seemed to be arguing that Congress had the power—as demonstrated in the Kansas-Nebraska Act—to set the rules for when the settlers of a territory could ban slavery. If so, then the issue was not one for the Supreme Court to decide. The Court could interpret the Kansas-Nebraska Act, perhaps concluding that Buchanan was correct that only at statehood could the settlers ban slavery, or concluding that under the 1854 act settlers could ban slavery at any time. But either conclusion would be based on the statute, not on the Constitution, and if Congress did not like that interpretation it could pass another law—a second Kansas-Nebraska Act—clarifying when popular sovereignty could be implemented.

But Buchanan also implied that the question of whether the power to ban slavery in a territory rested with the territory's settlers or with Congress was a constitutional one—a "judicial question, which legitimately belongs to the Supreme Court of the United States." That was in fact the issue before the Court in Dred Scott. Thus, Buchanan endorsed the Dred

Scott decision before it was announced, asserted his own view of the meaning of the Kansas-Nebraska Act, and invited the Supreme Court to reach a constitutional, not a statutory, resolution of the issue.

The Judicial Answer

Two days after the inauguration, Chief Justice Taney issued his opinion in *Dred Scott*. Speaking for a divided Court, Taney produced a remarkable opinion, covering more than fifty pages. Emphatically labeled as "the Opinion of the Court," Taney's opinion reached three major conclusions affecting free African Americans, slavery in the existing states, and slavery in the federal territories. First, he held that Scott had no standing to sue in federal court because blacks could *never* be considered citizens of the United States, even if they were considered citizens in the states where they lived. This conclusion shocked many. Taney wrote:

> The question is simply this: Can a negro, whose ancestors were imported into this country, and sold as slaves, become a member of the political community formed and brought into existence by the Constitution of the United States, and as such become entitled to all the rights, and privileges, and immunities, guarantied by that instrument to the citizen? One of which rights is the privilege of suing in a court of the United States in the cases specified in the Constitution.[35]

Taney argued that free blacks—even those allowed to vote in the states where they lived—could never be citizens of the United States and have standing to sue in federal courts. Here Taney set up the novel concept of dual citizenship. He argued that being a citizen of a state did not necessarily make one a citizen of the United States. Taney claimed that

> In discussing this question, we must not confound the rights of citizenship which a State may confer within its own limits, and the rights of citizenship as a member of the Union. It does not by any means follow, because he has all the rights and privileges of a citizen of a State, that he must be a citizen of the United States. He may have all of the rights and privileges of the citizen of a State, and yet not be entitled to the rights and privileges of a citizen in any other State.[36]

Taney based this novel argument entirely on race. He offered a slanted and one-sided history of the founding period which ignored the fact that free blacks had voted in a number of states at the time of the ratification of the Constitution. Ignoring this history, the chief justice nevertheless argued that at the founding of the nation blacks were either all slaves or, if free, without any political or legal rights. He declared,

> The words "people of the United States" and "citizens" are synonymous terms, and mean the same thing. They both describe the political body who . . . form the sovereignty, and who hold the power and conduct the Government through their representatives. . . . The question before us is, whether the class of persons described in the plea in abatement [people of African ancestry] compose a portion of this people, and are constituent members of this sovereignty? We think they are not, and that they are not included, and were not intended to be included, under the word "citizens" in the Constitution, and can therefore claim none of the rights and privileges which the instrument provides and secures to citizens of the United States. On the contrary, they were at that time [1787] considered as a subordinate and inferior class of beings who had been subjugated by the dominant race, and, whether emancipated or not, yet remained subject to their authority, and had no rights or privileges but such as those who held the power and Government might choose to grant them.

According to Taney, blacks were "so far inferior, that they had no rights which the white man was bound to respect."[37] Thus he concluded that blacks could never be citizens of the United States, even if they were born in the country and considered to be citizens of the states in which they lived.

This conclusion should have ended the case, because if Scott could never be a citizen of the United States and could not sue in diversity, then his case could not be before a federal court. If there was no case before the Court, then the Court had nothing to decide. Critics of Taney's opinion, such as Abraham Lincoln, would argue that everything Taney said after he concluded that Dred Scott could not sue was *dicta* and had no legal meaning. The *Chicago Tribune* declared that Taney's statements on black citizenship were "inhuman dicta," while Horace Greeley's *New York Tribune*, the nation's leading Republican paper, thought that Taney's decision had no more validity than the opinions that might be expressed in any "Washington bar-room."[38]

Taney, however, did not stop with his discussion of black citizenship. He next concluded that Congress had no power to ban slavery from the federal territories. Taney contended that "an act of Congress which deprives a citizen of the United States of his liberty or property, merely because he came himself or brought his property into a particular Territory of the United States, and who had committed no offence against the laws, could hardly be dignified with the name of due process of law."[39] Taney argued that no law could be constitutional if it arbitrarily denied a person his property, merely for taking that property into a federal territory. This analysis led to his conclusion that the Missouri Compromise was unconstitutional. So too was the Kansas-Nebraska Act to the extent that it allowed settlers in the territories to ban slavery. This position dovetailed with Buchanan's "individual opinion that under the Nebraska-Kansas act the appropriate period will be when the number of actual residents in the Territory shall justify the formation of a constitution with a view to its admission as a State into the Union."[40] Buchanan, it seemed, had predicted the outcome of *Dred Scott* before it was announced.

Finally, in a strained and illogical series of arguments, Taney asserted that Congress essentially had no power to govern the federal territories and that all Congress could do was set up a rudimentary government and let the citizens of the territories then run their own affairs. This part of his opinion did not carry all the majority justices and was so confused and illogical that it is not clear if anyone took it seriously. Moreover, it was utterly unnecessary for Taney's other holdings, namely, that slaves were a constitutionally protected form of property and that Congress could not ban slavery from the territories.

The Whisperings and the Conspiracy

As they digested Taney's opinion, Republicans began to articulate that it was part of a conspiracy to force slavery on the territories and maybe even into the North. Buchanan's brief conversation with Taney, before he gave his inaugural address, now took on new meaning. Senator William Henry

Seward of New York would later claim that the "whisperings" between Taney and Buchanan were part of a conspiracy to hang "the millstone of slavery" on the western territories.[41]

In his "House Divided" speech, Abraham Lincoln presented an elaborate analysis of this conspiracy. Lincoln argued that the Compromise of 1850—guided through Congress by his senatorial opponent Stephen A. Douglas—set the groundwork for undermining the Missouri Compromise. Then came the Kansas-Nebraska Act, which Douglas authored and Franklin Pierce signed. This law repealed most of the Missouri Compromise by allowing slavery in the territories west and northwest of Missouri. Buchanan's inaugural address followed and endorsed the outcome in *Dred Scott* before the decision's announcement. Finally came the decision itself.

Lincoln saw a conspiracy in this narrative. He described how the Supreme Court delayed giving an opinion in the case until after the election of 1856 and after Buchanan's inauguration. But he noted how "the *incoming* President in his inaugural address, fervently exhorted the people to abide by the forthcoming decision, *whatever it might be*. Then, in a few days, came the decision."[42] Thus Lincoln asked:

> Why was the court decision held up . . . till *after* the Presidential election? Plainly enough *now*: the speaking out *then* would have damaged the "*perfectly free*" argument upon which the election was to be carried. Why the *outgoing* President's felicitation on the indorsement? Why the delay of a reargument? Why the incoming President's advance exhortation in favor of the decision? These things look like the cautious *patting* and *petting* of a spirited horse preparatory to mounting him, when it is dreaded that he may give the rider a fall. And why the hasty after-indorsement of the decision by the President and others?[43]

As Lincoln saw it, the plan all along had been to open all the territories to slavery. It was a giant conspiracy between Stephen A. Douglas, Franklin Pierce, James Buchanan, and Roger B. Taney. Lincoln observed:

> We cannot absolutely *know* that all these exact adaptations are the result of preconcert. But when we see a lot of framed timbers, different portions of which we know have been gotten out at different times and places and by different workmen—Stephen, Franklin, Roger and

James, for instance—and when we see these timbers joined together, and see they exactly make the frame of a house or a mill, all the tenons and mortices exactly fitting, and all the lengths and proportions of the different pieces exactly adapted to their respective places, and not a piece too many or too few—not omitting even scaffolding—or, if a single piece be lacking, we see the place in the frame exactly fitted and prepared yet to bring such a piece in—in *such* a case, we find it impossible not to believe that Stephen and Franklin and Roger and James all understood one another from the beginning, and all worked upon a common *plan* or *draft* drawn up before the first lick was struck.[44]

Lincoln gave this speech as part of his campaign to win the U.S. Senate seat then held by Douglas. Thus, Lincoln's candidacy was the political solution to the problem created by Taney, Buchanan, and Douglas. Lincoln predicted that if his party did not control the national government, Buchanan, Taney, Douglas, and others would conspire to make slavery a national institution. He argued that the logical conclusion of Taney's opinion was that "what Dred Scott's master might lawfully do with Dred Scott, in the free State of Illinois, every other master may lawfully do with any other *one*, or *one thousand* slaves, in Illinois, or in any other free State."[45] He predicted that the conspiracy between "Stephen and Franklin and Roger and James" would soon lead to "another Supreme Court decision, declaring that the Constitution of the United States does not permit a *state* to exclude slavery from its limits."[46] The next *Dred Scott* decision would allow slavery in the North:

Such a decision is all that slavery now lacks of being alike lawful in all the States.

Welcome, or unwelcome, such decision *is* probably coming, and will soon be upon us, unless the power of the present political dynasty shall be met and overthrown.

We shall *lie down* pleasantly dreaming that the people of *Missouri* are on the verge of making their State *free*, and we shall awake to the *reality* instead, that the *Supreme* Court has made *Illinois* a *slave* State.[47]

Thus Buchanan's "whispering" on the podium, preceding his inaugural address, followed by Taney's opinion, created the appearance of a great conspiracy to nationalize slavery, making it "alike lawful in all the States."[48]

Buchanan's Own Conspiracy

In hindsight it is clear that no conspiracy existed to nationalize slavery. Nor were Buchanan and Douglas working closely together from 1850 through 1857, when Lincoln's conspiracy would have taken place, although in that period both supported allowing slavery to spread to the Mexican territories and the older territories left over from the Louisiana Purchase. In 1857 they may have disagreed about when popular sovereignty could prevent slavery in a territory, but they both believed slavery could legitimately spread to the existing federal territories. By 1858 Douglas and Buchanan were effectively at war with each other within the Democratic Party. But from the perspective of Lincoln and other Republicans, Douglas and Buchanan were fellow travelers and fellow doughfaces supinely acting on behalf of slavery and the South.

It is also extremely unlikely that Chief Justice Taney told Buchanan what the Court would decide in *Dred Scott* moments before the president-elect gave his inaugural address. Their public-yet-private conversation was far too brief, and Buchanan had, after all, written his inaugural address well before he gave it—and before chatting with Taney. Moreover, as will be made clear below, Buchanan already knew what the decision would be, Chief Justice Taney also *knew* that Buchanan knew, and Buchanan knew that Chief Justice Taney knew. There was no need for the chief justice to tell Buchanan of the Court's decision in *Dred Scott*.

But if Lincoln and Seward were wrong in arguing that Douglas and perhaps Pierce had conspired with Buchanan and Taney, they were correct in thinking that *Dred Scott* tainted the Court's integrity and that the new president corruptly used insider knowledge to endorse the decision before it was announced. In the month before the inauguration, and before the Court announced the result in *Dred Scott*, president-elect Buchanan corresponded with two members of the Court—John Catron of Tennessee and Robert Grier of Pennsylvania—about the upcoming decision. This correspondence would be considered an unpardonable breach of judicial ethics today and was surely questionable then.[49] In these letters, members of the Court not only told Buchanan how the case would be decided but enlisted his support for lining up votes in favor of the majority opinion.

Two points emerge from this correspondence. First, Buchanan clearly knew exactly how the Court would decide the case before he gave his inaugural address. Thus, when he pledged he would "cheerfully submit" to the decision "whatever this may be," he was not taking any risks. Duplicitously, he was agreeing to support the unknown outcome in a case where in fact he already knew the outcome. Second, in a breach of political and judicial ethics, Buchanan lobbied one member of the Court (his Pennsylvania colleague Justice Grier) to support the majority opinion striking down the Missouri Compromise.

The context of this lobbying—what Lincoln would call this "conspiracy"—is complicated. After the Court first heard arguments in *Dred Scott* a majority of the justices initially decided to affirm the lower-court result based on the Court's earlier decision in *Stader v. Graham*. In *Strader* the court had held that the states were free to determine for themselves if an African American was a slave or not. Had the Court followed *Strader* it would have quickly disposed of the case in a short opinion written by Justice Samuel Nelson of New York. Had the Court followed through on this resolution of the issues, the case would have been dismissed for want of jurisdiction because as a slave under Missouri law, Dred Scott could not sue in federal court. Nelson in fact drafted such an opinion and ultimately delivered it as a concurrence. However, after the Court heard re-arguments in December 1856 the five Southern justices agreed to a more comprehensive opinion, which would strike down the Missouri Compromise. The majority seemed to be headed for an overarching Opinion of the Court written by Taney and joined by four other Southerners, Daniel (Virginia), Wayne (Georgia), Campbell (Alabama), and Catron (Tennessee), a concurrence written by Nelson (New York) joined by Grier (Pennsylvania), and dissents by McLean (Ohio) and Curtis (Massachusetts).[50]

The votes were there to bring about the result Taney and the other Southerners wanted: to strike down the Missouri Compromise and to determine that free blacks could never be citizens of the United States. But the outcome would have been clearly sectional: five Southern justices supporting this outcome; two Northerners concurring in the result but not in any other part of the decision; and two Northerners dissenting. Taney and the other Southerners—especially the moderate John Catron of Tennessee—wanted to have at least one Northerner join them. Thus began the correspondence between Buchanan and Catron.

On February 3 Buchanan wrote to Justice Catron, asking whether the Court would decide *Dred Scott* before the inauguration. On the sixth, Catron replied that he had no clear notion of when the decision would come.[51] On the tenth, however, he told Buchanan that the Court would decide the case in four days, intimating that it would hold the Missouri Compromise unconstitutional. Catron thought this information would help Buchanan "in preparing your inaugural."[52] However, on the nineteenth Carton wrote again, noting that it might not be decided until after the inauguration. He then asked Buchanan to intervene by lobbying Justice Grier to join the majority opinion. Catron asked the president-elect to "drop Grier a line, saying how necessary it is—& how good the opportunity is, to settle the agitation by an affirmative decision of the Supreme Court." Catron wanted Grier to join the majority in declaring that the Missouri Compromise was unconstitutional to the extent that it banned slavery in the territories.[53]

Buchanan quickly wrote Grier, who responded on February 23, indicating that he had shown Buchanan's letter to Justice Wayne and to Chief Justice Taney. Grier's response was just what Buchanan (and Catron) wanted: "We [Grier, Wayne, and Taney] fully appreciate and concur in your views as to the desirableness at this time of having an expression of the court on this troublesome question."[54] Then, "with their [Taney's and Wayne's] confidence," Grier told Buchanan exactly what the opinion would hold, and that he (Grier) would concur with Taney's opinion. Grier explicitly told Buchanan that six or seven of the justices would declare the Missouri Compromise unconstitutional.[55]

The correspondence violated the integrity of the Court, while Buchanan's admonition to follow the forthcoming decision proved to be deeply disingenuous. He was not supporting the rule of law or the Court's right to interpret the Constitution in the abstract. Rather, he had lobbied at least one member of the Court to vote a certain way and had used his insider's knowledge of the forthcoming decision for political advantage. It was contrary to the ethics of the Court and the executive branch, and in the end it undermined Buchanan's administration from the moment he took office.

This correspondence shows that Lincoln's instincts were right. Buchanan had conspired directly with two members of the Court, and indirectly (through Grier) with Taney and Justice Wayne. Lincoln, Seward, and other Republicans could not name all the conspirators, but the improper communications were there, and so was the plan, by at least four members for the Court and the president-elect, to make sure a decision came out as Buchanan and Taney wanted. The conspiracy was both less elaborate than Lincoln believed, because Douglas was clearly not involved, but also more elaborate, because it involved at least four justices. Buchanan had worked with, communicated with, and indeed conspired with members of the Supreme Court to lay the groundwork for *Dred Scott*.

In his inaugural Buchanan had declared that however the issue of slavery was resolved—and whether it was resolved by the territorial legislature or when the territory wrote a Constitution in anticipation of statehood—"it is the imperative and indispensable duty of the Government of the United States to secure to every resident inhabitant the free and independent expression of his opinion by his vote. This sacred right of each individual must be preserved. That being accomplished, nothing can be fairer than to leave the people of a Territory free from all foreign interference to decide their own destiny for themselves, subject only to the Constitution of the United States."[56] But as president, he soon abandoned this position by supporting the Lecompton Constitution, which, as Nicole Etcheson shows elsewhere in this volume, was obviously not the will of the people and clearly the result of electoral fraud. In the end Buchanan offered the North capitulation to the proslavery fire-eaters at the national level and slavery in Kansas. His administration made a mockery of both popular sovereignty and democracy.

Ironically, Buchanan was perhaps the nation's last hope to avoid a civil war.[57] He was a Northerner who won fourteen of fifteen slave states in his campaign. He might have used his lifetime of political skills and contacts to soften the debate over the territories, to compromise the issues by giving something to both sides. But he did not. Instead he pushed a proslavery agenda, purging his party of those, like Douglas, who disagreed with him.[58] Buchanan left no room for compromise, no room for the fact that the majority of all Americans favored freedom and opposed slavery. His "whispering" companion, Chief Justice Taney, did the same.

By 1860 the best option for a majority of Northerners was Lincoln and the Republican Party. As one slave state after another left the Union, Buchanan stood by, doing nothing and unwilling to contemplate any action to hold the Union together. Thus, a man who served his country for almost half a century watched the nation collapse, paralyzed by his own inability to see that his own actions and those of his friend, the chief justice, more than those of any other individuals, had brought the nation to the brink of civil war.

This all began with Buchanan's conspiring with members of the Court and his dishonest posture of neutrality in his inaugural address. He urged the nation to accept the outcome of a case, publicly pretending he did not know what the outcome would be, when in fact he knew exactly how the Court would decide the case. The costs of Buchanan's actions were monumental. His "whisperings" with Taney, his endorsement of *Dred Scott* before it was announced, and his almost blind support for radical proslavery positions undermined his administration and set the nation on its last, final road to Civil War. Buchanan may have believed that all these actions were necessary to placate the South—to keep the South in the Union—but in doing so he vastly underestimated Northern revulsion of his proslavery positions and Taney's grotesque and extremist positions in *Dred Scott*. Thus, his administration began with a series of lies in his inaugural address and ended with a nation careening toward Civil War.

Notes

1. James Buchanan, Inaugural Address, March 4, 1857, in James D. Richardson, *A Compilation of the Messages and Papers of the Presidents*, vol. 5 (New York: Bureau of National Literature, 1897), 2961, 2962. Buchanan was quoting the Kansas-Nebraska Act, An Act to Organize the Territories of Nebraska and Kansas, Act of May 30, 1854, Chap. XLIX, 10 *Stat.* 277.

2. Nicole Etcheson, *Bleeding Kansas: Contested Liberty in the Civil War Era* (Lawrence: University of Kansas Press, 2004), 1.

3. Buchanan, Inaugural Address, 2962.

4. Ibid.

5. Millard Fillmore, running on the anti-Catholic Know-Nothing ticket, carried Maryland. See generally, Paul Finkelman, *Millard Fillmore* (New York: Times Books, 2011).

6. Buchanan, Inaugural Address, 2962.

7. *Dred Scott v. Sandford*, 60 U.S. (19 How.) 393 (1857).

8. See generally, Paul Finkelman, *Slavery and the Founders: Race and Liberty in the Age of Jefferson*, 2nd ed. (Armonk, N.Y.: M. E. Sharpe, 2001), chap. 2.

9. An Act to Provide for the Government of the Territory Northwest of the River Ohio, Act of August 7, 1789, Chap. VIII, 1 *Stat.* 50.

10. An Act for the Government of the Territory of the United States south-west of the River Ohio, Act of May 26, 1790, Chap. XIV, 1 *Stat.* 123.

11. An Act to authorize the people of the Missouri Territory to form a Constitution and State government, Act of March 6, 1820, Chap. XXII, 3 *Stat.* 548; An Act Establishing the Territorial Government of Wisconsin (April 20, 1836), 5 *Stat.* 10.

12. The politics of the first Wilmot vote are described in David M. Potter, *The Impending Crisis, 1848–1861* (New York: Harper and Row, 1976), 20–23.

13. For a discussion of Fillmore's role in the compromise, see ibid. and Finkelman, *Millard Fillmore.*

14. In his Pulitzer Prize–winning history of this period, *The Impending Crisis*, David Potter argued that the territorial settlement "contributed nothing to the strength of the 'slave power'" (100). This analysis is simply wrong, both as a matter of history and, more significantly, as a matter of geography. The Compromise of 1850 did more than just take the Wilmot Proviso off the table, which in itself was a major victory for the South. It also substantially undercut the Missouri Compromise. Much of the Mexican Cession—the present-day states of Nevada, Utah, most of Colorado, and a bit of Wyoming—lay north of the Missouri Compromise line. See also Finkelman, *Millard Fillmore*; and Paul Finkelman, "The Appeasement of 1850," in *Congress and the Crisis of the 1850s*, ed. Paul Finkelman and Donald R. Kennon (Athens: Ohio University Press, 2012), 36–79.

15. This area was larger than the total area of nine of the fifteen slaves, and could easily have been subdivided into at least six new slave states.

16. A few proslavery fanatics, such as John C. Calhoun, argued that Congress had no power to ban slavery in the territories—only to allow it. However, they were in a minority, even in the South.

17. Buchanan, Inaugural Address, 2962.

18. *Marbury v. Madison*, 5 U.S. (1 Cr.) 137 (1803).

19. In the Fugitive Slave Law of 1793, Congress authorized state officials to hear fugitive slave cases and issue certificates of removal to those claiming fugitive slaves. In *Prigg v. Pennsylvania*, 41 U.S. (16 Pet.) 359 (1842), the Court said that Congress could not *compel* the states to participate in the enforcement of the 1793 law, but the Court did not find any part of the law to be unconstitutional, and in fact urged state judges to help enforce it. See Paul Finkelman, "Story Telling on the Supreme Court: *Prigg v. Pennsylvania* and Justice Story's Judicial Nationalism," in *Supreme Court Review, 1994*, ed. Dennis J. Hutchinson, David A. Strauss, and Geoffrey R. Stone (Chicago: University of Chicago Press, 1995), 247.

20. *American Insurance Company v. Canter* (also cited as *American Insurance Company v. 356 Bales of Cotton*), 26 U.S. (1 Pet.) 511 (1828), at 542.

21. Buchanan, Inaugural Address, 2962.

22. Andrew Jackson, "Veto Message," July 10, 1832, Richardson, *Compilation*, 3:1139.

23. 17 U.S. (4 Wheat.) 318 (1819).

24. Jackson's position was perfectly reasonable and constitutional. As president, Jackson was obligated to enforce a ruling by the Supreme Court if a case required him to do so, and if the Court struck down a law the president would have been barred from trying to enforce it. But before a bill is signed into law, the president is always free to use his independent judgment on whether to sign it.

25. The first was in *The Passenger Cases*, 7 How. (48 U.S.) 283 (1849), which involved the right of the states to regulate immigration.

26. For a short history of this case, see Paul Finkelman, *Dred Scott v. Sandford: A Brief History* (Boston: Bedford Books, 1995). For a comprehensive history of the case, see Don E. Fehrenbacher, *The Dred Scott Case: Its Significance in Law and Politics* (New York: Oxford University Press, 1978). For a series of essays placing the case in historical and modern context, see David T. Konig, Paul Finkelman, and Christopher Alan Bracey, eds., *The Dred Scott Case: Historical and Contemporary Perspectives on Race and Law* (Athens, Ohio: Ohio University Press, 2010).

27. *Scott v. Emerson*, 15 Mo. 576, 586 (1852).

28. His name is misspelled in the official report of the case as Sandford.

29. See Kenneth C. Kaufman, *Dred Scott's Advocate: A Biography of Roswell M. Field* (Columbia: University of Missouri Press, 1996).

30. *Dred Scott v. Sandford*, 60 U.S. (19 How.) 393 (1857) at 393–94.

31. I believe that Wells was arguably incorrect in this ruling, and that under the law of Missouri Dred Scott was not a "citizen" of that state, even if he was free. Paul Finkelman, "Was Dred Scott Correctly Decided? An 'Expert Report' for the Defendant," *Lewis and Clark Law Review* 12 (2008): 1219.

32. *Strader v. Graham*, 10 Howard (U.S.) 82 (1851).

33. Buchanan, Inaugural Address, 2962.

34. Ibid.

35. *Dred Scott* at 403.

36. Ibid. at 405.

37. Ibid. at 404–5.

38. Quoted in Finkelman, *Dred Scott v. Sandford*, 46, 145.

39. *Dred Scott* at 450.

40. Buchanan, Inaugural Address, 2962.

41. *Congressional Globe*, 35th Congress, 1st Session, 941, quoted in Fehrenbacher, *Dred Scott Case*, 473.

42. "A House Divided," speech at Springfield, Illinois, June 16, 1858, in *The Collected Works of Abraham Lincoln*, ed. Roy P. Basler (New Brunswick, N.J.: Rutgers University Press, 1953), 2:461 at 463.

43. Ibid. at 465.

44. Ibid. at 465–66.

45. Ibid. at 464–65.

46. Ibid. at 466–67.

47. Ibid.

48. Ibid.

49. Recent scholarship suggests that contact between justices and politicians, lawyers, litigants, and members of the public was not uncommon at this time. In 1846 Justice McLean discussed a pending case with Salmon P. Chase, who was an attorney for one of the parties. In 1856 Justice Nelson told a lawyer he had won his case before the Court announced its decision. While Grier and Catron were communicating with Buchanan about the *Dred Scott* decision, Justice Curtis was telling his correspondents about the Court's deliberations. Prominent advocates before the Court often socialized with members of the Court and discussed pending litigation. Buchanan's correspondence was unusual and perhaps extreme, but not wholly outside the realm of common practice at the time. On the other hand, his pre-endorsement of the outcome in his inaugural address stepped over the line of normal behavior. See Rachel A. Shelden, "The Taney Court and the Problem of Judicial Ethics in the Nineteenth Century" (unpublished paper presented at the American Society for Legal History Annual Meeting, Atlanta, November 2011). For more discussion of this see Paul Finkelman, "Coming to Terms with *Dred Scott*: A Response to David A. Farber," *Pepperdine Law Review* 39 (2012): 495.

50. Fehrenbacher, *Dred Scott Case*, 310–11.

51. Catron to Buchanan, February 6, 1857, in Philip G. Auchampaugh, "James Buchanan, the Court and the Dred Scott Case," *Tennessee Historical Magazine* 9 (January 1926): 234.

52. Catron to Buchanan, February 10, 1857, ibid., 235.

53. Catron to Buchanan, February 23, 1857, ibid., 236, and in John Bassett Moore, ed., *The Works of James Buchanan, Comprising His Speeches, State Papers, and Private Correspondence*, 12 vols. (Philadelphia: J. P. Lippincott, 1910), 10:105–13.

54. Grier to Buchanan, February 23, 1857, in Auchampaugh, "James Buchanan, the Court and the Dred Scott Case," 236, and in Moore, *Works of James Buchanan*, 10:106.

55. Grier to Buchanan, February 23, 1857, in Auchampaugh, "James Buchanan, the Court and the Dred Scott Case," 236, and in Moore, *Works of James Buchanan*, 10:106. See also Fehrenbacher, *Dred Scott Case*, 312, and Jean H. Baker, *James Buchanan* (New York: Times Books, 2004), 83–87.

56. Buchanan, Inaugural Address, 2962.

57. Baker, *James Buchanan*, 1–2.

58. In 1858 Buchanan tried to bring Kansas into the Union as a slave state under the Lecompton Constitution, which had been written by an undemocratically elected convention and ratified in a patently fraudulent election. Stephen A. Douglas, who always claimed he did not care if slavery was voted "up or down," nevertheless opposed Kansas statehood under Lecompton, because this was clearly an undemocratic process. As a result, Buchanan had Douglas stripped of his position as chairman of the Senate Committee on the Territories and then tried to prevent his reelection to the Senate in 1858.

2

Prelude to Armageddon

James Buchanan, Brigham Young,
and a President's Initiation to Bloodshed

WILLIAM P. MACKINNON

Some of us would yet see "the red stuff run."

Mormon Bishop and Militia Brigadier General Aaron Johnson,
March 1857, in Salt Lake City *Valley Tan,* April 19, 1859

As James Buchanan became president on March 4, 1857, his major priorities were a mixture of the crucial and the prosaic: preserving the Union, curbing civil disorders in Kansas, advancing an expansionist foreign policy, completing his cabinet appointments, dispensing the federal patronage, and recovering from the gastrointestinal ravages of the "National Hotel disease" that had killed his secretary-nephew. Within two weeks a wholly different issue had unexpectedly catapulted to the top of Buchanan's agenda and had assumed crisis proportions: "the Mormon problem," or what to do about Brigham Young and the gigantic U.S. territory that he had governed controversially since 1847.

That Utah was not a front-rank national issue in early March is reflected in the fact that Buchanan's inaugural address made no mention of the territory, its governor, Mormonism, or polygamy. For that matter, the valedictory letter that outgoing president Franklin Pierce had privately read to his cabinet earlier that day to reprise their challenges and accomplishments was also silent on these subjects.[1]

By the end of March 1857 the new administration had made but not announced two fateful decisions about Utah: to supersede Young as governor and to provide his as-yet-undesignated successor with a substantial but

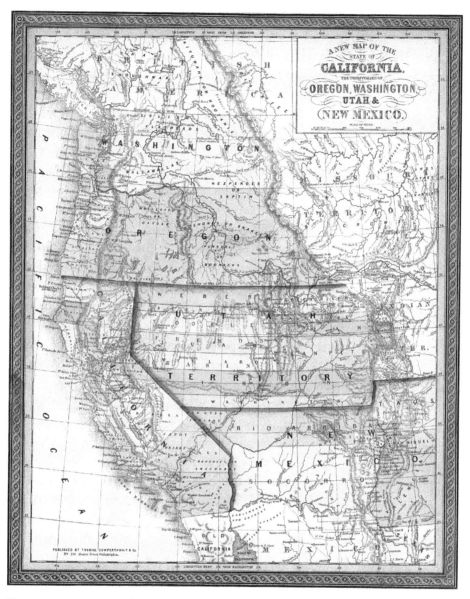

Figure 2.1. *A New Map of the State of California, the Territories of Oregon, Washington, Utah, and New Mexico* (Philadelphia: Thomas, Cowperthwait & Co., 1853). Carved from the Mexican Session in 1850, Utah was originally seven hundred miles wide and stretched from the crest of the Rocky Mountains to California. Partly as punishment for the Utah War, Congress reduced it six times during the 1860s to create or enlarge Nevada, Colorado, Wyoming, and Nebraska.

undefined military escort to restore federal authority. Within months the Utah crisis escalated into an armed confrontation that became the country's most extensive and expensive military undertaking during the period between the Mexican and Civil Wars—one that ultimately pitted the Utah territorial militia (Nauvoo Legion) against almost one-third of the U.S. Army.

Exploration of how this crisis developed and exploded into the Utah War of 1857–58 is undergoing a renaissance—one stimulated by the recent sesquicentennial commemoration of the conflict, the publication of long-simmering scholarly work by a phalanx of highly motivated historians, and a sea change in public access to the Mormon Church's indispensable archives (more extensive than even during the temporary openness stimulated by church historian Leonard J. Arrington in the 1970s).[2] Still neglected, though, is an assessment of how James Buchanan handled this unexpected intrusion into the opening months of his presidency and that subject's crucial linkage to the subject that has dogged his legacy since 1861: Buchanan's performance in the later part of his administration, especially in dealing with Southern secession.

The purpose of this essay is to probe the effectiveness of Buchanan's Utah War performance. It does so as a reconnaissance intended to stimulate a more complete assessment yet to come. Because of the extent to which Buchanan's presidential reputation has suffered from the twin scourges of vilification and neglect, this essay focuses on those aspects of Buchanan's handling of the Mormon problem that went positively, as well as on the even longer list of those crucial Utah issues before which his presidential skills-in-formation faltered. Among the latter are such major matters as the quality of his key Utah War appointments, intelligence gathering, effectiveness in using senior military advisers, communications style, ability to manage the war's financing in the face of a deep economic recession, and constancy of purpose.

Background: The Mormon Problem Develops

Because the Utah War is still understood so unevenly, at least minimal background on the conflict's origins is essential to assessing how well Buchanan handled this earliest aspect of his administration.[3]

The Utah War was the armed confrontation over power and authority between the civil-religious leadership of Utah Territory led by Governor Brigham Young and James Buchanan's administration. The war did not well up spontaneously because of a single critical incident. Instead, it was a confrontation nearly ten years in the making with Mormon-federal relations, already poor in Missouri and Illinois before the 1847 Mormon arrival in the Salt Lake Valley, steadily deteriorating immediately thereafter.

By Buchanan's inauguration on March 4, 1857, virtually every area of contact between the territorial and federal governments had become a test of wills. Tensions rose over such issues as the selection and performance of mail contractors for the routes connecting the Pacific Coast and Missouri River to the Salt Lake Valley; relations with and allegiances of Utah's Indian tribes; matters of landownership and the accuracy of federal surveys; financial stewardship of congressional appropriations for the territory; the administration of Utah's federal courts and criminal justice system; and perhaps most important, the background, competence, and behavior of appointees to federal office in Utah. At one point in the Utah War, Brigham Young's editorial "organ" complained that six of Buchanan's seven cabinet departments were engaged in persecuting the Latter-day Saints and then, upon reflection, added the missing Navy Department to the list after realizing that a floating military reconnaissance of southern Utah was then under way through an ascent of the Colorado River from the Gulf of California.[4]

In addition to these departmental pinch points, there were other highly public controversies over such incidents as the 1852 announcement of the Mormon principle of plural marriage (polygamy), a common practice but one aggressively denied by church leaders since the 1830s; the uneven treatment of non-Mormon emigrants passing through Utah to the Pacific Coast (welcoming by some accounts, predatory by others); responsibility for the massacre of the U.S. Army's Gunnison Expedition in 1853; a series of other uninvestigated, unprosecuted murders; repeated congressional rejection of petitions to replace Utah Territory with a Mormon State of Deseret; and a related controversy over whether Brigham Young was seeking Mormon independence outside the Union, an issue that would resonate with what Buchanan was to face with the South during the secession crisis of 1860–61. At the heart of these clashes was the conflict implicit in

Figure 2.2. Utah territorial governor Brigham Young. Courtesy of LDS Church History Library, Salt Lake City.

two radically different philosophies of governance: Brigham Young's vision of Utah as a millennially focused theocracy operating under his prophetic, autocratic leadership; and the U.S. government's view of Utah as just another territory, intended to function under republican principles as a ward of Congress through a federally sworn governor, appointed by the president.[5]

In the summer of 1856 these controversies entered the national presidential contest in an unexpected way, with the new Republican Party's adoption of a campaign platform plank calling for the eradication of polygamy and slavery, "the twin relics of barbarism," from the federal territories. It was an association that pleased neither the South nor Mormon Utah. The plank also intentionally created a vexing dilemma for the Democratic Party's standard-bearer, Buchanan, which required him to thread his way through the electoral minefield sown by fellow Democrat Stephen A. Douglas's intellectual hobbyhorse—the doctrine of popular sovereignty, by which territories were to choose their own "peculiar institutions." Notwithstanding today's view of the Republicans' "twin relics" plank as provocative and sensational, anti-Mormonism did not dominate the election of 1856. It was a platform plank drafted to respond less to a national political groundswell than to the idiosyncratic whim of a lone California delegate who conceived the phrasing as he strolled to the Republicans' Philadelphia convention hall one summer morning. The party's presidential candidate, John C. Frémont, did not campaign on the "twin relics" slogan; to the contrary, he felt indebted to the Utah Mormons who had rescued his imperiled exploring expedition during the winter of 1852–53.[6]

The presidential contest was settled in Buchanan's favor on November 4, 1856, but what came to be called "the Mormon problem" remained unresolved. There were ominous straws in the wind. President-elect Buchanan's predecessor, Pierce, had refused to reappoint Young when his four-year gubernatorial term expired in 1854, a decision that retained him in office only through the technicality of a day-by-day continuance. This arrangement would terminate automatically once a new appointee was designated, confirmed, and sworn. In September 1855, livid over the social misconduct in Salt Lake City of the U.S. Army's recently departed Steptoe Expedition, Young fumed to two Europeans visiting Salt Lake City that "the conduct of the American officers, [was] so abominable, that were they to return to the Salt Lake, war would immediately be declared against them, or if fresh troops were to come, the inhabitants would hold no communication with them, either in the way of social intercourse or trade."[7] Two months before Buchanan's inauguration, Mormon-federal relations had deteriorated to the point that Brigadier General Peter W. Conover of the Nauvoo Legion wrote a Mormon friend, who was a general of the California state militia. With a request emblematic of both tensions and war plans afoot, Conover asked that he

> bring or send as much [gun] powder as you can get hold of, for we shall need it by the time we can get it here. I want you to bring me 1000 lbs for my Brigade. . . . [I]f you could send a Keg by the mail every time they come it would be a good plan by that means we could be supplied at Uncle Sams expense. . . . [W]e are expecting some U.S. troops in here next summer, but we do not anticipate as much trouble from them as we do from the apostates that are here in our midst but from all appearances we will need powder and [percussion] caps

before long and if you cannot send it before you come be sure to bring it with you.[8]

Upon hearing of Buchanan's election, Young had tried to view the pending change optimistically. On January 31, 1857, he wrote to his closest non-Mormon friend in Philadelphia, "We are satisfied with appointment of Buchanan as future President, we believe he will be [a] friend to the good, that [President] Fillmore was our friend, but Buchanan will not be a whit behind."[9] But by Inauguration Day Young's hopes had faded, and he wrote to his mission president in Liverpool in a vein similar to General Conover's to inquire about potential British recruits for the Nauvoo Legion and to report on the status of his continuing quest for arms and munitions: "Can you inform us, what has become of the [Latter-day] Saints who were engaged as soldiers in the Crimean War? We have 8000 lbs [of ballistic] lead on the way from [our] Los Vegas [New Mexico] mines."[10]

The catalyst igniting this volatile, long-smoldering mix of damaged relationships and provocative behaviors was not only their cumulative weight but the receipt by cabinet officers from March 17 to March 20 of five documents portraying Utah as a violent, out-of-control place led by a disloyal, unaccountable governor. The language of one document, a January 6, 1857, memorial sent by Utah's legislative assembly to President-elect Buchanan, was couched in a cheeky, swaggering tone that characterized the political patronage system—Buchanan's preoccupation during his first two months in office—as "throwing a bone to satisfy this hungry hound and a crumb to that yelping cur"; unsatisfactory non-Mormon appointees to federal offices in Utah "shall not live in our midst . . . they must and shall leave this Territory," and their appointment constituted "fastening upon our necks the yoke of tyranny and oppression."[11] The phrasing of this memorial later prompted Secretary of the Interior Jacob Thompson to inform Utah's territorial delegate in Congress, Dr. John M. Bernhisel, that it was "a declaration of war." Fearful that uncontrolled political consequences, if not violence, might follow any public awareness of such volatile material, the Buchanan administration suppressed these documents rather than share them with Congress. Buchanan continued to do so even after a February 6, 1858, House resolution called for the disclosure of all documents bearing on the extent to which Utah was in a state of "rebellion." Secretary

Thompson instructed Bernhisel that neither he nor Young should publish the offending memorial if they wished to avoid major trouble.

By the end of March 1857 this chain of events had destroyed any remaining vestiges of political support in the cabinet for retaining Brigham Young, and there was an overarching alarm over a perceived loss of federal authority in Utah Territory. By the month's end Buchanan had launched the search for a new governor in tandem with the start of planning for his military escort. On April 15 all of Utah's federal appointees except Young and two Indian agents fled the territory for their lives—the second such mass exodus of Washington appointees in less than six years, one that Young dubbed "emetic." On May 28, Winfield Scott, the army's general in chief, announced the long-rumored creation of a twenty-five-hundred-man Utah Expedition to be drawn from infantry, artillery, ordnance, and dragoon units in New York, Florida, Minnesota, and Kansas. The army's orders for the first time described Utah as in a state of "rebellion." The war was on.[12]

Superseding Young: The Courage to Act as Pierce Had Not

Although few historians have bothered to analyze the matter, one aspect of Buchanan's handling of the Mormon problem for which he deserves credit was his most fundamental decision—to supersede Brigham Young as Utah's governor. Perhaps the best way to illustrate the courage with which Buchanan approached this challenge is to examine briefly the appalling way in which his predecessor had botched and then ignored the matter of Young's gubernatorial tenure.

In March 1853, realizing that his term would expire in a year, Young had sent his greetings to newly inaugurated Franklin Pierce along with the unsubtle suggestion that the president should reappoint him as governor. Young argued that Mormons were the most appropriate candidates for Utah's federal offices because they were qualified and available. Furthermore, only Latter-day Saints understood and could serve effectively for the long term in the territory's isolated, highly expensive, and culturally unusual environment. Young also shared with Pierce his belief that any non-Mormon easterner who accepted federal office in Utah was probably ipso facto dishonest if not incompetent.[13] Unstated in Young's letter—but shared by him publicly in his Sunday discourses—was his belief that

President Fillmore had first appointed him in 1850 as a matter of divine providence, and that he was unwilling to yield the gubernatorial chair unless relieved by the same authority. Five weeks after thus advising President Pierce on Utah's leadership, Young—still a federally sworn territorial governor—addressed a gathering of several thousand Latter-day Saints to dispense the inflammatory, irresponsible advice that in Utah thieves were to be dealt with through summary execution rather than through the legal formalities of arrest and trial.[14]

Pierce wrestled with his Brigham Young problem for more than a year. Deeply concerned by the cumulative weight of the disturbing controversies swirling around Young, by the fall of 1854 Pierce seriously considered replacing him, although success in identifying a suitable successor eluded the president. In November 1854 Pierce realized that the means for resolving his Young dilemma was serendipitously already on the scene in Salt Lake City. The candidate was Brevet Lieutenant Colonel Edward Jenner Steptoe, commander of an army battalion wintering over in Utah on its way to California. Steptoe, a comrade-in-arms from the Mexican War, had defended Pierce's reputation at a crucial point during his 1852 presidential campaign. In mid-December, without consulting Steptoe, the president sent his nomination to the Senate, which immediately confirmed Steptoe and sent his commission to Salt Lake City. There, Colonel Steptoe quietly agonized for months over two dilemmas: whether to resign from the army to accept the governorship, and whether as a non-Mormon he would be able to govern a population of Latter-day Saints. In the spring of 1855— still undecided—Steptoe and his troops left Utah for the Pacific Coast, where he eventually decided *not* to take the oath of office, a non-action that had the practical effect of continuing Young as governor.[15]

Although Pierce and others had viewed Steptoe as sympathetic to the Mormons, the colonel wrote to the army's adjutant general upon leaving Salt Lake City, "I am highly gratified at being able so early to leave this city[,] for the growing ill-feeling of the inhabitants towards the troops was fully reciprocated by the latter—gave me constant uneasiness. A [Christmas day] street riot some 4 mo[nths] ago in which more than 100 men on each side were engaged. I have not felt assured of quiet for a single moment."[16] Embarrassed and unwilling to risk further political capital by sending another nomination for Utah to the Senate, Pierce let the matter lay for resolution by his successor.[17]

Resolve it Buchanan did, although he had not foreseen the Mormon problem as a priority for his administration. In Utah there were doubters in the small community of non-Mormons about Buchanan's appetite for dealing with such a contentious issue. The day after the president took office, a pseudonymous *New-York Daily Times* correspondent wrote from Salt Lake City:

> Yesterday, as we suppose, James Buchanan was inaugurated President of the United States, and entered upon the discharge of his high functions as chief magistrate of the Nation. To-day, a trembling band of American citizens, here in this remote quarter of American dominion, vibrates anxiously between hope and distrust as we wonder whether Utah will be deemed by him to be included in the country wherein he has sworn to maintain the constitution and the laws—whether he will practically regard our peace, prosperity and lives worth an effort for their preservation against lawless violence. Looking back upon the history of the past seven years, and the course of the national Administration during that time, what wonder that we have little confidence in the future.[18]

In assessing Buchanan's earliest confrontation with the specter of disunion, a number of issues bearing on his presidential performance remain subject to debate. For example, how qualified and effective was Alfred Cumming, Buchanan's choice as Brigham Young's successor? Was a large military escort needed? How competent were the Buchanan-appointed leaders of the State and War Departments to deal with such a long-standing and geographically distant challenge? How effectively did communications and the best military advice available flow to the White House, and with what effect? The balance of this essay explores these issues, often critically. Nonetheless, it is evident that Buchanan's decision to supersede Brigham Young was considered carefully and was quite bold, certainly relative to Pierce's fecklessness, with dramatic, long-term consequences. Buchanan's shift in the political leadership of Utah was a warranted sea change, an action that altered forever the balance of power and authority in the territory and the character of Mormon-federal relations.

That Buchanan was able to make such a change—and to do so while holding at bay those forces in American society straining to turn the Utah War into a religious or anti-polygamy crusade against a reviled Mormon people—should be to his credit. Few commentators—professional historians, members of Congress, and the laity—have seen it this way. There have been two interrelated factors at work undercutting any interpretation of Buchanan's actions in superseding Young as necessary or justified: ridicule and revulsion.

First came a largely successful Mormon image campaign—begun during the Civil War—to portray the entire Utah War as a heavy-handed blunder brought on by ineptness as well as by plotting among proto-Confederates in Buchanan's cabinet actively planning disunion as early as 1857. Implicit in the depiction of the Utah War as "Buchanan's blunder"—a label still used by Mormon commentators—was the notion that the entire confrontation, including the removal of Young as governor, was unnecessary. Here Buchanan was cast in the role of a sort of misguided, if not malevolent, Sheriff of Nottingham playing to Brigham Young viewed as a nimble, misunderstood Robin Hood.[19]

Accompanying the development of this campaign was a widespread public revulsion over the Civil War's carnage. This corrosive force largely destroyed Buchanan's reputation and with it the willingness of most commentators to assess his presidential performance in balanced fashion. In the process, awareness that there had even been a Utah War at the beginning of his administration receded into obscurity. No memorial would be erected to Buchanan in Washington until Herbert Hoover's administration; the Commonwealth of Pennsylvania is still unwilling to see Buchanan honored in the Capitol's Hall of Statuary as one of its most prominent native sons, as Utah has done for Brigham Young.[20] The impact of these twin forces of ridicule and revulsion over the past 150 years has been the degradation of Buchanan's image into a highly unattractive blend of cartoonish bumbler on barely understood Utah matters and pro-Southern chief executive presiding over a national slide into the bloodbath of disunion.

On December 8, 1857, Buchanan's first and virtually only public utterance about the Utah War defended his decision of the previous spring on grounds that "This is the first rebellion which has existed in our Territories; and humanity itself requires that we should put it down in such a manner that it shall be the last." Secretary of War John B. Floyd went further, noting Utah's key location astride the nation's transcontinental emigration routes to the Pacific Coast and Brigham Young's unacceptable attempt to close this flow with his September 15, 1857, proclamation of martial law.[21] Buchanan's commissioner of Indian Affairs, James W. Denver, had already entered the fray in November 1857 with a scathing note to Young written in blunt language of the sort he may not have heard in decades:

> In addition to this [alleged tampering with the allegiances of Utah's tribes], you have been denouncing this government and threatening an armed resistance to the authorities sent out by the president. Indeed, unless you and your coadjutors are most grossly misrepresented, and your language misquoted, the appearance of those authorities among you is all that is necessary to prompt you to an overt act of treason.... But, when, convinced of the existence of such facts, the chief executive has no alternative left but to crush out rebellion; and for this purpose all the powers of the government are placed under his control.[22]

A month later, when a disillusioned, Buchanan-betrayed Governor Robert J. Walker resigned in Kansas, the president sent Denver west as his successor. In selecting Denver for gubernatorial responsibilities, he may have chosen the right man but the wrong territory.[23]

Flawed Appointments: Nothing as Expensive as Bad Leadership

If Buchanan's decision to supersede Young was an appropriate, even necessary, one, there is little in the quality of his subsequent actions that enhances his reputation. Among the most significant aspects of Buchanan's decision making about the Utah War warranting criticism are his selections for the confrontation's senior civilian and uniformed leaders. In this respect, Buchanan's travails somewhat resemble the early ones of Abraham Lincoln. But, unlike Lincoln, Buchanan showed little apparent capacity to recognize and therefore learn from his mistakes so that he might take corrective action.

In some respects, Buchanan's problems started with the gaps in his own background. Except for a few days spent along the perimeter of Baltimore during the War of 1812 with a pick-up group of young gentlemen-adventurers, Old Buck had no military experience. It is conceivable that he may have learned something about warfare as secretary of state in Polk's Mexican War cabinet, but Buchanan lacked the practical leadership lessons that so many of his predecessors and successors acquired from service in uniform.

Compounding this lack of pertinent experience was the fact that the two cabinet officers on whom Buchanan should have been able to lean mightily with respect to territorial and military matters, Secretary of State Lewis Cass and Secretary of War Floyd, were distinctly ill-suited for their assignments. Cass's advanced age, ill health, and poor standing in Buchanan's eyes rendered nugatory his earlier background as a successful general and territorial governor. This circumstance prompted Buchanan the micromanager to ignore Cass from the beginning with the informal but clear understanding that the president would serve as his own secretary of state. That Buchanan had never traveled west of Pittsburgh no doubt further handicapped his grasp of the territorial aspects of the State Department's, if not the president's, responsibilities.[24]

Floyd was substantially younger than Cass, and he entered the cabinet in good standing, albeit with a back problem that sometimes kept him from the War Department for weeks. By background an attorney and unsuccessful planter-speculator, Floyd lacked administrative skills. He had no military experience other than brief responsibility for Virginia's militia as a one-term governor. From his first day as secretary, Floyd bore responsibility for the nation's most complex and only continental organization—one engaged in combat operations from Florida to the Pacific Northwest. His was a military-management portfolio demanding at least two prerequisites that he lacked: executive skill and, in the view of some critics, a rigorous sense of probity. The looseness of Floyd's administrative style was such that within months of taking office he had provoked mini-uproars and congressional investigations over the army's construction of the Washington Aqueduct, renovation of the Capitol, sale of Fort Snelling, Minnesota Territory, and the acquisition of land on which to construct Fort Totten, New York. By contrast, Buchanan refused to secure a West Point appointment for his own nephew and reprimanded his niece-hostess when he perceived that she had abused use of a government revenue cutter.[25]

Floyd and Cass were two of Buchanan's earliest, most unfortunate cabinet selections. With the advent of the Utah War, such flawed leaders among Buchanan's most senior civilian counselors constituted the equivalent of a self-inflicted wound in terms of missing advice, bad counsel, the worries of scandals-in-formation, and additional strain on an ailing, aging president.

Among the army's officer corps, the problem of inadequate leadership started at the top with Brevet Lieutenant General Winfield Scott, the general in chief. At age seventy, weighing over three hundred pounds, unable to mount a horse, and at times barely able to walk, Scott was valorous, strategic, but notoriously prickly and vain. In the late 1840s he had unilaterally moved the army's headquarters from Washington to New York in a fit of pique following the presidential election of his Mexican War rival, Zachary Taylor. There his small entourage shuttled on a seasonal basis between two rented rooms in lower Manhattan and Scott's beloved West Point. Throughout the Pierce administration Scott conducted a running correspondence with Secretary of War Jefferson Davis so corrosive in its language that when published at Congress's insistence the letters created a near-scandal.[26]

With Davis's replacement by Floyd in March 1857, Scott went through the motions of offering to move his headquarters back to Washington. Floyd chose not to seize the opportunity, preferring instead to deal with Scott long-distance by mail or by episodically summoning him to the War Department for brief face-to-face meetings. Floyd intended to provide military advice to Buchanan with only minimal involvement by Scott. That Buchanan chose to retain Scott as general in chief under these circumstances and to tolerate Floyd's unwillingness to access Scott's expertise only served to aggravate the other limitations with which Buchanan approached military problems.[27]

The retention and toleration of Scott paled as a flawed presidential decision in comparison to Buchanan's initial choice to command the Utah Expedition, Brevet Brigadier General William S. Harney, commander of the swaggering Second U.S. Dragoons. By its nature the Utah assignment required a leader with not only military competence but maturity, tact, and consummate good judgment. Instead, Buchanan selected a highly experienced, brave officer with a track record for volatility, brutality, and impulsiveness that by the time of the Utah War had prompted the army to court-martial him four times, with a civilian court trying (and acquitting) him a fifth time for bludgeoning to death a defenseless female slave. It was emblematic that one Sioux band dubbed Harney "Mad Bear" while whites

Figure 2.3. Brevet Brigadier General Albert Sidney Johnston. Principal commander of the Utah Expedition, which ultimately involved nearly one-third of the army. He is uniformed here in the rank to which the Buchanan administration promoted him in 1858. Engraved etching (New York: Charles Barmore, 1896) from a pen-and-ink sketch by artist Jacques Reich. Probably based on a contemporary photograph. Courtesy of Yale Collection of Western Americana, Beinecke Library.

nicknamed him "Squaw Killer." As news of both Harney's Utah appointment and his dramatic but unauthorized boasts about summary execution for any captured Mormon leaders drifted west through Brigham Young's effective intelligence network, Mormon determination to prevent federal entrance into the Salt Lake Valley rose commensurately and needlessly. Although impossible to quantify, Harney's selection galvanized Mormon resistance as effectively as Young's addition of several Nauvoo Legion regiments.[28]

When the military demands of Kansas's Governor Walker made Harney's retention at Fort Leavenworth essential, Colonel Albert Sidney Johnston of the Second Cavalry, then in Texas, superseded Harney in late August 1857. With this choice Buchanan made a first-rate selection for the Utah Expedition's command, but as the war unfolded the president allowed Floyd and Scott to jeopardize Johnston's morale and effectiveness. Three times in January, April, and May 1858 they subordinated Johnston to a mixed bag of senior but not necessarily more competent officers—Brevet Major General John E. Wool, Brevet Major General Persifor F. Smith, and (again) Harney. Johnston's understandable pleas for relief from command were denied repeatedly until he was reassigned from Utah to California on March 1, 1860.[29]

In terms of the Utah War problem, Buchanan's most significant leadership appointment—a devastating one—was that of Alfred Cumming to succeed Young. To say that he was the president's last choice, perhaps the final candidate among a group of as many as ten men who declined Buchanan's offer, speaks volumes about Cumming's suitability for the role. For Kansas, Buchanan had immediately sought out and recruited Robert J. Walker, a successful Mississippi planter with Pennsylvania origins whom he knew well as Polk's secretary of the treasury. Cumming, however, was an obscure figure, then serving as Indian Affairs superintendent of the Upper Missouri agency based in St. Louis after mixed and undistinguished earlier experiences as mayor of Augusta, Georgia, and sutler to a Mexican War regiment. Had Buchanan scrutinized Cumming's recent record as an Indian Affairs superintendent, what should have surfaced as a cautionary note would have been his severe 1855 conflict with Washington Territory's strong-willed governor, Isaac I. Stevens. This clash was a warning sign ignored during the summer of 1857 with a price to be paid once Cumming and Albert Sidney Johnston came together and served at close quarters at Fort Bridger in late November.[30]

Cumming and Johnston, his designated protector, were soon at sword's point, a disastrous circumstance for any government attempting to forcibly restore its authority long-distance in the midst of a wilderness. Weighing more than four hundred pounds and probably alcoholic, Cumming was physically ill-suited for the task he faced during the Utah War.[31] When Young later succeeded in playing on this Cumming-Johnston enmity to co-opt a vulnerable Cumming, and after Cumming, in turn, helped gull Buchanan into believing, by the summer of 1858, that Young was at heart a cooperative leader, the stage was set for decades of counterproductive intrigue and plotting in Utah. Here was a divisiveness in federal authority that undercut what the president had set out to accomplish in March 1857.

Acting without Understanding: Buchanan's Avoidance of Military Intelligence and Advice

As inexperienced or flawed as Buchanan's principal civilian and military advisers were, the new president made poor use of them. At times he seemed to avoid their counsel, while at other important junctures he simply overruled them, imposing his poorly informed political judgment in place of their professional military assessments.

Having properly decided to supersede Brigham Young and set out to recruit his successor, the president immediately moved by the end of March to the debatable assumption that the new governor would need a very substantial army escort. Was such a force necessary or even practical in the summer of 1857? In July 1857, when General Harney dispatched quartermaster Captain Stewart Van Vliet to Salt Lake City in an attempt to supply the Utah Expedition, Van Vliet traveled across the plains and into the Rockies with a thirty-man army escort, but finished the last leg of the twelve-hundred-mile trip alone. When Colonel Johnston left Fort Leavenworth in early September in a forced march to catch up with his new command, he traveled with a guard of about forty dragoons. Why an as-yet-undesignated governor would require a brigade-strength expeditionary force drawn from five regiments does not seem to have been carefully discussed within the cabinet.

Also apparently unexamined was the feasibility of an alternate way to install Young's gubernatorial successor. For example, Buchanan could have sent this officer west accompanied by a smaller but highly symbolic detachment sufficiently large to deter Indian attack and, if necessary, serve as a posse comitatus, but not of a size to reawaken Mormon fears of persecution. In thinking about such an alternative, the powerful, informal slogan of the Texas Rangers comes to mind ("One Riot, One Ranger"), as does the lean operational model by which the Royal Canadian Mounted Police would later function to the north. Such an approach would, of course, have placed tremendous pressure on the quality of the new governor's judgment and diplomatic skills. Notwithstanding Winfield Scott's quirks and foibles, a civilian of his caliber would have commanded the requisite respect in Salt Lake City, even from an irascible Young. Two years later Buchanan indeed used "Old Fuss 'n' Feathers" for precisely such a purpose when he sent Scott—accompanied by a single aide—to the Pacific Northwest by sea to relieve Harney of command in Oregon and negotiate with the Royal Navy over his belligerent behavior in an 1859 border confrontation with Great Britain. Whether Alfred Cumming had the experience, inner resources, and presence to execute such an approach in Utah is highly questionable, again evoking the specter of his appointment as not only a presidentially self-inflicted wound but also the stuff from which self-fulfilling prophecies of failure arise.[32]

If Buchanan did not spend his first month in office encouraging spirited cabinet debate over the appropriate role of the army in addressing the Mormon problem, April and May were spent in discussing matters of size—whether the new governor's escort should be a single regiment of about a thousand men or a multi-regiment force of brigade strength. At this point Scott grew alarmed because he viewed the rumored size of the contemplated expedition as inadequate and the timing for its launch perilously late by two months for campaigning in the deteriorating weather of the West. Accordingly, on May 26, 1857, Scott wrote a remarkable memorandum in New York to Floyd arguing that a campaign in Utah would be ill-fated unless postponed until the spring of 1858. He pleaded that if there must be a military move on Utah during 1857, that he would need about four thousand men to prosecute it, but acknowledged that he could still campaign with as few as twenty-five hundred troops.[33]

Although by May 27 Scott had traveled to Washington and probably hand-delivered this paper to the War Department, Floyd never acknowledged receiving it and Buchanan subsequently commented that he had not seen the memo.[34] Interestingly, General Harney, Scott's arch-enemy, would independently echo these same recommendations a few weeks later.[35] Notwithstanding his counsel to Floyd for delay, on May 28 Scott announced to the army's staff departments that there was to be a twenty-five-hundred-man Utah Expedition and tasked them with its immediate support, although he was unable to explain this force's mission. What happened to unsettle Scott's world and overrule his last-minute advice of May 26 is one of the intriguing mysteries surrounding the Utah War's origins.

In his 1864 memoirs General Scott further clouded the issue—of why and how the Buchanan cabinet decided to launch the Utah Expedition—by introducing Secretary of War Floyd's 1857 behavior. Scott did so in the midst of the Civil War, with his remarks constituting an episode in a public joust with former president Buchanan over their roles in the secession crisis of 1860–61, and occurring after Floyd had become a Confederate brigadier general. With his 1864 comments, Scott added fuel to a Utah War conspiracy theory first advanced by Brigham Young in 1857. This view held that at the heart of the Utah Expedition was the Buchanan administration's corrupt desire to enrich commercial friends such as the western freighting firm of Russell, Majors, and Waddell. Scott wrote:

> The expedition set on foot by Mr. Secretary Floyd, in 1857, against the Mormons and Indians about Salt Lake was, beyond a doubt, to give occasion for large contracts and expenditures, that is, to open a wide field for frauds and peculation. This purpose was not comprehended nor scarcely suspected in, perhaps, a year; but, observing the desperate characters who frequented the Secretary, some of whom had desks near him, suspicion was at length excited. Scott protested against the expedition on the general ground of inexpediency, and specially because the season was too late for the troops to reach their destination in comfort or even in safety. Particular facts, observed by different officers, if united, would prove the imputation.[36]

Former president Buchanan probably recognized the accuracy of Scott's criticism about the expedition's timing and chose not to rebut that point. However, he did challenge Scott's accusation about corruption, although

defending Floyd in 1864 was difficult because of his wartime status as traitor. Furthermore, Floyd's subsequent irregularities in financing the Utah
War had forced his resignation from the cabinet in December 1860 and
prompted his indictment for malfeasance in office.[37]

Notwithstanding Harney's herculean early efforts in Kansas to organize the Utah Expedition, Secretary Floyd grew uneasy about his prospects for success as June turned into July. Belatedly sensing disaster, Floyd
turned for help to a fellow Southerner and Democrat, Ben McCulloch of
Texas, who happened to be in Washington. On July 8 Floyd asked Mc-
Culloch to visit Harney at his Fort Leavenworth headquarters and to assess the effectiveness of his preparations for the Utah campaign. Among
the list of questions that Floyd asked McCulloch to probe were three that
dramatically illustrated how little the Buchanan administration, including its secretary of war, understood of the military campaign that it had
already launched: "What is the reported condition of the route of travel,
as to grazing, roads &c? What is likely to be the reception the troops will
meet with in Utah? Any reliable information concerning the condition of
the Mormons, their disposition &c?"[38] Equally unprobed were the tactical
implications of the administration's decision to deny the Utah Expedition
the protection of its mounted regiment, the Second Dragoons, in order to
accommodate Governor Walker's insistence that he retain that unit (along
with its commander, Harney) to preserve order in Kansas. The costly
consequences of this trade-off became dangerously clear when mounted
Cheyenne and Mormon raiders attacked the Utah Expedition in August
and October, respectively.

Irrespective of whether a twenty-five-hundred-man Utah Expedition
constituted excessive force or a half measure, first news from the West of
Mormon resistance to the army forced Buchanan to reconsider the matter
in mid-November 1857. Especially shocking to both the public and the administration were reports that Brigham Young had declared martial law on
September 15, 1857, and had sealed Utah's borders, ordered the destruction
of much of the grass and natural forage in what is now southwestern Wyoming, burned the civilian trading posts and settlements at Fort Bridger and
Fort Supply, and on the night of October 4–5, 1857, burned seventy-six
undefended army supply wagons containing irreplaceable matériel worth
more than $1 million.[39] By November 24 Secretary Floyd was searching
for new military advice, a quest that immediately yielded a response from

Brevet Major General Persifor F. Smith, commander of the Department of the West, who unlike Scott happened to be in Washington. Smith recommended a gargantuan expansion of the army to double its size, with the additional troops to move on Utah in three columns from Kansas, California, and Oregon.[40]

When news of General Smith's recommendations leaked into the newspapers, General Harney gratuitously entered the fray by pelting the president at month's end with an out-of-channels recommendation of his own. Harney called for reinforcements about two-thirds the size of Smith's proposed force—all of which was to be commanded by him.[41] Whether General Scott was aware of his subordinates' recommendations to Floyd and Buchanan is unclear, but it was widely perceived that the general in chief was hostile to two of the key notions that they had advanced without his approval: a thrust against Utah from the Pacific Coast and the extensive use of volunteer as well as regular troops.

In the end, Buchanan and Floyd—acutely aware of the Utah Expedition's alarming cost within the context of the then-accelerating Panic of 1857—ratcheted downward all of these recommendations and drafted the president's December 8 first annual message to Congress to request only four new regiments, an army increase of about 20 percent, to finish the job in Utah.[42]

Too Clever by Half: The Cost of Erratic Communications and Presidential Cunning

Communications skills are far from a military commander's only qualification, but in matters of life and death they are crucial as well as revelatory about the leader's effectiveness.[43] Notwithstanding James Buchanan's superb portfolio of senior governmental experiences, his writings betray the military neophyte catapulted into an ill-fitting role. Like those instructions issued by Brigham Young, Buchanan's suffered from ambiguity and indirection at important times. Throughout the Utah War, Young feared postal interception—a practice in which he himself engaged—and felt the need to conceal many of his purposes. The phrasing of Buchanan's messages was driven by a different motivation—a crabbed, lawyerly desire to avoid political criticism by splitting hairs and changing directions. Buchanan frequently hedged mightily in his communications—most of which he wrote

himself with the help of a single secretary. At times this was a quirky, politically adroit, but manipulative communications style—one that the British might dub "too clever by half." For example, in October 1855 John F. T.
Crampton, the British plenipotentiary in Washington, confided to Foreign
Secretary Lord Clarendon that "the Buck"—as he called Buchanan—"is
a very cunning old gentleman and a great schemer in matters of private
interest."[44] Buchanan's communications style and behavior played a part
in destroying his personal and political relationships with a long list of
intimates: John C. Breckinridge (his vice-president), J. Buchanan Henry
(nephew and personal secretary), John W. Forney (decades-long acolyte
and newspaper editor), George Plitt (political ally and his niece's former
guardian), James C. Van Dyke (his closest political adviser in Philadelphia), and Robert J. Walker (governor of Kansas).

The result was serious communications and decision-making shortfalls
with respect to the conduct of the Utah War and other administration
business. The May 1857 decision to send an expeditionary force to Utah
without fully consulting Winfield Scott, the general in chief, has already
been discussed. Simultaneously, Buchanan committed an equally serious communications lapse in failing to inform Young that he was replacing him. This appalling omission, aggravated by the fact that Buchanan's
search for a new governor was an open secret reported in the nation's newspapers, gave Young the motive and wherewithal to assert for the next year
that he remained governor and that the approaching Utah Expedition was
an armed mob rather than a legitimate part of the federal government's
regular army. In June Buchanan also created a nightmarish organizational
conflict by promising General Harney and his dragoon regiment to both
Governor Walker in Kansas and to Scott for the Utah Expedition—si-
multaneous missions to be performed, somehow, twelve hundred miles
apart.

Because of their operating style and Scott's self-imposed absence in
New York, Buchanan and Floyd at times reassigned regiments to the Utah
Expedition without telling Scott until after the fact. Buchanan was the
principal draftsman for the State Department's instructions to Utah's
new governor, Alfred Cumming, that overlapped with but differed in essential ways from those issued three weeks earlier (also drafted by Buchanan, as well as Floyd and Scott) by the War Department to Harney,
the commander charged with escorting and protecting Cumming. In these

all-important Utah War orders for Harney, the administration's drafting committee included an instruction that it characterized as "a suggestion—not an order, nor even a recommendation," the least definite, most opaque guidance for a commander issued during the entire war.[45] Emblematically, it took the administration months to realize that, in canceling the Mormon mail contract for the Missouri River–Salt Lake City route effective June 1, 1857, it had unwittingly severed communications with its own army in the field—another self-inflicted wound. It took until the spring of 1858 for the administration to respond fully to Scott and Johnston's apoplectic demands for a replacement mail service.[46]

Incomprehensibly, between the launch of the Utah Expedition in late May 1857 and Buchanan's first annual message to Congress on December 8, seven months later, he made no public statement about the campaign. By today's standards this silence would be viewed as extraordinarily weak presidential communications skills. Historian David Herbert Donald provides some context in arguing that, in the traditional nineteenth-century view, "the President, once elected, had no direct dealings with the public. His job was to administer the government and to report his activities and wishes to the Congress. Presidents rarely left the capital city, except for brief vacations; they almost never made public addresses; and they maintained, in theory, a sublime indifference to public opinion and political pressures."[47] Yet as Matthew Pinsker notes, strong presidents like Andrew Jackson had always found ways to break with the inhibitions of tradition to communicate directly with the people.[48] Even Buchanan had taken the case for his Kansas policy to the public in an open letter of August 1857, a time at which he significantly remained silent about Utah. Furthermore, when Buchanan finally did communicate through his December message to Congress, near-contiguous paragraphs referred to Mormon "rebellion" and "insurrection," then backtracked by asserting that "unless he [Young] should retrace his steps the Territory of Utah will be in a state of open rebellion." Congressmen could well be pardoned for being confused, if not cynical, about whether Utah was, in fact, in rebellion. Buchanan's congressional opponents began calls for relevant documents and moved to an investigatory posture.[49]

Young allegedly believed, as he later asserted, that he could have prevented the Mountain Meadows Massacre—the appalling slaughter of 120 defenseless men, women, and children by Nauvoo Legionnaires and

Indian auxiliaries—by using a telegraph line that did not yet exist. In a similar vein, Buchanan told Delegate Bernhisel that a few hours' face-to-face meeting with Young could have averted the whole Utah conflict. Historian Richard D. Poll agreed that "a transcontinental telegraph or railroad" would have obviated the expedition "because the facts," which could have been thus easily determined, "did not support the alarms of either party."[50] I am less optimistic, given the ten-year history of escalating tensions between the territorial and federal governments and the grossly different temperaments, worldviews, and communication styles of their leaders. These what-if conjectures were the musings of Buchanan and Young retrospectively rueful about the impact of their decisions and wholly unrealistic about their ability to change their own deep-seated decision-making and communications behavior.

It would, of course, be unfair to attribute every communications lapse within the army's Utah Expedition to President Buchanan or even to Secretary Floyd and General Scott. On the other hand, the communications behaviors—including the absurdities—of an organization's most senior leaders tend to cascade into the ranks with commensurate impact on its tone. Consequently, in thinking about how President Buchanan dealt with his early Mormon crisis, it is relevant to consider the understandings of the Utah Expedition's leaders in early October 1857, as that force regrouped along Hams Fork of the Green River just west of the Continental Divide. There, in the absence of both the old expeditionary commander (Harney) and his west-bound successor (Johnston), the senior officer, Colonel Edmund Brooke Alexander, made a remarkable confession to his subordinates: that he was unaware of not only his commander's identity and location but also of the Utah Expedition's very mission. To those officers east of South Pass struggling to catch up to his brigade's main force while fending off Mormon raiders, Alexander wrote plaintively: "No information of the position or intentions of the commanding officer has reached me, and I am in utter ignorance of the objects of the government in sending troops here, or the instructions given for their conduct after reaching here."[51]

It would be easy to dismiss the ambiguities besetting Colonel Alexander as the harmless lamentations of an overly passive, incurious leader lacking the respect of his own troops ("the old woman"), a man whose inadequacies had been identified by Ben McCulloch for Secretary Floyd in July and for President Buchanan by General Harney in August. Yet in early October Alexander was the senior officer in the field standing between an armed brigade of the U.S. government and Brigham Young. That he was in such a command is further evidence of Buchanan's standards in choosing and retaining unsuitable key leaders. Given Alexander's dilemma it is not surprising that at about the same time one of his subordinates, coincidentally Governor Cumming's West Pointer nephew and namesake, reported to his mother in Georgia that, "Such is a kind of rough outline of the positions in which we are in at present. Of course no one in the camp from the Colonel down to the lowest corporal, knows *what* is to be done, or *when* it is to be done, though be sure every man delivers his own views with great volubility of what *ought* to be done."[52]

Aside from the murkiness of his annual message to Congress on the crucial matter of whether a "rebellion" was or was not under way in Utah, Buchanan created another problem in his recommendations to Congress by leaving open the important matter of whether the four regiments to reinforce the Utah Expedition would be regular troops, state-raised volunteers, or a combination of both forces. It was a debatable issue in terms of the rapidity, cost, and quality of recruitment involved but not a neutral matter. Surely the president and secretary of war had a point of view on this issue, although they never expressed one publicly. General Scott had been overtly jaundiced about the performance of volunteers since the Mexican War, if not earlier, yet virtually every state governor in the country felt otherwise. They viewed the organization of volunteer regiments for federal service as a wonderful opportunity for both political plums and local contracting boodle.

By remaining silent on this subject in December 1857, the administration may have felt that it was avoiding a Hobson's choice. In the process the ambiguity of Buchanan's message inadvertently triggered spontaneous organizing and recruiting activity on a grand national scale in such mixed venues as California mining camps—aflame with anti-Mormon indignation over the Mountain Meadows Massacre in September—and in Pennsylvania cities, where political bosses were anxious to support what they assumed were the wishes of their man in the White House. If, in dealing with the Mormon problem, Buchanan was trying to avoid uncontrolled mob action of the type most dreaded by Young, his unwitting creation of the volunteers-versus-regulars furor was counterproductive. Meanwhile, musters and elections to form volunteer units continued apace on a free-lance basis. In one rural Kentucky tavern there was a fatal brawl between would-be officers and gentlemen over who would hold command. As news of such bellicose, rough-and-tumble behavior drifted west to Utah, it permitted Young to continue his charade that the Utah Expedition was not a creature of the U.S. government's regular army but rather was an uncontrolled mob to be ignored if not resisted.[53]

Perhaps the best example of Buchanan's manipulative administrative and communications style is one heretofore unanalyzed by historians of his presidency and its Utah War—the use of General Scott as an unwitting pawn in a secret plan to induce a mass Mormon exodus from Utah to northern Mexico by directing military pressure on the Salt Lake Valley from the Pacific Coast. As Buchanan discussed his intentions in confidence with Sir William Gore Ouseley, a British plenipotentiary in Washington, during January and February 1858, the purpose of this gambit was twofold: to bring about the creation of an American colony in a portion of Mexico which Buchanan hoped to annex as the United States had previously done with Texas; and, through an even more convoluted chain of events, to facilitate the president's long-standing interest in seizing or buying Cuba from Spain. The linchpin for this plan was to be the dispatch of General Scott to the Pacific Coast for purposes of establishing a second front in the Utah War, which, in turn, was to stimulate Young's flight into Mexico.

Scott, unaware of the plan's broader intent, objected to the military practicality of a second front but agreed to steam for California on February 4, 1858, a move that was canceled abruptly on the eve of his departure when Congress—also unaware of Buchanan's plan—unwittingly refused to finance such a thrust. As Ouseley reported to British foreign secretary Lord Clarendon, "The [presidential] intention as to the Mormons was to bring about their emigration to Sonora and thus to turn their rebellion to account by making them pioneers for future annexation under a quasi-military colonial system, that General Scott was partly to inaugurate without however being aware of the full scope of the project for the execution of which he was to be one of the instruments. [Buchanan] deems absolute silence to be as yet necessary. He will find other ostensible motives to cover his real [Cuba] object."[54]

Paying the Piper: Destroying Federal Creditworthiness

In assessing the effectiveness of Buchanan's handling of the Utah War, one hunts in vain for an explanation of how he financed the conflict. James L. Huston has thoroughly analyzed the Panic of 1857, the severe economic downturn that began as the Utah Expedition marched west, and Leonard J. Arrington has surveyed the impact of the campaign on Utah's cash-starved economy.[55] But how Buchanan chose to pay for the country's most expensive military commitment of the antebellum period—and even the magnitude of the conflict's cost—remain largely unexplored. These are subjects worth probing because they shed light on why Secretary Floyd resigned in disgrace during the secession crisis and how Buchanan's financial policies hobbled President Lincoln's support of the Union army soon thereafter.

When Buchanan took office the federal budget he inherited included no provision for a military move on Utah, nor did the new president anticipate the need for one. As indicated above, Buchanan's March 4, 1857, inaugural address made no mention of "the Mormon problem." Accordingly, Congress adjourned a few days later oblivious to the daunting economic disaster and financial needs that would beset the nation during its nine-month absence. First signs of what lay ahead came with the failure in July 1857 of one of the country's major financial institutions, an Ohio life insurance company. Rippling from this collapse came the closure of multiple banks and a Wall Street stock market crash of unprecedented severity in October 1857. There soon followed the deepest recession in twenty years, a contraction that soon devastated not only the national economy but also the U.S. government's revenue stream. By November 2, 1857, conditions had deteriorated so rapidly that Utah's territorial delegate in Congress reported to Brigham Young: "There has recently been a tremendous crash among the banks, brokers and mercantile establishments throughout the country. Every bank east of the Rocky mountains (I am not aware that there is a single exception,) has suspended specie [gold] payments, and the failures among the brokers and merchants throughout the length and breadth of the land are very numerous, and in many instances very heavy."[56]

Compounding these problems was awareness in Washington during mid-November that during September and October Young had declined to leave Utah's governorship, declared martial law, and attacked a large portion of the army's supply trains, destroying in the process $1 million in matériel. This shocking news raised the specter of a long, expensive guerrilla war. Several of Buchanan's generals advised a doubling of the army's size to reinforce the Utah Expedition.

This essay cannot provide a comprehensive account of how President Buchanan and Secretary Floyd improvised to support the army during first Congress's adjournment and then its protracted 1858 debate over the size of military appropriations. After initiating the Utah War in May 1857 without congressional authorization or awareness, Buchanan continued to escalate the campaign even after a dismayed, truculent Congress reconvened in early December 1857. In the process the president quietly permitted Floyd to finance the Utah War by issuing to military contractors millions of dollars in "acceptances," promissory notes authorized by the secretary of war but unbacked by either a congressional appropriation or even the Treasury's rapidly declining cash balances.

When Buchanan as well as contractors and bankers grew queasy about this practice, the president ordered Floyd to stop issuing War Department acceptances. Driven by the need to support an army in the field, Floyd ignored Buchanan's directive and continued to generate his IOUs in secret. Eventually, Floyd was compromised by the misguided attempt of a distant relative to provide collateral for overdue obligations by "abstracting" $870,000 in state bonds from an unrelated Interior Department trust fund. When Buchanan became aware of the bond peculation and the scope of Floyd's rogue financing arrangements for the Utah War in December 1860, he reluctantly forced the secretary's resignation, with a consequent destruction of Floyd's reputation and indictment in early 1861 for malfeasance in office.[57]

The scope and character of such Utah War financing measures during the late 1850s contributed substantially to the unprecedented deficit spending that devastated the nation's creditworthiness and drained the U.S. Treasury. By the time Abraham Lincoln took office in March 1861 the country's largest military garrison was in the desert forty miles southwest of Salt Lake City, and the new administration could neither buy stationery nor meet the federal payroll. The two circumstances were not unrelated.

The most compelling description of the process by which Buchanan mismanaged federal finances, including (but not confined to) his support for the Utah War, is a recent one—Jane E. Flaherty's article "'The

Exhausted Condition of the Treasury' on the Eve of the Civil War."[58] Here Flaherty traces the precipitous 37 percent decline in federal revenues from $74.0 million in 1856 to $46.6 million in 1858, a drop accompanied by an 8 percent increase in annual expenditures during the same period from $68.7 million to $73.9 million. Consequently, the federal budget moved from a net surplus of $5.3 million for 1856 to an unprecedented deficit of $27.3 million in 1858. For 1861 the national budget deficit stood at a level of $25.2 million. Absent a thorough analysis of the Utah War's cost—a daunting challenge that even Flaherty avoids—historians have used unsupported expense estimates for the federal side alone that range widely between $14 million and $40 million.[59]

In presenting these data Flaherty argues that Buchanan's poor financial stewardship seriously handicapped Lincoln. Historians, she adds, often fail to connect Civil War financial legislation with the condition of the prewar Treasury. By 1860, she explains, "the 'Buchaneers' had created the largest debt ever accumulated by an administration without engaging in war." The Union's "exhausted Treasury and poor credit" created "the need for an unanticipated revolution in American fiscal policy."[60]

The antebellum financial problems of the federal government were not as serious as the secession crisis of 1860–61, but they were nonetheless formidable. The cost of the Utah War—imprecise as its dimensions still are—contributed mightily to this distraction in terms of both its scope and the ruinous manner in which the Buchanan administration spent and borrowed to prosecute the war. So ruinous was Buchanan's financial management and so substantial was the Utah War's negative impact on the nation's financial condition that once the Civil War began, conspiracists argued that proto-Confederates in Buchanan's cabinet—usually identified as Secretaries Floyd, Cobb, and Thompson of Virginia, Georgia, and Mississippi—had deliberately launched the Utah Expedition to undermine the U.S. government's financial ability to combat secession. Brigham Young was even quicker off the mark in discerning economic plots, noting as early as the summer of 1857 that commercial friends of the administration such as the freighting firm of Russell, Majors, and Waddell would reap millions of dollars from the Utah Expedition.[61] Unsupported as such conspiracy theories are, their very advancement indicates the extent of the economic problems inherited by Buchanan's successor.

In his postwar memoirs, written in detached third-person voice, Buchanan rationalized the debacle created by his lax supervision of Floyd. He did so in the face of General Scott's accusations of secretarial corruption by invoking the self-serving, age-old defense employed by beleaguered, if not derelict, chief executives—delegation of authority and its abuse by poorly performing subordinates: "Nearly eight years after these events had passed into history, Mr. Buchanan was no little surprised to discover that General Scott, in his autobiography, published in 1864, asserts that . . . it [the Utah Expedition] was set on foot by Secretary Floyd, 'to open a wide field for frauds and peculation.' . . . The President had, as a matter of course left the military details of the movement to the Secretary of War and the Commanding General of the Army."[62]

Buchanan's Urge to Declare Victory in Utah: A Troublesome Legacy

By the spring of 1858 James Buchanan had ordered nearly one-third of the U.S. Army to Utah, yet the president also faced daunting Indian campaigns in the Pacific Northwest and New Mexico Territory. Taken together with the economic shock of the Panic of 1857, the total cost of such military involvements was unsustainable. Compounding this military-economic problem was a political worry—the fact that Congress, never consulted or even briefed on the need for a Utah Expedition, had assumed an aggressively accusatory posture when it returned to Washington in December 1857. Consequently, Congress was still debating the size of budgetary support for the campaign and whether to reinforce the Utah Expedition at all in the spring of 1858.

To relieve these pressures the president chose a gambit that nearly unraveled the value of his only defensible accomplishment in the war—his decision to replace Brigham Young as Utah's governor and to restore federal authority through armed intervention. In effect, as Albert Sidney Johnston and his Utah Expedition marched through Salt Lake City on June 26, 1858, the president declared victory, unilaterally proclaimed a blanket pardon for Utah's entire population, quietly signaled that he might be able to "work" with Young, and rapidly diverted several of the regiments originally assigned to reinforce Johnston to other western military posts.[63]

Although a substantial portion of the army remained at Camp Floyd until the onset of the Civil War, the politically driven change in Buchanan's attitude toward Young, and Young's skill in co-opting his alcoholic successor (while dividing the other federal appointees into conflicting factions), had an unsettling effect. These dynamics delayed for decades the process of recasting Utah into a conventional American territory, let alone a state. Also delayed, if not lost entirely, was justice for those summarily executed at Mountain Meadows, Utah, on September 11, 1857, by Nauvoo Legion troops and Indian auxiliaries. The president's apparent lack of concern over this unprecedented atrocity and acceptance of a delayed, obfuscating account of what had happened at whose hands was perhaps the worst aspect of the clever, if not Faustian, bargain that Buchanan struck to extricate himself from the expense and distraction of his Utah morass. In his memoirs one of the Utah Expedition's subalterns characterized this presidential approach as "accomplished to the shame of the United States, and the Mormon criminals went unpunished for the treason, murder and robbery, and grew rich off of the very expedition which were prepared to punish them. This Mormon War brought out no great men. All in all, it was a very expensive and wasteful expedition and its only use was in the instruction the troops received in campaigning on the plains."[64]

Conclusions and Reflections

In February 1962, while hosting a meeting of historians assembled to discuss prior administrations, President John F. Kennedy grew testy, if not defensive, as the discussion turned to performance rankings for his predecessors. As the conferees bored in to criticize what conventional wisdom had dubbed the most hapless presidents on the list, politeness and Kennedy's tolerance for second-guessing abandoned him. According to the late historian David Herbert Donald, the president snapped: "No one has a right to grade a President—not even poor James Buchanan—who has not sat in his chair, examined the mail and information that came across his desk, and learned why he made decisions."[65]

For far too long, many of us have not done what President Kennedy urged in 1962, especially with respect to Buchanan's first real brush in Utah Territory with the possibility of disunion, if not outright rebellion and bloodshed. This armed and bloody confrontation in the Rockies was a far different affair than either the violent civil unrest already afoot on Kansas's plains—where separatism and opposition to the federal government were not issues—and the secession crisis that followed among southern states, not western territories. Yet different as it was, "the Mormon problem" and Buchanan's attempt to deal with it in 1857–58 provide part of the context for understanding what unfolded in the even more important later years of his presidency. In pursuit of this context, it is time for scholars of the American presidency and Civil War to park their inhibitions about entering the admittedly exotic worlds of Western Americana, Mormonism, and heretofore restricted LDS sources to exploit this opportunity to glimpse the decision making of a pivotal president's earliest days.

Recognizing this context might remind historians that Secretary of War John B. Floyd's December 1860 resignation did not stem from his disagreement over the reinforcement of southern forts. Instead, Floyd hoped to avoid publicizing his distant relative's involvement in an as-yet-unrevealed scandal over Floyd's financing of the Utah War. Buchanan understood Floyd's emotional attempt to salvage his family's honor, and so he permitted Floyd to use the fortress issue to cover his soon-scandalous cabinet exit.[66]

Given his high threshold for judging presidential performance, President Kennedy probably would have accepted the assessment of Theodore Roosevelt, who "classified presidents as Lincoln types and Buchanan types." Yet in commenting about Buchanan as he did, historian-president Roosevelt sometimes got it wrong. For example, in 1906 Roosevelt was on the defensive to explain why, in the absence of Congress, he had intervened militarily in Cuba following a governmental collapse in that young republic. Casting about for an example antithetical to his own well-known action urges, Roosevelt seized on what he viewed as Buchanan's fecklessness during the secession crisis of 1860–61. To a senator from Ohio, Roosevelt argued, "I am sure you will agree with me that it would not have been wise to summon Congress to consider the situation in Cuba, which was changing from week to week and almost from day to day. . . . You, my dear Senator, are the last man to advocate my playing a part like President Buchanan or failing to take the responsibility that the President must take if he is fit for his position."[67] Apparently lost on Roosevelt (himself born in the midst of the Utah War) was the fact that, in the opening months of the Buchanan administration, the fifteenth president had indeed taken vigorous action to change the government in a faraway place while intervening with unprecedented military force. Old Buck, like Theodore Roosevelt who followed, had done so with Congress absent, leaving the legislative branch unconsulted and uninvolved. In neither case was Congress amused.

As this volume's introduction and concluding conversation between Michael Holt and William Freehling make clear, historians have disagreed whether Buchanan had been simply a passive and feckless president or, to the contrary, an energetic yet largely ineffective one. I believe that at various times Buchanan had displayed presidential leadership of both types. In assessing his presidency one needs to look at the entire four years, including his decisions in the administration's earliest days. Surely that period includes Buchanan's involvement with, and endorsement of, the *Dred Scott* decision and the dispatch of Governor Robert J. Walker to Kansas, but it should also sweep in the unanticipated Utah crisis about which we still have so much to learn. The key but still unexamined question is whether Buchanan's wariness in the wake of the controversial, economically ruinous Utah War discouraged creativity and boldness three years later when seceding slave states were the problem. Such difficult actions—requiring strength of character and wisdom—are not apt to flow from a chief executive whose style was simply "too clever by half."

One of President Buchanan's last official acts in March 1861 was to carve large areas from Utah's western and eastern flanks to create the territories of Nevada and Colorado and to enlarge Nebraska. As President Lincoln took office to deal with the southern secession crisis, the nation's biggest army garrison was in the desert forty miles southwest of Salt Lake City, and the U.S. Treasury had been nearly drained by the cost of the Utah War. By then the killings in Utah had reached a scale roughly equivalent to those that had earned her eastern neighbor the enduring label "Bleeding Kansas." One of these atrocities—Utah's Mountain Meadows Massacre of September 1857—would alone stand as the greatest American incident of organized mass murder of unarmed civilians until the Oklahoma City bombing of 1995. Another, the November 1857 execution of the six-man Aiken party crossing Utah from California, would rival the scope and ferocity of John Brown's earlier rampage at Osawatomie Creek, Kansas.[68] In Utah—amidst the Rockies rather than in South Carolina—James Buchanan received his earliest introduction to the realities of bloodshed and potential disunion. With respect to resolution of "the Mormon problem,"

Buchanan deserves credit for doing what a brooding Franklin Pierce had not accomplished in superseding Brigham Young, but not for much more.

Notes

Chapter copyright 2011 by William P. MacKinnon

Chapter epigraph: Johnson quoted in affidavit of Joseph Bartholomew, March 29, 1859, Salt Lake City *Valley Tan*, April 19, 1859.

1. Buchanan, Inaugural Address, March 4, 1857, John Bassett Moore, ed., *The Works of James Buchanan, Comprising His Speeches, State Papers, and Private Correspondence*, 12 vols. (Philadelphia: J. B. Lippincott, 1910), 10:105–13; Franklin Pierce to Cabinet, March 4, 1857, J. Pierpont Morgan Library, New York.

2. A review of the Utah War's recent and likely future historiography appears in William P. MacKinnon, *Predicting the Past: The Utah War's Twenty-First Century Future* (Leonard J. Arrington Mormon History Lecture Series No. 14) (Logan: Utah State University Press, 2009). The most recent narrative of the war is David L. Bigler and Will Bagley, *The Mormon Rebellion: America's First Civil War, 1857–1858* (Norman: University of Oklahoma Press, 2011). For examples of the documents recently published for the first time from the church's collections, see William P. MacKinnon, *At Sword's Point, Part 1: A Documentary History of the Utah War to 1858* (Norman, Okla.: Arthur H. Clark, 2008), and Richard E. Turley Jr. and Ronald W. Walker, eds., *Mountain Meadows Massacre: The Andrew Jenson and David H. Morris Collections* (Provo and Logan, Utah: Brigham Young University Press and Utah State University Press, 2009).

3. The following summary of Mormon-federal tensions and the multiple non-governmental controversies leading to the Utah War is adapted from William P. MacKinnon, "And the War Came: James Buchanan, the Utah Expedition, and the Decision to Intervene," *Utah Historical Quarterly* 76 (Winter 2008): 24–25; and David L. Bigler, "A Lion in the Path: Genesis of the Utah War, 1857–1858," *Utah Historical Quarterly* 76 (Winter 2008): 4–21. For the most recent (and pointed) discussion of federal appointees to Utah during this period see Thomas G. Alexander, "Carpetbaggers, Reprobates, and Liars: Federal Judges and the Utah War (1857–1858)," *The Historian* 70 (Summer 2008): 208–38.

4. "Expedition against Utah," editorial, Salt Lake City *Deseret News*, October 7, 1857.

5. See note 4 as well as David L. Bigler, "Sources of Conflict: Mormons and Their Neighbors, 1830–90" (unpublished lecture, Salt Lake [City] Theological Seminary, July 25, 2003) and *Forgotten Kingdom: The Mormon Theocracy in the American West, 1847–1896* (Spokane, Wash.: Arthur H. Clark, 1998).

6. MacKinnon, *At Sword's Point, Part 1*, 56. In-depth discussion of the Mormon issue in national politics, especially the 1856 presidential campaign, appears in Richard D. Poll, "The Mormon Question Enters National Politics, 1850–1856," *Utah Historical Quarterly* 25 (April 1957): 16–44; Norman F. Furniss, *The Mormon Conflict, 1850–1859* (New Haven: Yale University Press, 1960); and Sarah Barringer Gordon, *The Mormon Question: Polygamy and Constitutional Conflict in Nineteenth-Century America* (Chapel Hill: University of North Carolina Press, 2001).

7. Jules Remy and Julius Brenchley, *A Journey to Great-Salt-Lake City*, 2 vols. (London: W. Jeffs, 1861), 1:206–7.

8. Conover to Jefferson Hunt, January 8, 1857, Brigham Young Collection, Church History Library, Church of Jesus Christ of Latter-day Saints, Salt Lake City [hereafter LDS Church Archives].

9. Young to Thomas L. Kane, January 31, 1857, ibid.

10. Young to Orson Pratt, March 1, 1857, ibid. For a summary of the deterioration in Mormon-federal relations between Buchanan's election and inauguration and the mounting pressures on Young, see MacKinnon, *At Sword's Point, Part 1*, 61–82.

11. For the text of this memorial and an assessment of its impact on the Buchanan cabinet's view of affairs in Utah, see MacKinnon, *At Sword's Point, Part 1*, 67–73, 100–107.

12. MacKinnon, "And the War Came," 22–37, and *At Sword's Point, Part 1*, 99–138.

13. Young to Pierce, March 30, 1853, LDS Church Archives.

14. Young, Discourse of May 8, 1853, *Deseret News*, May 14, 1853.

15. William P. MacKinnon, "Sex, Subalterns, and Steptoe: Army Behavior, Mormon Rage, and Utah War Anxieties," *Utah Historical Quarterly* 76 (Summer 2008): 236–39.

16. Steptoe to Adjt. Gen. Samuel Cooper, April 25, 1855, Dale L. Morgan research notes, McQuown Collection, Marriott Library, University of Utah, Salt Lake City.

17. For an assessment of Pierce's subsequent disinterest in Utah affairs, see Steptoe to Elias Blackburn, November 3, 1855, LDS Church Archives.

18. "Utah," Dispatch of March 5, 1857, "Highly Interesting from Utah," *New-York Daily Times*, May 19, 1857.

19. Elsewhere I have compared this image campaign by Mormon leaders to degrade Buchanan's reputation to that by which after the Civil War former Confederate generals created the myth of the Lost Cause and, in the process, virtually canonized Robert E. Lee. See William P. MacKinnon, "Epilogue to the Utah War: Impact and Legacy," *Journal of Mormon History* 29 (Fall 2003): 217.

20. Ibid., 190–93, 198.

21. The Utah-relevant portions of Buchanan's December 8, 1857, first annual message to Congress and Floyd's annual report for 1857 may be found in MacKinnon, *At Sword's Point, Part 1*, 481–85.

22. Denver to Young, November 11, 1857, quoted in "Utah Expedition," U.S. Cong.,

House, 35th Cong., 1st Sess., *House Ex. Doc.* 71, Serial 956, 186–87. A month later Young was indicted for treason by a federal grand jury sitting at Fort Bridger, a prosecution that was quashed by a suborned U.S. attorney after the Utah War in 1859.

23. For the tensions and eventual rupture in the relationship between Buchanan and Walker see George D. Harmon, "President James Buchanan's Betrayal of Governor Robert J. Walker of Kansas," *Pennsylvania Magazine of History and Biography* 53 (1929): 51–91; and Pearl T. Ponce, "Pledges and Principles: Buchanan, Walker, and Kansas in 1857," *Kansas History: A Journal of the Central Plains* 27 (Spring–Summer 2004): 87–99.

24. Until later in the nineteenth century, the secretary of state was the cabinet officer principally responsible for the oversight of territorial affairs as well as international relations.

25. Floyd's only full-length biography is a somewhat sympathetic one: Charles Pinnegar, *Brand of Infamy: A Biography of John Buchanan Floyd* (Westport, Conn.: Greenwood Press, 2002). During the 1930s, Robert M. Hughes, a Floyd relative, wrote a series of journal articles defending his conduct as secretary of war. For articles by non-relatives, see Philip G. Auchampaugh, "John B. Floyd and James Buchanan," *Tyler's Quarterly Historical and Genealogical Magazine* 4 (April 1923): 381–88; and John M. Belohlavek, "The Politics of Scandal: A Reassessment of John B. Floyd as Secretary of War," *West Virginia History* 31 (April 1970): 145–60. Notwithstanding his middle name, Floyd was not related to the president.

26. Allan Peskin, *Winfield Scott and the Profession of Arms* (Kent, Ohio: Kent State University Press, 2003), 206–28.

27. MacKinnon, *At Sword's Point, Part 1*, 95–97.

28. George Rollie Adams, *General William S. Harney: Prince of Dragoons* (Lincoln: University of Nebraska Press, 2001), 159–81; MacKinnon, *At Sword's Point, Part 1*, 166–68.

29. William P. MacKinnon, "'Who's in Charge Here?': Utah Expedition Command Ambiguities," *Dialogue: A Journal of Mormon Thought* 42 (Spring 2009): 30–64.

30. MacKinnon, *At Sword's Point, Part 1*, 180.

31. For a discussion of Cumming's alcohol problem during the Utah War period see Thomas L. Kane to Young, July 24, 1859, and Young to Kane, December 15, 1859, both LDS Church Archives. Young's and Buchanan's own substantial but under-studied health problems, especially at the beginning of the war, are described in MacKinnon, *At Sword's Point, Part 1*, 63–64, 83–85, 90–95, 102, 328.

32. That Cumming did enter Salt Lake City to assume the governorship in early April 1858 accompanied only by civilian mediator Thomas L. Kane and two servants was more a reflection of the flow of events and Kane's influence with Brigham Young than an indicator of Cumming's ability to have accomplished such a feat in 1857.

33. Brevet Lt. Gen. Winfield Scott, "Garrison for Salt-Lake City," Memorandum for Secretary of War, May 26, 1857, Headquarters of the Army, Letters Sent (Record

Group 108), National Archives, Washington, D.C. The only published text of this important memo appears in M. Hamlin Cannon, "Winfield Scott and the Utah Expedition," *Military Affairs: Journal of the American Military Institute* 5 (Fall 1941): 109–11; and MacKinnon, *At Sword's Point, Part 1*, 130–32.

34. James Buchanan, *Mr. Buchanan's Administration on the Eve of the Rebellion* (New York: D. Appleton, 1866), 238–39.

35. Harney to Floyd, June 7, 1857, U.S. Army, Records of Adjt. Gen's Office, Letters Received (Record Group 94), National Archives.

36. Winfield Scott, *Memoirs of Lieut.-General Scott, L.L.D., Written by Himself*, 2 vols. (New York: Sheldon, 1864), 2:604. Scott, like Buchanan, wrote his memoirs in the third person.

37. William P. MacKinnon, "125 Years of Conspiracy Theories: Origins of the Utah Expedition of 1857–58," *Utah Historical Quarterly* 52 (Summer 1984): 212–30. Within a few months of leaving office, Buchanan was so skeptical of Scott's memoranda and letters to newspapers that he told one editor, "[it] has been often said of the gallant general that when he abandons the sword for the pen, he makes sad work of it." Buchanan to Gerard Hallock, June 29, 1861, quoted in William H. Hallock, *Life of Gerard Hallock, Editor of the New York Journal of Commerce* (1869; reprint, New York: Arno Press, 1970), 242.

38. Floyd to McCulloch, July 8, 1857, U.S., Secretary of War, Letters Sent (Record Group 107), National Archives; MacKinnon, *At Sword's Point, Part 1*, 173–78.

39. MacKinnon, *At Sword's Point, Part 1*, 415–23.

40. Smith to Floyd, November 24, 1857, Persifor Fraser Smith Papers, Historical Society of Pennsylvania, Philadelphia.

41. Harney to Buchanan, November 29, 1857, James Buchanan Papers, Historical Society of Pennsylvania, Philadelphia.

42. MacKinnon, *At Sword's Point, Part 1*, 481–85.

43. The following discussion of Buchanan's communications style and its impact is adapted from William P. MacKinnon, "'Lonely Bones': Leadership and Utah War Violence," *Journal of Mormon History* 33 (Spring 2007): 162–75.

44. Crampton to Clarendon, October 2, 1855, reprinted in James J. and Patience P. Barnes, eds., *Private and Confidential: Letters from British Ministers in Washington to the Foreign Secretaries in London, 1844–67* (Selinsgrove, Penn.: Susquehanna University Press, 1993), 138–39.

45. Lt. Col. George W. Lay to Harney, June 29, 1857, "The Utah Expedition," *House Ex. Doc.* 71, 7–9.

46. MacKinnon, *At Sword's Point, Part 1*, 177 n. 61.

47. David Herbert Donald, *Lincoln* (New York: Simon & Schuster, 1995), 440.

48. Professor Pinsker's observation was made informally during the Educators In-Service Enrichment Workshop, The President James Buchanan National Symposium, Lancaster, Pennsylvania, September 20, 2008. His point, and that of the late

Professor Donald about Buchanan and other nineteenth-century presidents, are argued extensively by other scholars throughout Martin J. Medhurst, ed., *Before the Rhetorical Presidency* (College Station: Texas A&M University Press, 2008).

49. For Buchanan's December 8, 1857, first annual message to Congress see note 21 above.

50. The best and most recent scholarship about this atrocity is Juanita L. Brooks, *The Mountain Meadows Massacre*, 2nd ed. (1950; Norman: University of Oklahoma Press, 1962); Will Bagley, *Blood of the Prophets: Brigham Young and the Massacre at Mountain Meadows* (Norman: University of Oklahoma Press, 2002); Ronald W. Walker, Richard E. Turley Jr., and Glen M. Leonard, *Massacre at Mountain Meadows* (New York: Oxford University Press, 2008); David L. Bigler and Will Bagley, *Innocent Blood: Essential Narratives of the Mountain Meadows Massacre* (Norman, Okla.: Arthur H. Clark, 2008); Turley and Walker, *Mountain Meadows Massacre*. Young's assertion about the telegraph appears in Josiah Rogerson, "The Guilt of John D. Lee," 18, in Mountain Meadows File, LDS Church Archives; John M. Bernhisel, untitled memo of conversations with Buchanan, June 1859, Brigham Young Collection, LDS Church Archives; Richard D. Poll, "The Utah War," in *Utah History Encyclopedia*, ed. Allan Kent Powell (Salt Lake City: University of Utah Press, 1994), 607.

51. Alexander to the officers of the United States Army commanding forces en route to Utah, October 8, 1857, LeRoy R. and Ann W. Hafen, eds., *Mormon Resistance: A Documentary Account of the Utah Expedition, 1857–1858* (1958; reprint, Lincoln: University of Nebraska Press, 2005), 66–69.

52. Capt. Alfred Cumming to mother, September 23, 1857, Cumming Family Papers, Augusta Richmond County Historical Society and Special Collections, Reese Library, Augusta [Georgia] State University.

53. Daniel N. Rolph, "Kentucky Reaction & Casualties in the Utah War of 1857–58," *Journal of Kentucky Studies* 4 (September 1987), 89–96. For an exposition of Young's treatment of the Utah Expedition as a mob, see Young, Discourse of October 18, 1857, Salt Lake City *Deseret News*, October 28, 1857.

54. William P. MacKinnon, "Buchanan's Thrust from the Pacific: The Utah War's Ill-Fated Second Front," *Journal of Mormon History* 34 (Fall 2008): 246–49; Ouseley to Clarendon, February 15, 1858, in Barnes and Barnes, *Private and Confidential*, 193–94. A more complete discussion of Buchanan's hope to use reinforcement of the Utah Expedition from the Pacific Coast to advance military intervention in Mexico and acquisition of Cuba appears in William P. MacKinnon, "'Not as a Stranger': A Presbyterian Afoot in the Mormon Past," *Journal of Mormon History* 38 (Spring 2012): 21–39; and William P. MacKinnon, "Hammering Utah, Squeezing Mexico, and Coveting Cuba: James Buchanan's White House Intrigues," *Utah Historical Quarterly* 80 (Spring 2012): 132–51.

55. James L. Huston, *The Panic of 1857 and the Coming of the Civil War* (Baton Rouge: Louisiana State University Press, 1987); Leonard J. Arrington, *Great Basin*

Kingdom: An Economic History of the Latter-day Saints, 1830–1900 (Cambridge: Harvard University Press, 1958), 161–203; Leonard J. Arrington, "Mormon Finance and the Utah War," *Utah Historical Quarterly* 20 (July 1952): 219–38.

56. Bernhisel to Young, November 2, 1857, LDS Church Archives.

57. The most recent and extensive discussions of Floyd's service at the War Department and his resignation appear in Pinnegar, *Brand of Infamy*, and Belohlavek, "Politics of Scandal," 145–60.

58. Jane Flaherty, "'The Exhausted Condition of the Treasury' on the Eve of the Civil War," *Civil War History* 55 (July 2009): 244–77.

59. Ibid., 245, 253; MacKinnon, "125 Years of Conspiracy Theories," 219–22. Flaherty recognizes the cost of the Utah War (unspecified) as a component of Buchanan's "excessive" spending, but she lacks an appreciation of the conflict's scope, referring to it merely as a case of "the march into Utah against the Mormons." Accordingly, Flaherty discusses spending levels during the Buchanan administration as being unprecedented for peacetime, an unusual characterization of a period during which nearly one-third of the army drawn from ten regiments was committed to Utah.

60. Flaherty, "'Exhausted Condition of the Treasury,'" 245–47.

61. MacKinnon, "125 Years of Conspiracy Theories."

62. Buchanan, *Mr. Buchanan's Administration*, 238–39.

63. This discussion of the change in Buchanan's approach to Utah after the spring of 1858 and its impact is adapted from MacKinnon, "Epilogue to the Utah War," 190, 243–47.

64. 1st Lt. David S. Stanley quoted in Samuel W. Fordyce IV, ed., *An American General: The Memoirs of David Sloan Stanley* (Santa Barbara, Calif.: The Narrative Press, 2004), 104.

65. Donald, *Lincoln*, 13.

66. MacKinnon, "125 Years of Conspiracy Theories." Rather than personally demanding Floyd's resignation, Buchanan chose to delegate the task to Attorney General Jeremiah S. Black—an action reminiscent of Buchanan's sending Floyd to repair the president's damaged relationship with John C. Breckinridge in April 1857. Floyd's mission to Breckinridge kept the vice-president from returning to Kentucky but was not enough to bring about a private meeting between Buchanan and Breckinridge for another three years. For the rupture in relations between Buchanan and Breckinridge and the personal communications incident that caused it, see Kenneth M. Stampp, *America in 1857: A Nation on the Brink* (New York: Oxford University Press, 1990), 71; Mark O. Hatfield (with Senate Historical Office), "Strained Relations with Buchanan," "John C. Breckinridge (1857–1861)," *Vice Presidents of the United States, 1798–1993* (Washington, D.C.: U.S. Government Printing Office, 1997), 193–99n11; Floyd to Breckinridge, March 25, 1857, Jeremiah S. Black Papers, Manuscript Division, Library of Congress, Washington, D.C.

67. Richard Norton Smith, "Taking Up the Mantle," in *A New Birth of Freedom*, ed. Don Wycliff (Washington, D.C.: Abraham Lincoln Bicentennial Commission, 2009), 68–71; Edmund Morris, *Theodore Rex* (New York: Modern Library, 2002), 459.

68. David L. Bigler, "The Aiken Party Executions and the Utah War, 1857–1858," *Western Historical Quarterly* 38 (Winter 2007): 451–70. For a comprehensive analysis of violence and bloodshed in Utah connected to the Utah War see MacKinnon, "'Lonely Bones.'"

3

General Jackson Is Dead

James Buchanan, Stephen A. Douglas, and Kansas Policy

NICOLE ETCHESON

In the winter of 1857, a controversy arising out of Kansas Territory once again convulsed Congress and the nation. A constitutional convention sitting in the territorial capital, Lecompton, had submitted a proslavery constitution to Congress, requesting admission to the Union as a slave state. Despite serious problems with how the convention had been formed, conducted its proceedings, and structured ratification, President James Buchanan decided to endorse this constitution. Stephen A. Douglas, the powerful Illinois senator under whose Kansas-Nebraska Act the territory had been formed, however, opposed it.

In early December, Douglas called at the White House. He may have been angry that the president had decided to support Lecompton without consulting him, ignoring his role as a key formulator of Kansas policy. Or perhaps he felt that the courtesy of explaining his disagreement with the president might avert a split in their party. In any case, the interview between the two powerful Democrats was unpleasant. Finally, President Buchanan threw down the gauntlet. He told the senator, "Mr. Douglas, I desire you to remember that no Democrat ever yet differed from an Administration of his own choice without being crushed. Beware the fate of Tallmadge and Rives." The president was referring to two Democrats who had disagreed with Andrew Jackson and been politically destroyed. The threat failed to cow Douglas, who replied, "Mr. President, I wish you to remember that General Jackson is dead!"[1]

Figure 3.1. Senator Stephen Douglas. Abraham Lincoln Presidential Library and Museum, Springfield, Illinois.

Buchanan as Jacksonian

Biographer Jean H. Baker has called Buchanan's Kansas policy "one of the greatest of presidential blunders in American history." At the same time, however, she points out that Buchanan was the president with the most "impressive credentials" since James Madison. He was more widely experienced than his predecessors, with previous office at the state, national, and international level. She asks the natural question: How did a man seemingly so qualified for the highest office of the land come to be ranked by historians as one of the United States' worst presidents? Baker's answer is that Buchanan was "tone-deaf to the kind of compromises that might have fulfilled his intentions."[2]

There are many reasons for Buchanan's Kansas blunder. He was too close to Southerners. He took seriously—some thought too seriously—Southern threats to secede over Lecompton. And he did not take seriously enough the prospect that bringing Kansas in as a slave state would hurt the Democratic Party in the North. The president, however, shared with Douglas a moral tone-deafness on the issue of slavery, and a tendency to condemn abolitionists as troublemakers while overlooking how Southerners exacerbated sectional problems. Buchanan felt no strong commitment to popular sovereignty, the doctrine that territorial settlers would decide whether to have slavery, under which Kansas Territory had been organized. He also heartily disliked popular sovereignty's leading advocate, Douglas. Confronted with the dilemma posed by the Lecompton Constitution, Buchanan, like many pro-Lecompton Southerners, took refuge in a law-and-order rationale the proslavery party used as it tried to force its will on the free-soil settlers of Kansas.

But what scholars have not noted is the impact of the Jacksonian era on Buchanan. The president's reference to Tallmadge and Rives is revealing. At a time when many Americans longed for an Andrew Jackson—the tough Old Hickory who had destroyed the monster Bank and faced down the South Carolina nullifiers—James Buchanan thought he could be Andrew Jackson. And Stephen Douglas was right—James Buchanan was no Andrew Jackson.

Andrew Jackson had little but contempt for James Buchanan. As a young congressman in the winter of 1824–25, Buchanan had tried to play go-between between Henry Clay's supporters and General Jackson in the disputed presidential election that went into the House of Representatives. Buchanan suggested that Jackson announce his intention to replace John Quincy Adams as secretary of state, explaining that Clay's friends would see that action as a hint that Jackson might appoint Clay to that post, thereby securing Clay's votes for Jackson in the House. Not only was Jackson outraged at the idea that he would try to buy Clay's support, but Buchanan's eye condition appeared to have him winking conspiratorially at General Jackson—all of which proved unfortunate for Buchanan.[3]

Because Buchanan had helped Jackson carry Pennsylvania in the 1828 election, the new president rewarded him by making him minister to Russia. Michael J. Birkner points out that this appointment amounted to exile and suggested Jackson's distrust of Buchanan. Buchanan was thus abroad during crucial periods of the Jackson administration—the Bank War and nullification crisis. In his ministerial post, he even had difficulty getting access to the newspapers, about which he complained repeatedly to the administration.

In Congress—before and after his sojourn in Russia—Buchanan made speeches about contentious issues: the Cumberland Road and internal improvements; duties on molasses, woolens, iron products, and other items subject to tariffs; Native Americans; and banking. Except for protective tariffs, important to his Pennsylvania constituents, Buchanan was a consistent supporter of Democratic Party policies. Even while abroad, he managed to follow events at home well enough to comment on the Tariff of 1832 and on "Bankism" as well as to explain the nullification controversy to his Russian counterparts. His letters from St. Petersburg reveal that he spent considerable time discussing South Carolina's defiance of the federal government with European observers.

It would be the nullification crisis, of course, that would provide the model of Andrew Jackson as staunch defender of the Union. When South Carolina defied the federal government by refusing to enforce the tariffs of 1828 and 1832, thereby nullifying them, President Jackson acted decisively. He issued a "Proclamation" rejecting the legitimacy of nullification, sent troops to Charleston, and asked Congress to pass the so-called Force Bill: the power to use federal troops and state militia to disperse the nullifiers if they seized U.S. property. At the same time, members of Congress—including Jackson's old foe, Henry Clay—put together a compromise tariff which would gradually give the nullifiers the lower tariffs they desired.

Facing this combination of stick and carrot, the nullifiers backed down and rescinded their ordinances of nullification, but they defiantly nullified the Force Bill.

Although the long-term implications of South Carolina's stance were ominous, for the time being Jackson had stood up for the Union against Southern disunionists and prevailed. Historians have argued about whether his handling of nullification was successful. Richard E. Ellis believes there was a backlash against Jackson's Nullification Proclamation and threats of force. Ultimately, South Carolina succeeded in getting a lower tariff and enshrining states' rights as a tool to protect the South. But the Civil War generation overlooked these details and longed for Jackson's firmness of purpose.[4] It would be against this memory that Buchanan's contemporaries would judge his performance.

Certainly, Buchanan had come of age during the Jacksonian era. Kenneth M. Stampp characterized Buchanan as a "loyal party man" and "a firm believer in the principles of Jacksonian Democracy." He was a hardworking politician but lacked the charisma of a Jackson or the legislative abilities of a Douglas. More than two decades later, when he ascended to the presidency, Buchanan chose cabinet members who came of age in the period or earlier. Significantly, none were Northern advocates of popular sovereignty, except Secretary of State Lewis Cass. The elderly Cass could claim the title "Father of Popular Sovereignty," having advanced that position in his 1848 candidacy for the presidency. Although Cass occasionally differed with Buchanan about interpreting the doctrine, Cass suppressed his qualms and deferred to the president. Cass supported the Lecompton Constitution without reservation. Almost a decade younger than Cass, Buchanan was sixty-five when inaugurated and, at the time, the second-oldest man elected president. Peter Knupfer points out that Buchanan's nickname, the "old public functionary," highlighted how out of touch the president was with the concerns of a new political generation.[5]

Buchanan, Douglas, and Popular Sovereignty

Buchanan was familiar with the dilemma posed by slavery and its expansion. As senator in the 1830s, he became chairman of the committee to consider the prohibition of slavery and the slave trade in the District of Columbia. This committee was the target of antislavery petitions that

Southerners preferred to suppress. Buchanan did not want to curtail the right of petition, but he viewed the abolitionists as dangerous to the Union. A decade later he served as secretary of state during the presidency of James K. Polk. When the acquisition of the Mexican Cession first reopened the problem of slavery in the territories, Buchanan's preferred solution was to extend the Missouri Compromise line across the cession to the Pacific Ocean. Congress, however, allowed California to come in as a free state but provided for no restriction on slavery in Utah and New Mexico Territories.[6]

Stephen A. Douglas would later claim that the 1850 compromise's no-restriction policy was really popular sovereignty, the principle of his Kansas-Nebraska Act four years later. In actuality, the situation was somewhat different. The 1850 bills organizing New Mexico and Utah said they might be admitted "with or without slavery" and affected only those territories. In 1854, Douglas was attempting—once again—to organize the territory west of Iowa. The 1820 Missouri Compromise prohibited slavery in this territory. For that reason, Missouri politicians made it clear to Douglas that he could not get Southern votes to organize the territory. To placate Southerners and secure their votes, Douglas's legislation, the Kansas-Nebraska Act, used language similar to the New Mexico and Utah bills but also explicitly repealed the Missouri Compromise restriction on slavery and replaced it with the people's right "to form and regulate their domestic institutions in their own way, subject only to the Constitution of the United States," that is, popular sovereignty. When challenged, Douglas maintained that no repeal had taken place because the 1850 compromise had already superseded the Missouri one.

Few were fooled by Douglas's sleight-of-hand. Most Northerners objected that the Missouri Compromise was a "sacred compact" (black abolitionist Frederick Douglass scoffed at such talk, as the 1820 compromise legalized slavery in the southern part of the Louisiana Purchase; the South's pressure to repeal the Missouri Compromise, Douglass thought, "shows the danger of ever making compacts with wrong"). Despite the ensuing political storm, the Kansas-Nebraska bill passed, creating the new territories of Kansas and Nebraska.[7]

Whatever Buchanan may have thought of the merits of popular sovereignty—he was out of the country again as U.S. minister to Great Britain—it was settled Democratic Party policy when he was nominated for the presidency in 1856. According to biographer Philip Shriver Klein, Buchanan disliked the Kansas-Nebraska Act's unsettling of the Compromise of 1850.[8] The Cincinnati convention that nominated Buchanan for the presidency, however, unanimously adopted a resolution endorsing "the principles" of the Kansas-Nebraska Act "as embodying the only sound and safe solution of the 'slavery question' upon which the great national idea of the people of this whole country can repose in its determined conservatism of the Union—NON-INTERFERENCE BY CONGRESS WITH SLAVERY IN STATE AND TERRITORY."[9] As candidate, Buchanan professed to "heartily approve" of the platform. He expressly endorsed the Kansas-Nebraska Act.[10]

Buchanan may have been committed to the popular sovereignty plank of the Cincinnati platform, but that did not mean he had to like it—or its author, Senator Douglas. After all, Buchanan had only emerged as the compromise choice of the convention after Douglas's candidacy had sputtered. Douglas was a powerful rival for leadership of the party. Although Douglas worked for Buchanan's election, it became clear very quickly that he would have limited influence over the new administration.[11] At the president-elect's request, Buchanan and Douglas met before the inauguration, at which time Douglas learned that the patronage decisions for the Midwest had already been made—and that at the direction of Indiana senator Jesse D. Bright, a Douglas foe. "I am an out sider," Douglas reported. "My advice is not coveted nor will my wishes probably be regarded."

Although the open break with the administration would not come until Lecompton, Douglas was already determined to fight for his rights. If "the power of the administration is to be used either for plunder or ambition I shall return every blow they may give."[12] Buchanan did not even consult Douglas about lucrative federal patronage in Illinois, and he appointed Douglas's father-in-law to a position against Douglas's wishes. Douglas complained that after he spent $42,000 of his own money to elect Buchanan in 1856, Buchanan addressed the thank-you letter to "Samuel" A. Douglas.[13] While doubtless a careless error by the busy president-elect, it boded ill for their future relationship.

Despite their policy differences, both Buchanan and Douglas accepted the paternalist model of slavery as the norm in the South, and they failed to understand Northerners' moral objections to it. Buchanan had indentured former slaves working for him. Baker compares Buchanan's estate,

Wheatland, to a Southern plantation. It was so presented in a campaign biography aimed at Southern voters. Baker contends that Buchanan admired the life of a Southern gentleman and believed that slavery civilized African Americans. At Wheatland, Buchanan acted as a patriarch to a large family of orphaned or poor nieces and nephews.

The bachelor Buchanan's closest friendship was with William King of Alabama. Buchanan and King boarded together in Washington, D.C., during Buchanan's years as congressman and senator. One congressman referred to Buchanan and the handsome King as "Buchanan & his wife." Their surviving correspondence—both their nieces destroyed their letters to each other—resemble those of other same-sex yet heterosexual friends in the nineteenth century. It is certainly possible that Buchanan and King were lovers, but a homosexual relationship is impossible to prove definitively with the surviving evidence. It is definitely the case, however, that King, Buchanan's most intimate friend, warned the Pennsylvanian that abolitionism would foment disunion.

Douglas also had strong ties to the South. His first wife, Martha Martin, was the daughter of a North Carolina planter and inherited a Mississippi plantation with more than one hundred slaves. Douglas profited from the income from this property, which later passed to his sons when his wife died. When Douglas remarried after Martha's death, it was to another Southerner: Adele Cutts was a Washington belle from a Maryland family.[14]

Both men had shown a definite pro-Southern tilt. Douglas might offer popular sovereignty as *the fundamental principle of self-government*, but it served Southern interests by opening to slavery territory that had previously been closed.[15] Popular sovereignty not only garnered Southern votes to organize the Kansas and Nebraska Territories but also won Douglas Southern support. In fact, many disgruntled Northerners suspected that Douglas's Kansas-Nebraska Act was merely a plot to win the ambitious senator Southern support for a presidential bid. Buchanan's cabinet consisted of four Southern slaveowners and three Northerners, none of whom were free-soil Democrats. Moreover, Southerners Howell Cobb of Georgia and Jacob Thompson of Mississippi were Buchanan's favorites, at least until the secession crisis caused him to rely more heavily on fellow Pennsylvanian Jeremiah Black.[16]

Whatever their sectional sympathies, the Lecompton controversy forced both Buchanan and Douglas to choose between North and South. Although Douglas's Kansas-Nebraska Act had been a boon to the South, the Illinois senator's allegiance was to popular sovereignty as an ideology. The proslavery Lecompton Constitution, which many Northerners believed to be the result of rigged delegate and ratification elections, was too egregious a violation of that ideology for Douglas to endorse. In addition, his political popularity in Illinois, which had already been strained by the Kansas-Nebraska Act, might be irrevocably lost if he supported Lecompton. He chose the North.

Buchanan had neither Douglas's stake in popular sovereignty nor the need to be reelected in a Northern state. He chose the South. In addition, Buchanan had a long-standing fear of Southern secession and a loathing of Northern antislavery. During the 1856 campaign, Buchanan argued that the election of Republican John C. Frémont would lead to the dissolution of the Union. Such declarations were more than campaign hyperbole, and Buchanan insisted that Northerners needed to be alerted to the disunionist threat. He deplored the *National Intelligencer* for taking a "neutral position" between him and Frémont: "This opinion they have expressed, notwithstanding I am in the daily receipt of letters from the South which are truly alarming; & these from gentlemen who formerly opposed both nullification and disunion. They say explicitly that the election of Fremont involves the dissolution of the Union, & this immediately." Buchanan thus took office with a profound sense of the threat to the country if Northerners were to carry out Black Republican "outlawry" against the Southern states.[17]

Although Buchanan believed that conflict between "a combined North against a combined South on the question of slavery" was the most dangerous for the Union, it was not the South's threat to the North that concerned him. "With the South it is a question of self-preservation, of personal security around the family altar, of life or of death." Buchanan spoke of no threat to the North from the South.[18] In a letter after his election, he pledged, "The great object of my administration will be to arrest, if possible the agitation of the Slavery question at the North & to destroy sectional parties." He did not speak of stopping Southern agitation, and by "sectional parties" he meant the Republicans. He repeated these themes in his inaugural address: the danger of "geographical parties," and the threat that slavery "agitation . . . may eventually endanger the personal safety of a large portion of our countrymen where the institution exists."[19] Southern threats to secede if Kansas was not admitted under Lecompton played powerfully on the president's existing fears of disunion.

As Paul Finkelman explains within this volume, Buchanan had expected agitation over slavery to cease because of the U.S. Supreme Court's *Dred Scott* decision—one that he knew of in advance, thanks to his correspondence with Justice Robert C. Grier.[20] More importantly, the Court's decision in *Dred Scott* would practically invalidate Northern Democrats' interpretation of popular sovereignty by ruling that slave property could not be kept out of the territories. Buchanan evidently had little trouble reconciling *Dred Scott* with popular sovereignty. When justifying his administration's Kansas policy to Connecticut citizens, Buchanan quoted the Kansas-Nebraska Act's promise that territorial residents would be "perfectly free" to decide about slavery. He then continued, "Slavery existed at that period and still exists in Kansas, under the Constitution of the United States. This point has at last been finally decided by the highest tribunal known to our laws.... If a confederation of sovereign States acquire a new territory at the expense of their common blood and treasure, surely one set of the partners can have no right to exclude the other from its enjoyment, by prohibiting them from taking into it whatsoever is recognized to be property by the common Constitution."

How, then, were the territorial residents to exercise their perfect freedom to prohibit slavery? The president's answer was that when they "proceed to frame a State constitution, then it is their right to decide the important question for themselves whether they will continue, modify, or abolish slavery."[21] Buchanan proposed no way in which settlers might prohibit slavery while still a territory. Although the president might find it possible to reconcile *Dred Scott* with popular sovereignty, the decision would not only fail to quiet slavery agitation in the North but would also invigorate the proslavery party inside and outside Kansas, strengthening its conviction that slavery had a permanent place in Kansas Territory.

In contrast, Stephen Douglas sought to reconcile *Dred Scott* with popular sovereignty by insisting settlers still had the ability to reject slavery during the territorial period. His most famous enunciation of this position came during the 1858 senatorial race against Abraham Lincoln. Lincoln posed a set of questions during their debate at Freeport, Illinois. The second question was, "Can the people of a United States Territory, in any lawful way, against the wish of any citizen of the United States, exclude slavery from its limits prior to the formation of a State Constitution?" *Dred Scott* would seem to suggest not. Douglas pointed out that he had answered this question "a hundred times from every stump in Illinois," but his answer would nonetheless come to be known as the Freeport doctrine. This doctrine said that the people could prohibit slavery "for the reason that slavery cannot exist a day or an hour anywhere, unless it is supported by local police regulations." If settlers of a territory failed to pass laws to enforce slavery, it would not exist.[22]

While the president and senator struggled to incorporate *Dred Scott* into Democratic Party doctrine, the African American community focused as much on the Supreme Court's attack on black citizenship as on the territorial aspects of the decision. In speaking three years earlier against the Kansas-Nebraska Act, Frederick Douglass had asserted his citizenship by arguing that the Constitution delineated only citizens and aliens—and he was not the latter. A convention of black men in Troy, New York, called the decision's rejection of black citizenship and its assertion that blacks had no rights "a bold and infamous lie . . . in striking contrast with the sacred guarantees for liberty, with which the Constitution abounds." James McCune Smith, a prominent African American physician and abolitionist, authored a lengthy treatise on "Citizenship" to prove that blacks were citizens. African Americans also focused on how *Dred Scott* threatened the right of Northern states to exclude slavery. Douglass reprinted in his newspaper a piece from the *Utica Herald* warning that *Dred Scott* "makes Slavery national and human bondage legal in every State of the Union." Although African Americans were less interested in the territorial ramifications of *Dred Scott*, the proslavery party welcomed the decision as a justification for its efforts to make Kansas slave.[23]

The Lecompton Constitution

Dred Scott contributed to the intransigence of proslavery men in Kansas and exacerbated the Lecompton controversy. The territorial government of Kansas at the time of the *Dred Scott* decision was in the hands of proslavery men. Before Buchanan's inauguration, Democrats had suppressed the guerrilla fighting in Kansas Territory. The president-elect declared that there was nothing left but for Kansas to "slide gracefully into the Union."

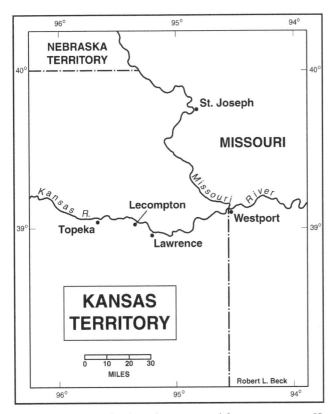

Figure 3.2. Divided by their slave-state and free-state origins, Kansas settlers aligned with either the slave-state capital in Lecompton or the free-state capital in Topeka. The Buchanan administration lost many political allies in pushing for Kansas statehood under a proslavery constitution framed in Lecompton. Map created by Robert L. Beck, Department of Geography, Indiana University–Purdue University Indianapolis.

Kansas admission, after the struggles in the territory the preceding two years, would not only be a policy success for the new administration but would—some Democrats thought—kill the new Republican Party by depriving it of its key issue.[24] Unfortunately, there would be nothing graceful about the struggle for Kansas admission during Buchanan's administration. The new president's reading of *Dred Scott* meant the citizens of Kansas had only a narrow window—the writing of the state constitution—in which to forbid slavery. The proslavery party in the territory was determined to close that window.

In 1857, Kansas held a constitutional convention. The problems with the constitutional process were many and severe. The proslavery-dominated territorial legislature mandated the call for the convention and election of delegates, to which free-staters accorded no legitimacy because voting irregularities had marred the election of those legislators. Free-staters complained that proslavery territorial officials left them off the rolls of those who could vote for convention delegates, and, despite the objections of territorial governor John Geary, the convention was not required to submit its work for ratification by Kansas settlers.

Free-staters boycotted the election for delegates, which made the constitutional convention in Lecompton solidly proslavery. Meanwhile, a new Buchanan-appointed territorial governor, Robert J. Walker, sought to bring the free-staters back into the process. A good friend of the president, Walker thought he had Buchanan's backing that the constitution should be endorsed by Kansans. Walker succeeded in reincorporating free-staters into Kansas politics in that the free-staters decided to participate in the election of a new territorial legislature. There was some attempt at fraud by the proslavery party, but Walker threw out the returns from Oxford and McGhee County, which were inflated with false proslavery votes, and the free-staters secured control of the territorial legislature. The Lecompton delegates had been watching this election closely. They had even suspended their convention to see how the elections came out. When they reconvened, they were torn by their desire to make Kansas a slave state and by the expectation that the constitution they produced would be subject to a popular ratification.[25]

Members of Buchanan's administration did their best in lobbying the delegates at the Lecompton constitutional convention to provide for the document's final approval in a plebiscite. In a way, the administration's behind-the-scenes role in the Lecompton Constitution was akin to the secret role Buchanan had played in lobbying Justice Grier for a suitable vote on *Dred Scott*. The convention's chairman, John Calhoun, knew that the administration would face sharp criticism in the North if the convention bypassed voter ratification of their final document. But proslavery delegates adamantly opposed submitting their constitution to Kansas voters, knowing that the free-state majority in the territory would kill it. Calhoun finally persuaded the convention delegates to accept a compromise. Kansans would be able to vote for the Lecompton Constitution "with or without slavery." The former meant that Kansas would be a slave state; the latter, however, meant only that there would be no further importation of slaves into Kansas—slave property already there would be protected. And voters were not allowed to reject the entire constitution.[26]

Senator Douglas was initially hesitant to reach a conclusion about these proceedings, writing, "The only question is whether the Constitution formed at Lecompton is the act & will of the people of Kansas, [or] whether it be the act and will of a small minority, who have attempted to cheat & defraud the majority by trickery & juggling."[27] Douglas was also receiving political advice from friends in Illinois. James Washington Sheahan warned him, "To admit Kansas as a Slave State would be destructive of everything in Illinois. We could never recover from it. . . . Remember that the *only* fight of 1858 will be in Illinois."[28] Between his review of the official record of the Lecompton proceedings and the political winds in the state where he would, within a year, stand for reelection, Douglas concluded that Lecompton was a "Fraud." "We will nail our colors to the mast and defend the right of the people to govern themselves against all assaults from all quarters," he vowed.[29] Buchanan, however, decided to support Lecompton. In his annual message to Congress on December 8, 1857—two days after Douglas vowed to nail the colors to the mast to fight for popular sovereignty—the president endorsed the convention's actions.[30]

Buchanan used the words "fair" and "legal" frequently in this December 1857 annual message. He reviewed the law creating the convention and judged it "in the main fair and just." If a "large proportion" of Kansans had decided not to vote for delegates, the opportunity had nonetheless been "fairly afforded" them and "their refusal to avail themselves of their right could in no manner affect the legality of the convention." Although he would have preferred full ratification, Buchanan noted that the Kansas-Nebraska Act did not require it—only that the main question, that of slavery, be submitted to the territory's voters. The convention had "fairly and explicitly" sent the important question to the people "whether they will have a constitution 'with or without slavery.'"

When Buchanan communicated to Congress, two weeks yet remained before that vote would be taken. The president hoped to persuade the free-staters to participate in this election, or at least warn them of the consequences of staying away. Again, he noted that the ratification election "will be held under legitimate authority, and if any portion of the inhabitants shall refuse to vote, a fair opportunity to do so having been presented, this will be their own voluntary act, and they alone will be responsible for the consequences."

Whether Kansas came in "with or without slavery," the president reminded Kansans that they had the power to change the constitution "within a brief period." Even though "without slavery" meant the retention of some slaveholding, Buchanan noted that there were few slaves in the territory. Furthermore, "the highest judicial tribunal of the country" had decided that during the territorial phase "both equality and justice demand that the citizens of one and all of them [sovereign states] shall have the right to take into it whatsoever is recognized as property by the common Constitution. To have summarily confiscated the property in slaves already in the Territory would have been an act of gross injustice." In any case, Buchanan asserted in this message, if Kansas were simply admitted under Lecompton, "the excitement beyond her own limits will speedily pass away, and she will then, for the first time, be left, as she ought to have been long since, to manage her own affairs in her own way."[31]

Buchanan's efforts failed. Governor Walker was horrified at the Lecompton ratification process and angry that administration officials had operated behind his back in talking to members of the convention. He went east to Washington to see his old friend the president. Unable to prevail on Buchanan to repudiate Lecompton, Walker resigned. The free-staters refused to participate in the ratification election on December 21. Lecompton with slavery was ratified by a 90 percent margin, in a very low turnout.

Douglas was not the only Northern Democrat unhappy with Lecompton. Between the ratification in December and the submission of Lecompton to Congress at the beginning of February, other Northern congressmen pleaded with the president not to insist on Lecompton. James P. France, the editor of the Springfield, Illinois, Democratic newspaper, wrote Senator William Bigler, a close political ally of Buchanan, that "Gen. Jackson rising from the dead and advocating the Lecompton constitution would not receive one hundred votes in Illinois."[32] The Northern press, including Frederick Douglass's newspaper, followed the efforts in Congress to rally votes for Lecompton. But Buchanan did not listen, at least not to Northerners. Instead, Buchanan seems to have been more concerned about what he was hearing from Southerners. Georgia and Alabama were committed to holding state conventions "for the purpose of determining what course they shall pursue" if Kansas were denied admission under the Lecompton Constitution. That course, presumably, would be secession.[33]

At the beginning of February, having officially received the Lecompton Constitution from Calhoun, the convention's presiding officer, Buchanan presented it to Congress with his recommendation that it be accepted. Buchanan spent the first two pages of that message arguing that the free-state movement in Kansas was a "revolutionary" one. He invoked Governor Walker in making this case, referring to Walker's insistence on having troops in Kansas to preserve "the regular [territorial] government and the execution of its laws." Buchanan argued that the free-staters had refused to vote for constitutional convention delegates, not because the process was flawed, but because they "refused to sanction or recognize any other constitution than that framed at Topeka." In contrast to the extralegal Topeka or free-state movement, the Lecompton process had been carried out with "regularity," the convention was "lawfully constituted," and there had been "a fair opportunity" for the free-staters to vote on ratification. Governor Walker had urged the free-staters to vote for delegates and warned them of the consequences if they did not.

That the convention had not submitted the entire constitution hardly mattered. Only the slavery question was at issue. The president maintained that when he instructed Walker that the constitution must be submitted, he really was thinking only of "the all-absorbing question of slavery." Buchanan expected "domestic peace" to return if Kansas were admitted, but otherwise the dissension over slavery would "be renewed in a more alarming form." Even if Kansas were admitted as a slave state under Lecompton, the president argued, free-staters could still make Kansas a free state: they had merely to amend the constitution or write a new one.[34]

Douglass editorialized that the message was "a tissue of palpable inconsistencies and base falsifications, almost every paragraph abounding with evidence of moral stultification." Rather than being ashamed, as a president from a free state ought to be, at this triumph of slavery, the "President alludes in a rather exultant tone than otherwise, to the presence of slavery in Kansas." The message was a "deliberate insult to the people of the Free States." Douglass's assessment of the message was exactly that of many Northerners. Even though the president insisted "that the people of Kansas were consulted, and their wishes expressed, as to forming a Constitution," Douglass noted, "Every body knows this to be false."[35]

Senator Douglas also had decided it was false. Just as Buchanan had constructed a legal rationale for supporting Lecompton, Douglas had formulated his own reasons for opposing it. The newly elected free-state-dominated territorial legislature had called for an up-or-down ratification vote on Lecompton. Kansans voted on January 4, 1858, and resoundingly defeated the Lecompton Constitution. Douglas pointed to this election to show that Lecompton "does not embody the popular will of that [Kansas] Territory." Lecompton was illegitimate for two reasons. First, the Lecompton convention lacked the sovereign power necessary to put its constitution into force. That power had to come from the people. Second, the territorial legislature had now held a ratification election that nullified the Lecompton Constitution.[36]

The English Compromise

Despite intense lobbying by the Buchanan administration, which Frederick Douglass referred to as "bribes and threats," the president failed to win passage for the bill to admit Kansas under the Lecompton Constitution. Although Lecompton passed the Senate, it foundered in the House of Representatives. Pro-administration Democrat William English of Indiana urged a conference committee as a "courtesy" to the Senate. According to one report, Buchanan so feared the humiliation to his administration if Lecompton failed that he cried while speaking to a Pennsylvania congressman. When the vote on creating a conference committee tied, the Speaker of the House, James L. Orr, broke the tie in the administration's favor.[37]

The conference committee nearly deadlocked. It finally produced a compromise that took English's name, although the compromise was largely the work of Alexander Stephens of Georgia. The compromise decreased the size of the land grant Kansas would receive and, with that development as a pretext, sent the constitution back to Kansas for another ratification vote. Northern Democrats could claim this compromise as a victory. Free-staters in Kansas would be given the opportunity to vote Lecompton down in its entirety (not all Northern Democrats supported the English compromise, as Stephen Douglas voted against it). Southerners, however, could argue that it was not slavery that had forced the resubmission but the land grant. Douglass merely used the commonplace Northern term of "the English swindle" to label the bill, although he improved it cleverly in his newspaper as the "*Anglicized* Lecompton Swindle": "It offers the People of Kansas a Bribe of five millions of acres of Land if they will sanction the Lecompton constitution; and threatens them with years of Territorial pupilage if they refuse!"

Despite assertions that the English compromise punished Kansans if they rejected Lecompton—they would have to wait for their territorial population to reach ninety-three thousand before applying again—enough Northern congressmen switched sides to allow the compromise to pass the House. The Senate also voted for it. On August 2, 1858, Kansans got another chance to vote on the Lecompton Constitution. Although Frederick Douglass predicted the proslavery party would rig this election as it had others, Kansans resoundingly rejected Lecompton, 11,300 votes to 1,788.[38]

Buchanan never forgave Stephen Douglas for his opposition to the Lecompton Constitution. While he congratulated himself, after the passage of the English bill, "that my administration has been so successful in pacifying the Country on the Kansas question," Buchanan lamented the role that Douglas had played: "Had Mr. Douglas been successful in defeating the Legislation on the subject [of Kansas], the Country would have been in a terrible condition. . . . [T]he Union would have been shaken to its centre." He added: "[H]ow Douglas . . . or any other person who had ever been a Democrat could have preferred the do-nothing policy . . . to the English Bill, which leaves to the people of Kansas to decide their own destiny, I am utterly at a loss to imagine."[39] Douglas complained "that the administration is more anxious for my distruction [*sic*] than they are for the harmony & unity of the Democratic Party." Buchanan ordered Douglas supporters be removed from their patronage positions and had his administration work to defeat the Illinois senator's reelection.[40]

With the passage of the English bill, Buchanan observed that "the Kansas question as a national question is at an end."[41] In his annual message to Congress at the end of 1858, Buchanan emphasized this point. Kansas "now appears to be tranquil and prosperous," for which Buchanan gave credit to his administration's policy. He had no regrets about backing Lecompton. When Congress reacted differently, he "cordially acquiesced" in the English compromise. He acknowledged that under the terms of that legislation, Kansas was now required to wait until its population reached ninety-three thousand. Citing a need for fairness, he recommended legislation requiring this population requirement for future territories considering statehood.

But he saw no reason why Kansas could not wait. The Kansas question had preoccupied Congress in the last two sessions. Surely the country deserved a rest. "By waiting for a short time, and acting in obedience to law, Kansas will glide into the Union without the slightest impediment."[42] As a matter of fact, this time Buchanan was right. Kansas did glide into the Union in 1861 under yet another constitution—it only took the secession of the Southern states to remove the impediment.[43]

The president viewed his Kansas policy as a success, but he failed to recognize the damage he had done his party. "A few more triumphs such as Nebraska and Lecompton, and the Black Oligarchy will have fought its last battle," Frederick Douglass slyly noted. Rather than despond over the English bill's passage, Douglass exulted at the attention being drawn to antislavery: "The slave is at length heard." Not everyone agreed. Charles L. Remond, a black abolitionist from Massachusetts, speaking to the annual meeting of the American Anti-Slavery Society, concluded that abolitionist activity had failed. Not only had the slave population quadrupled since the Revolution, but "this Kansas controversy has been carried on . . . in reference to the white men in that Territory . . . and that the sin of American slavery has not been touched." Remond lamented that opposing slavery's extension to Kansas, but not its existence in the South, the Republican Party's position, qualified one as a "good anti-slavery man." Remond's despair contrasted with Douglass's insistence that "We shall yet triumph."[44]

Indeed, the Buchanan Democrats were soundly punished at the polls in the fall 1858 elections. Buchanan told his niece, "This I have anticipated for three months & was not taken by surprise except as to the extent of our defeat." He and several others dined together and "had a merry time of it, laughing among other things over our crushing defeat."[45] But rather than drawing from that electoral defeat the recognition that many Northerners would never accept his pro-Southern definition of popular sovereignty, Buchanan instead became more determined to defeat Stephen Douglas. More than a year before the 1860 election, he was planning the "attack" against Douglas's candidacy for president.[46] He still expected Northerners to make concessions to proslavery Southerners, arguing that settlers from both the North and the South were equal in the territories, as the *Dred Scott* decision had affirmed.

Buchanan's assertions were consistent with the emerging Southern insistence on a slave code for the territories. Such a code would assert political equality with Northerners by requiring the federal government to allow and protect slave property in the territories. Any Northern insistence on keeping slavery out violated that equality. "Whilst the South cannot surrender their rights as co-equal States in the Confederacy," Buchanan asked, "what injury can it possibly do to the Northern States to yield this great Democratic principle?"[47] For proslavery Southerners to yield was "self-degradation"; for free-soil Northerners to yield was submission to the Constitution. But acceptance of a slave code required Northern Democrats to abandon the last vestiges of popular sovereignty, the premise that slavery could be kept out of a territory.[48]

Buchanan supported his vice-president, John C. Breckinridge, for president in 1860. Breckinridge had been nominated by a splinter faction of Southern Democrats. The president justified his failure to support Stephen Douglas, whom Northern Democrats nominated after Southerners had walked out of one convention, on the legalistic ground that neither Breckinridge nor Douglas had been nominated by the Democratic Party's two-thirds rule. This split left Democrats free to choose, Buchanan argued. Breckinridge "sanctions and sustains the perfect equality of all the States within their common Territories, and the opinion of the Supreme Court of the United States, establishing this equality." Douglas, in clinging to his original interpretation of popular sovereignty—namely, that slavery exclusion could be carried out during the territorial period—advocated what Buchanan now dismissed as lawless "squatter sovereignty."[49]

During the secession crisis, Americans longed for a return of Andrew Jackson. They feared that, as Douglas had pointed out during the Lecompton controversy, Buchanan "was no man for the emergency, no Jackson."[50] While popular memory credits Jackson with having ended nullification by threatening South Carolina with force, it was in fact Henry Clay's compromise tariff that allowed the nullifiers a face-saving way to back down. Jackson did not save the Union in perpetuity. Nullification festered for another thirty years, until it produced the even greater crisis of secession. Yet Americans remembered Jackson as having saved the Union. Like Clay, William English gave southerners wedded to Lecompton a face-saving way to lose. The English compromise did not save the Union either, and only provided a window of three years—not enough time for Buchanan to be remembered for his toughness.

Baker writes that Buchanan's Kansas policy was based on "the arrogant, wrongheaded, uncompromising use of power."[51] This statement might just as easily describe Jackson's efforts to destroy the Bank, or to force the submission of the Southern nullifiers. But while Buchanan failed to bring Kansas into the Union until the waning days of his term, Jackson succeeded in both destroying the Bank and repressing nullification.

Kenneth Stampp points out that Buchanan almost got Lecompton through Congress. One might add that Buchanan almost destroyed Stephen Douglas. Douglas only narrowly retained his Senate seat against his Republican challenger, Abraham Lincoln, in 1858, and failed to unify the Democratic Party in 1860. But Buchanan did not get Lecompton passed, and he did not keep Douglas from reelection in 1858. If Jackson had threatened to break Douglas, one inclines to believe Old Hickory would have succeeded. In addition, there was another difference between Presidents Jackson and Buchanan. Jackson stood up to the Southern disunionists in 1833. By contrast, almost thirty years later, Buchanan delivered a convoluted presidential message in the midst of the secession crisis, declaring secession illegal but denying that the federal government had any power to stop it. Republicans saw this position as cowardly if not treasonous.[52] Not only did Buchanan lack Jackson's toughness, but it was not even clear on which side he stood.

In his play, *Buchanan Dying*, John Updike reprises the scene between Buchanan and Douglas with which this chapter began. When Douglas issues his crushing rejoinder that "General Jackson is dead!," Updike's Buchanan is bewildered. "*Lights go out.* BUCHANAN *is alone, and repeats, puzzled*; Dead?"[53] A product of the Jacksonian era, Buchanan misjudged both the extent of presidential power and his own ability to wield it as effectively as Old Hickory once had.

Notes

1. Philip Shriver Klein, *President James Buchanan* (University Park: Pennsylvania State University Press, 1962), 300–301; David M. Potter, *The Impending Crisis, 1848–1861* (New York: Harper & Row, 1976), 316.

2. Jean H. Baker, *James Buchanan* (New York: Times Books, 2004), 1–6. A 1982 poll of historians put Buchanan at the bottom, with only Richard M. Nixon, Ulysses S. Grant, and Warren G. Harding listed as worse presidents. William E. Gienapp, "'No Bed of Roses': James Buchanan, Abraham Lincoln, and Presidential Leadership in the Civil War Era," in *James Buchanan and the Political Crisis of the 1850s*, ed. Michael J. Birkner (Selinsgrove: Susquehanna University Press, 1996), 95.

3. Robert V. Remini, *The Life of Andrew Jackson* (New York: Harper & Row, 1988), 152–53.

4. Michael J. Birkner, "Introduction: Getting to Know James Buchanan, Again," 17–36, in Birkner, *James Buchanan and the Political Crisis of the 1850s*, 23; John Bassett Moore, ed., *The Works of James Buchanan, Comprising His Speeches, State Papers, and Private Correspondence*, 12 vols. (New York: Antiquarian Press, 1960), 1:274–75, 313–14, 318–29, 330–63, 382–95, 398–418; 2:11–12, 48–49, 437–38; James Buchanan to Edward Livingston, August 9, 1832, ibid., 2:221–30; James Buchanan to General Jackson, December 20, 1832, ibid., 306–8; James Buchanan to Edward Livingston, ibid., 317–19. For evaluations of Jackson's handling of nullification, see Sean Wilentz, *The Rise of American Democracy: Jefferson to Lincoln* (New York: Norton, 2005), 379–89; Richard E. Ellis, *The Union at Risk: Jacksonian Democracy, States' Rights, and the Nullification Crisis* (New York: Oxford University Press, 1987). For the Civil War generation's admiration of Jackson's firmness in the nullification crisis, see Sean Wilentz, "Abraham Lincoln and Jacksonian Democracy," in *Our Lincoln: New Perspectives on Lincoln and His World*, ed. Eric Foner (New York: Norton, 2008), 62–79, esp. 76–79.

5. Kenneth M. Stampp, *America in 1857: A Nation on the Brink* (New York: Oxford University Press, 1990), 46–47, 62; Klein, *President James Buchanan*, 280; Willard Carl Klunder, *Lewis Cass and the Politics of Moderation* (Kent: Kent State University Press, 196), 296–301; Peter Knupfer, "James Buchanan, the Election of 1860, and the Demise of Jacksonian Politics," in Birkner, *James Buchanan and the Political Crisis of the 1850s*, 147–70.

6. Klein, *President James Buchanan*, 148–50, 200–201; Potter, *Impending Crisis*, 56–57, 115–16.

7. Michael F. Holt, *The Fate of Their Country: Politicians, Slavery Extension, and the Coming of the Civil War* (New York: Hill and Wang, 2004), 96, 100–105; Act of September 9, 1850, ch. 49, 9 *Stat.* 447; Act of September 9, 1850, ch. 51, 9 *Stat.* 453; John R. Wunder and Joann M. Ross, *The Nebraska-Kansas Act of 1854* (Lincoln: University of Nebraska Press, 2008), 195, 205; "The Nebraska Controversy" and "The Kansas-Nebraska Bill" in Philip S. Foner, ed., *The Life and Writings of Frederick Douglass*, vol. 2, *Pre–Civil War Decade, 1850–1860* (New York: International Publishers, 1950), 276–79, 316–32. See also Nicole Etcheson, *Bleeding Kansas: Contested Liberty in the Civil War Era* (Lawrence: University Press of Kansas, 2004), 9–27.

8. Klein, *President James Buchanan*, 263.

9. *Official Proceedings of the National Democratic Convention Held in Cincinnati, June 2–6, 1856* (Cincinnati: Enquirer Co., 1856), 26, 29.

10. Speech, June 9, 1856, in Moore, *Works of James Buchanan*, 10:81; James Buchanan to the Committee of Notification, June 16, 1856, ibid., 81–85.

11. Klein, *President James Buchanan*, 255; S. A. Douglas to James Buchanan, September 29, 1856, in Robert W. Johannsen, ed., *The Letters of Stephen A. Douglas* (Urbana: University of Illinois Press, 1961), 367–68.

12. S. A. Douglas to Samuel Treat, February 5, 1857, in Johannsen, *Letters of*

Stephen A. Douglas, 372. David E. Meerse disagrees with the argument that Douglas was slighted on patronage at the beginning of the Buchanan administration. Meerse, "Origins of the Buchanan-Douglas Feud Reconsidered," *Journal of the Illinois State Historical Society* 67 (April 1974): 154–74.

13. Klein, *President James Buchanan*, 283–84; Michael J. Birkner, Don Fehrenbacher, Kenneth M. Stampp, Robert Johannsen, and Elbert Smith (discussants), "The Presidency of James Buchanan: A Reassessment," in Birkner, *James Buchanan and the Political Crisis of the 1850s*, 188.

14. William W. Freehling, *The Road to Disunion*, vol. 2, *Secessionists Triumphant, 1854–1861* (New York: Oxford University Press, 2007), 98; Baker, *James Buchanan*, 25–26, 47, 137–38, 141; James L. Huston, *Stephen A. Douglas and the Dilemmas of Democratic Equality* (Lanham: Rowman & Littlefield, 2007), 53–54, 122.

15. Huston, *Stephen A. Douglas*, 105. Sean Wilentz calls Douglas the leader of the "Northern doughface Democrats." Wilentz, "Abraham Lincoln and Jacksonian Democracy," 73. Jean Baker says that Lewis Cass was "like Buchanan, a northern man with southern principles," i.e., a doughface. Baker, *James Buchanan*, 55.

16. In the 1856 convention, Douglas had stronger support from Southern delegates than from any other region (Klein, *President James Buchanan*, 255, 276–78; Geo. Sanderson to James Buchanan, February 24, 1854, James Buchanan Papers, Historical Society of Pennsylvania, Philadelphia; Baker, *James Buchanan*, 79–80). Regarding Buchanan's relationships with his cabinet members, see Daniel W. Crofts's essay in this volume.

17. James Buchanan to Nahum Capen, August 27, 1856, in Moore, *Works of James Buchanan*, 10:88–89; James Buchanan to William B. Reed, September 14, 1856, ibid., 91–92.

18. Speech at Wheatland, November 6, 1856, ibid., 96. John Brown's attack at Harpers Ferry, Virginia, which Buchanan discussed in his Third Annual Message to Congress in December 1859, seemed to bear out his warnings of the threat to Southerners. He used the same language as he had in 1856 about "the personal safety" of Southerners, the threat to "the mothers of families," and the Southern need for "self-preservation." But he also hoped the raid had shown Americans the need to avoid "the possible peril to their cherished institutions," the Constitution and the Union. Third Annual Message, December 19, 1859, ibid., 339–41.

19. James Buchanan to John Y. Mason, December 29, 1856, ibid., 100; Inaugural Address, March 4, 1857, ibid., 108–9.

20. Inaugural Address, March 4, 1857, ibid., 105–6. For the *Dred Scott* decision, see also Don E. Fehrenbacher, *Slavery, Law, and Politics: The Dred Scott Case in Historical Perspective* (New York: Oxford University Press, 1981); and Paul Finkelman, *An Imperfect Union: Slavery, Federalism, and Comity* (Chapel Hill: University of North Carolina Press, 1981).

21. Reply to a Memorial of Citizens of Connecticut on Kansas, August 15, 1857, in Moore, *Works of James Buchanan*, 10:120–21. Later, Buchanan would distinguish

between "squatter sovereignty" and "popular sovereignty." The former meant "the revolutionary attempts of the first squatters in a new Territory to abolish Slavery or prevent its introduction into the Territory through the agency of a Territorial Legislature." The latter was "the Constitutional & quiet exercise of the rights of Sovereignty by the people of a Territory in the formation of a State Constitution, with or without domestic Slavery as they may determine. In the mean time slave holders take their property to the Territory, & whilst in a territorial condition it is protected by the Constitution and the Dred Scott decision." Of course, what the president now denigrated as "squatter sovereignty" had been popular sovereignty as understood at the passage of the Kansas-Nebraska Act. Buchanan to Robert Tyler, June 27, 1859, ibid., 325.

22. Robert W. Johannsen, *The Lincoln-Douglas Debates of 1858* (New York: Oxford University Press, 1965), 79, 88.

23. "The Kansas-Nebraska Act," in Foner, *Life and Writings*, 2:316–32; *Frederick Douglass' Paper*, September 24, 1858, March 18, May 13, 1859.

24. Speech at Wheatland, November 6, 1856, in Moore, *Works of James Buchanan*, 10:97; Stampp, *America in 1857*, 10.

25. Etcheson, *Bleeding Kansas*, 141–55.

26. Ibid., 155–56.

27. S. A. Douglas to John A. McClernand, November 23, 1857, in Johannsen, *Letters of Stephen A. Douglas*, 403–4.

28. Johannsen, *Letters of Stephen A. Douglas*, 404.

29. S. A. Douglas to Charles H. Lanphier and George Walker, December 6, 1857, ibid., 405.

30. Etcheson, *Bleeding Kansas*, 156–60.

31. First Annual Message, in Moore, *Works of James Buchanan*, 10:145–51. The Lecompton Constitution allowed for the Kansas state legislature to alter or amend the constitution in 1864 or thereafter. The time preceding 1864 was what Buchanan meant when he referred to the "brief period" that free-staters might have to wait to change the slavery provision of the Lecompton Constitution. Daniel W. Wilder, *Annals of Kansas* (Topeka: Geo. W. Martin, 1875), 189.

32. France quoted in Stampp, *America in 1857*, 288. See also Etcheson, *Bleeding Kansas*, 159–66.

33. *Frederick Douglass' Paper*, February 12, 1858; James Buchanan to J. W. Denver, March 27, 1858, in Moore, *Works of James Buchanan*, 10:201; James Buchanan to Wm. B. Reed, ibid., 225.

34. Message on the Constitution of Kansas, February 2, 1858, in Moore, *Works of James Buchanan*, 10:179–92; Klein, *President James Buchanan*, 300–312.

35. *Frederick Douglass' Paper*, February 12, 1858.

36. S. A. Douglas to John W. Forney et al., February 6, 1858, in Johannsen, *Letters of Stephen A. Douglas*, 408–10.

37. *New York Times*, April 2, 1858; *Frederick Douglass' Paper*, May 6, 1858; Etcheson, *Bleeding Kansas*, 168–76.

38. Etcheson, *Bleeding Kansas*, 179–84; Huston, *Stephen A. Douglas*, 140; Frederick Douglass, "Freedom in the West Indies," in John W. Blassingame et al., eds., *The Frederick Douglass Papers, Series 1, Speeches, Debates and Interviews*, vol. 3, *1856–63* (New Haven: Yale University Press, 2009), 235–36; *Frederick Douglass' Paper*, May 6, 1858.

39. James Buchanan to Wm. B. Reed, in Moore, *Works of James Buchanan*, 10:225.

40. S. A. Douglas to Samuel Treat, February 28, 1858, in Johannsen, *Letters of Stephen A. Douglas*, 418; David E. Meerse, "Buchanan, the Patronage, and the Lecompton Constitution: A Case Study," *Civil War History* 41 (December 1995): 291–312; Robert W. Johannsen, *Stephen A. Douglas* (Urbana: University of Illinois Press, 1997), 648–50.

41. James Buchanan to Wm. B. Reed, in Moore, *Works of James Buchanan*, 10:225.

42. Second Annual Message, December 6, 1858, ibid., 235–42.

43. Kansas was admitted to the Union on January 29, 1861, while Buchanan was still in office. Absent Southern senators and congressmen, who had resigned as their states seceded, allowed for the statehood bill's passage. Etcheson, *Bleeding Kansas*, 224.

44. *Frederick Douglass' Paper*, May 6, 1858; "Speech by Charles L. Remond," in C. Peter Ripley et al., eds., *The Black Abolitionist Papers*, vol. 4, *The United States, 1847–1858* (Chapel Hill: University of North Carolina Press, 1991), 382–90.

45. Buchanan to Harriet Lane, October 15, 1858, in Moore, *Works of James Buchanan*, 10:229.

46. James Buchanan to Robert Tyler, June 27, 1859, ibid., 326. Philip Klein blamed the feud on Douglas because Douglas judged it politically advantageous to reject Buchanan's efforts at reconciliation. Klein, *President James Buchanan*, 328–30. For Buchanan in the election of 1860, see Johannsen, *Stephen A. Douglas*, 685, 751, 755.

47. James Buchanan to C. Comstock, July 5, 1860, in Moore, *Works of James Buchanan*, 10:456–57.

48. Speech, July 9, 1860, ibid., 461. For the link between Buchanan's ideas and a Southern slave code see Potter, *Impending Crisis*, 403–4; Michael F. Holt, *The Political Crisis of the 1850s* (New York: Norton, 1978), 207, 242.

49. Speech, July 9, 1860, in Moore, *Works of James Buchanan*, 10:457–60.

50. Kenneth M. Stampp, *And the War Came: The North and the Secession Crisis, 1860–1861* (Baton Rouge: Louisiana State University Press, 1950), 11, 50, 54, 68.

51. Ellis, *Union at Risk*, 178–98; Baker, *James Buchanan*, 148–49.

52. Birkner et al. (discussants), "The Presidency of James Buchanan: A Reassessment," 190; Stampp, *And the War Came*, 54–57. Allan Nevins contrasts Buchanan's dithering and timidity in the secession crisis with Jackson's handling of nullification in *The Emergence of Lincoln*, vol. 2, *Prologue to Civil War, 1859–1861* (New York: Scribner, 1950), 344–47.

53. John Updike, *Buchanan Dying: A Play* (New York: Knopf, 1974), 90.

4

In Defense of Doughface Diplomacy

A Reevaluation of the Foreign Policy of James Buchanan

JOHN M. BELOHLAVEK

In his recent Pulitzer Prize–winning study of the early American republic, *What Hath God Wrought*, Daniel Walker Howe easily distinguishes the forces of good from the forces of evil. Two visions contested each other for the heart, mind, and future of nineteenth-century America. The Whig view embodied technology, factories, urbanization, and immigration—a partnership between business and government to build railroads and canals—in a word, "progress." The competing view, represented by the Democrats, reflected an older, simpler time of independent farmers, with or without slaves, seeking to extend their dream of the Jeffersonian republic spanning the continent. Paradise appeared as a well-plowed field, loving family, and sturdy cabin mirrored in the waters of a still pond. While ultimately, of course, Whiggery has prevailed in the twenty-first century, Howe deeply regrets the shortsightedness of Americans in more broadly choosing the Democratic over the Whig vision in the antebellum era.[1]

Whether or not Americans ultimately made the "right" choice to opt for a place in the line at a Lowell mill over a sixty-acre farm, certainly many politicians of the era knew the critical nature of geographic expansion—not only for U.S. security, but also to keep alive an economic and social dream embraced by most Americans. Andrew Jackson, John Tyler, James K. Polk, Franklin Pierce, and certainly James Buchanan acted upon this phenomenon. Should Americans settle in California or Cuba, Nebraska or Nicaragua, millions believed that the destiny of America might send the eagle soaring over the Caribbean, Central America, and even out into the Pacific.

The intention of this essay is not to attack or defend James Buchanan on the issue of the drift toward civil war. Instead, the objective is to reexamine several major aspects of his diplomacy in the light of their aims, triumphs, and failures and to argue that his policies, actions, and sound judgment often benefited the nation. Even those instances of failure reflected a genuine and realistic concern for American security and commercial goals that would be pursued by later administrations.

Historian Robert May has pointed out that presidential success is often related to timing. Polk, for example, settled troubling domestic problems connected to the tariff and banking in 1846 without having them hinder the primary goal of his presidency, Manifest Destiny—the continental expansion of the United States into the Northwest and Southwest. With impeccable timing, Polk triumphed, and the nation benefited mightily at the expense of Mexico and Great Britain. Buchanan, his secretary of state, attempted a similar course of action, but in a markedly different era.[2]

Much had changed in America in the decade following the Mexican War. The year 1857 was not kind to "Old Buck." Quelling a rebellion of hostile Mormons required a military expedition. Meanwhile, sectional tensions heightened, agitated by fugitive slaves and the passions of "Bleeding Kansas." The president hoped to allay the concerns of his Southern constituents by the passage of the strikingly low (17 percent average) Hunter tariff of 1857 as well as meddling in the now infamous Supreme Court *Dred Scott* case. That decision infuriated Yankees of all stripes. Domestic matters became even more troubled when the economy crashed in the fall in a "panic" for which Buchanan had no remedy.

"The Sage of Wheatland" had never been a master of domestic policy. His legendary blunder in calling for the daily wage of an American workingman to rival that of his European counterpart—a dime!—earned him the unflattering sobriquet "ten-cent Jimmy." No wonder the president hoped to focus the nation's attention on foreign affairs. His party shared that view. The 1856 platform demanded that the "sacred principles" of the Monroe Doctrine be applied with "unbending rigidity." The Democratic Party also pledged itself to "insure our ascendancy in the Gulf of Mexico." To further that end, the later 1860 platforms of both Northern and Southern Democrats endorsed the concept of the acquisition of Cuba on terms "honorable to ourselves and just to Spain."[3]

Ironically, Buchanan dedicated very little of his inaugural address to foreign policy. Content to mouth platitudes about never interfering in the domestic concerns of another country unless motivated by "the great law" of self-preservation, he emphasized that Americans' history forbade the nation from adding future territory unless sanctioned by "the laws of justice and honor." Such brevity was replaced by detailed discussions of foreign affairs, which consumed more than half of his annual messages to Congress in 1858 and 1859.[4]

The rising Republican Party contested Buchanan at every turn. Antebellum Republicans have fared much better in the eyes of historians than have Democrats. Even those scholars who embrace the notion of a "blundering generation" that led us into Civil War find more "blunderers" among the Democrats than among the Republicans. Perhaps too often, scholars have dwelled upon the uprightness of the Republicans of the 1850s. They chose the moral high road of antislavery, but their rigid path on expansion could only end in secession. Meanwhile, historians have sometimes marginalized the Democrats, especially the so-called doughfaces, who sought compromise and desperately wanted to preserve the country.

Buchanan attempted to rejuvenate Manifest Destiny—to refill old wine into new bottles in an effort to advance the Democratic vision of America, expand the commercial and physical boundaries of the nation, save the Union, and perhaps even add luster to his presidency. While a combination of foreign and congressional resistance limited his success, he should receive recognition for his efforts. Importantly, too, Buchanan almost alone deserves credit (or blame) for his course of action. He complained to British foreign secretary Lord Clarendon that he felt obliged to give his personal attention to matters of the least importance. Unfortunately, the responsibilities of the president had increased twenty-fold and were "now so onerous that no man can very long bear the burden. There must be some change [he lamented]; but innovation is the difficulty."

Cleary, shifting those burdens to the secretary of state was not an option. Few would maintain that Lewis Cass determined strategy. Roy Franklin Nichols observed that "senility was creeping up on the obese, indolent Lewis Cass." who was "worse than useless." Most historians concur. Cass's recent biographer is more flattering. While acknowledging that Buchanan made policy, Willard Klunder emphasizes that the two men agreed on most issues and the secretary of state was more than a figurehead. Perhaps so. Accordingly, an examination of several problems will help define the Buchanan presidency in foreign affairs.[5]

Latin America and Great Britain

The Monroe Doctrine, first asserted in 1823, was under fire in the 1850s from the Spanish, English, and French, each of whom saw territorial or commercial prospects in the Western Hemisphere—Spain in the Dominican Republic, England in Central America, and France in Haiti and Mexico. Congress had declined to respond to a possible European threat in the Yucatán in 1848, but Buchanan reacted to a very minor transgression in remote Paraguay in 1858. When Paraguayans fired upon an unarmed American naval vessel charting the waters of the Parana River, a sailor was killed. This incident in combination with the arbitrary seizure of property held by Americans in the country prompted the president to demand action. Congress approved the appropriation of $1,350,000 to purchase five steamers to be utilized in an expedition against Paraguay, and the president forthwith dispatched a commissioner accompanied by a fleet of nineteen ships of two hundred guns manned by twenty-five hundred sailors and marines. Clearly, this was overkill against a landlocked nation, although it did produce the desired results of prompt concessions from Asunción.

Jean Baker, however, contends that this was "a ludicrous assertion of American power," and Elbert B. Smith caustically notes, "no insult, real or implied, against the U.S. escaped Buchanan's attention. . . . No significant trade developed with Paraguay and the expedition probably cost several hundred thousand dollars, but American honor was vindicated." Instead, it could be reasoned that by sending a fleet to highly visible Montevideo, Uruguay, Buchanan delivered a message asserting American sea power and commercial interests to an audience of Latin Americans and European diplomats. While not exactly the "Great White Fleet" of Teddy Roosevelt, the intended meaning was parallel.[6]

Buchanan had to contend with the omnipresence of Great Britain in Latin America. As the United States sought to extend itself territorially and commercially, the Mighty Lion continually reared his massive head. "Old Buck" was no stranger to the intrigues and nuance of Anglo-American relations. While serving as U.S. minister to London prior to his presidency, he had befriended the powerful Lord Clarendon, who acted as foreign secretary through the spring of 1858. Their relationship produced a number of intimate and revealing letters in which Buchanan candidly chided his comrade about topics ranging from the British occupation of India ("it could be improved"), the Crown's protégés in Central America (they should be kept "in better order"), and any denial of American access across the isthmus ("To this I shall not submit"). Amid Anglophobic denunciations, especially in the Senate, of British imperialism, Buchanan sounded the cry of reason and mutual benefit. He predicted to Clarendon, "there's a better day-a-coming" in Anglo-American relations. "The material interests of both [nations] are essentially involved in the welfare of the each other; & according to the old Scotch proverb, 'blood is thicker than water.' This will shew itself some day."[7]

In the meantime, Buchanan held the line on three key issues. First, in Central America, the United States had signed the Clayton-Bulwer Treaty of 1850, an accord that many Americans, including Buchanan, felt obligated the Crown to abandon its possessions in Honduras and Nicaragua. The British government took exception, claiming the treaty only committed them to take no *additional* land. While they would not agree to abrogate the recent pact, which Buchanan desired, the English did negotiate treaties with Honduras (November 1859) and Nicaragua (January 1860) that conceded some territorial sovereignty back to the Latin Americans.[8]

Meanwhile, the great "Pig War" in the American Northwest almost produced a transatlantic conflict. On June 15, 1859, Lyman Cutler, an American farmer, shot and killed a boar rooting out his well-tended potato patch. The animal belonged to the Hudson's Bay Company, which also held land on jointly occupied San Juan Island, off the coast of Vancouver. In spite of Cutler's apologies, both sides took the issue seriously. Oregon commander General William Harney overreacted, landing a company of troops under Captain George Pickett in July (to save the Americans' bacon). With tempers flaring and the possibility of the British sending Royal marines ashore, Buchanan faced yet another potential crisis. He defused the San Juan crisis by removing General Harney from command and dispatching Winfield Scott as a peacemaker. While the issue remained unresolved until after the Civil War, scholar Scott Kaufman praises the president's calm demeanor and sound judgment: "he [Buchanan] deserves credit for wading through a potential storm of troubles."[9]

The Slave Trade

Third, tensions also arose over the Royal Navy's repeated searches of vessels purportedly engaged in the African slave trade that flew the U.S. flag. The practice of "search and seizure" played out very prominently in Anglo-American relations. Although Congress banned the international trade to the United States in 1808, the traffic had continued illegally to the South and legally to Spanish Cuba. Recognizing the unwillingness of Washington to permit the search of American vessels by European navies, many slavers hid their cargoes within the folds of the Stars and Stripes. The Anglo-American Webster-Ashburton Treaty of 1842 provided a compromise that committed the United States to post ships totaling a minimum of eighty guns off the coast of Africa to restrict the trade. Either from an absence of dedication to the principle or perhaps due to an inadequate maritime force, administrations from Tyler through Pierce had generally failed to meet the obligation. Unscrupulous captains and merchants took advantage of the situation with as many as eighty-five vessels fitting out for the nefarious traffic in New York harbor between February 1859 and July 1860.[10]

Early in his political career Buchanan personally found slavery offensive—in 1826 he referred to it in a speech in Congress as a "great political and a great moral evil"—and thanked God that the institution did not exist in Pennsylvania. Slavery, however, did not especially exercise Buchanan. He viewed slavery as rather benign and considered blacks generally as "well fed, well clothed, and not overworked." They were treated with "kindness and humanity." Like chief executives before him, whether out of political or constitutional considerations, he ignored the broader issue. The mounting evidence of the illicit international slave trade demanded his attention, however, and Buchanan responded, ushering in a rather dramatic change in American policy. In his December 1859 annual message he argued against the reopening of the trade and lamented its negative impact on African society and civilization. He identified the Cuban market as the chief culprit, and while he still cast a envious eye on the island, there existed a "Christian and moral" concern about the notion of the illegal commerce.[11] Historian Robert Ralph Davis says that Buchanan did more than raise moral objections as a matter of conscience; he acted in a practical manner.

He centralized the enforcement of the slave trade legislation in the hands of the Department of the Interior and urged an increase in congressional appropriations for the navy. His perpetuation of "a largely successful effort to perfect naval enforcement of the laws demonstrates Buchanan's genuine desire to end the African slave trade to the United States."[12]

Accordingly, the navy and the Buchanan administration became more aggressive and opportunistic than their predecessors when dealing with the issue. Still, the five U.S. naval vessels plying the African coastline were too few, too old, and too slow to do much damage to slavers sailing smaller, faster craft. For example, the *Echo*, a brig carrying some 475 slaves (almost 150 died en route), had sailed from West Africa in the summer of 1858 but was captured by the USS *Dolphin* off the coast of Cuba on August 21. The Africans were brought to Charleston, South Carolina, and placed in the custody of U.S. Marshal Daniel Hamilton. Buchanan become personally involved and ordered the marshal, a physician, to properly care for the slaves. On October 8 they sailed back to Africa aboard the USS *Niagara* under the auspices of an agent of the Colonization Society, arriving a month later at Monrovia, Liberia. Sympathetic judges and juries, however, found both the captain and the crew of the *Echo* not guilty in trials in Charleston and Key West in 1859.[13]

In late November 1858 the yacht *Wanderer* arrived off Jekyll Island, Georgia. Built in New York in 1857, the fast (twenty knots), luxurious ship could outrun almost any vessel on the high seas. Within a year, she had been sold and re-outfitted on Long Island. The activity prompted an investigation by federal officials, who suspected the conversion would produce either a ship conducive to filibustering or slave-running. When nothing incriminating was discovered, Captain William Corrie sailed the *Wanderer* to Charleston, where he declared his intention to continue on to his Trinidad plantation.[14]

The ship next appeared in October 1858 off the African coast, where, even with some 350 slaves aboard, she easily outran the USS *Vincennes*, which could make only half her speed. Six weeks later, the slaver arrived near privately owned Jekyll Island and landed her cargo during the night. While the slaves were quickly disbursed to plantations in the area, rumors filtered into Savannah and the event was widely reported in local newspapers. The *New York Times* reprinted columns of the *Albany Statesman*,

Savannah Republican, Augusta Chronicle, and *Edgefield (S.C.) Advertiser,* all of which recounted the *Wanderer's* voyage while attacking the legality of the slave trade and opposing its renewal in the South.[15]

A prompt investigation by U.S. Attorney Joseph Ganahl in Savannah produced the arrest of the captain and the seizure of the ship. Buchanan and Attorney General Jeremiah Black lent their support, urging that the perpetrators and the slaves should be identified and apprehended. In February 1859 a federal judge ruled that the *Wanderer* had been engaged in the illegal traffic and was henceforth forfeit to the U.S. government and would be sold at auction.[16] The captain and crew of the *Wanderer* enjoyed the same Southern sympathy as their brethren aboard the *Echo.* Trials were held, but by mid-1860 an exasperated Attorney General Black and the federal judge in Charleston indicated they wanted the charges to be dropped.[17]

Meanwhile in the autumn of 1859, the eighty-six-foot-long, copper-hulled, two-masted schooner *Clotilde* succeeded in reaching Mobile Bay with a cargo of about 116 Africans purchased in Ghana in May. Federal authorities had learned of the voyage and were prepared to seize the vessel upon its arrival in Alabama. A cautious Captain William Foster landed at night at Twelve Mile Island and transferred the slaves to their potential masters before his ship could be discovered. The evidence—the *Clotilde*—was summarily burned and sank. Although the federal government attempted to prosecute the vessel's owner, Tim Meaher, the case was dismissed out of court; the charges of "importing Africans for the purpose of slavery" could not be proved. Besides, when the case arrived in court in the spring of 1861, Alabama had seceded from the Union and the state was no longer under federal law. This incident was arguably the last known successful attempt to bring slaves into the United States illegally.[18]

Certainly, the voyages of the three vessels reopened the ugly scar of the international slave trade. The issue became hotly political. While Southerners denied their support and claimed adherence to the law, the *New York Times* offered a conspiracy theory: perhaps a small but vigorous band of radicals was intentionally embarking on the trade to unite the North and elect a Republican as president in 1860.[19] Such a choice would guarantee secession. New York senator and White House aspirant William Seward seized the moment—and the stage—by introducing a resolution calling for "the number and character of American vessels engaged in the trade with Africa" and demanding the chief executive's correspondence relative to the case of the *Wanderer*.[20]

Buchanan knew that although the number of slavers had not spiraled out of control, the issue posed both a domestic political problem and an embarrassment in relations with Great Britain. The administration newspaper, the *Washington Union*, mirrored Buchanan's viewpoint. Some Southerners were either sympathetic or turned a blind eye to the slave trade. Since federal authorities could do little once the blacks had been landed, action must be taken "to suppress the traffic wholly on the high seas, where their jurisdiction is complete." Consequently, the government moved by 1859 to strengthen the U.S. Navy by adding four steamers in the Caribbean off Cuba, introducing faster steamers of war and eight more vessels to the African squadron, and cooperating with the British as a tactic to halt the slave trade. The strategy bore fruit: eighteen ships were seized as slavers in 1860 and twelve were prosecuted—a dramatic increase over the total of twenty-four ships taken in the previous three years of the Buchanan administration.[21]

To ensure that his strategy worked, the president dispatched Benjamin F. Slocumb, an Interior Department agent, to travel the entire South secretly for two months in September–November 1859 to investigate the extent of the foreign slave trade. Slocumb scoured Dixie and heard rumors of the *Wanderer*'s blacks, but informed Washington that "since the landing of the *Wanderer*, there is no convincing evidence that any other landing of Africans has been effected upon our southern coast." Apparently, word of the *Clotilde* had not reached Slocumb. Buchanan felt comfortable, however, informing Congress in his 1860 annual message that no additional Africans had been landed since 1858 and that the government was effectively pursuing its mission to end the trade. Even so, skeptical Republican Henry Wilson of Massachusetts introduced a Senate resolution in March 1860, seeking an inquiry into whether the treaty with Great Britain to suppress the traffic had been executed and whether any further legislation was necessary on the subject. Ultimately, in the three critical situations that emerged with Whitehall in the late 1850s, Buchanan's approach redounded to the advantage of the United States.[22]

Southern Expansion: Cuba and Mexico

Buchanan the expansionist expressed territorial interest in both Cuba and Mexico. Given its strategic location and lucrative commerce, Cuba had been a target of the United States dating back to the early 1800s. The Southern pulse quickened when the Spanish added more than 165,000 slaves to the island in the late 1830s. Buchanan had moved in 1857 to make inquiries in Madrid about the possible sale of Cuba. No luck—apparently the Spanish were not interested. New minister William Preston of Kentucky was instructed, however, to try to utilize $30 million to "facilitate negotiations." Concurrently, in his second annual message of December 1858 Buchanan noted the unpaid property claims—$128,000—owed U.S. citizens by Spain generally related to Cuban-based violations. Cuba "in its existing colonial condition" was "a constant source of injury and annoyance to the American people." The slave trade had caused serious tensions between the United States and Great Britain over the right of search and promoted chaos in Africa itself. The trade would "instantly disappear," the president promised, if the island were ceded. "We would not, if we could, acquire Cuba in any other manner."[23]

Buchanan compared the purchase of Cuba to that of Louisiana from Napoleon in 1803, noting that neither possession was of as great a value to the European power as to the United States. Congress promptly followed up in January 1859 with Louisiana senator John Slidell proposing $30 million to commence the negotiations. We can assume that a larger sum, possibly as much as $150 million, would have been in the offing. Slavery quickly became the consuming issue, however, and Republicans relentlessly attacked the measure in both houses. After lengthy, spirited debate, Slidell acknowledged defeat and withdrew the bill in late February. This debate was as close as the president would come to success. He recommended the purchase of the island briefly in his succeeding 1859 and 1860 messages, but must have known that the idea had no future, particularly in the Republican-dominated House of Representatives.[24]

The case can be made that Buchanan had a reason for his aggressive posture (some might claim "obsession") with Cuba. Carving out several additional slave states from the island would clearly boost the South's declining base in Congress and perhaps stabilize the shaky Union. Politically, annexation might reunite a Democratic Party divided between

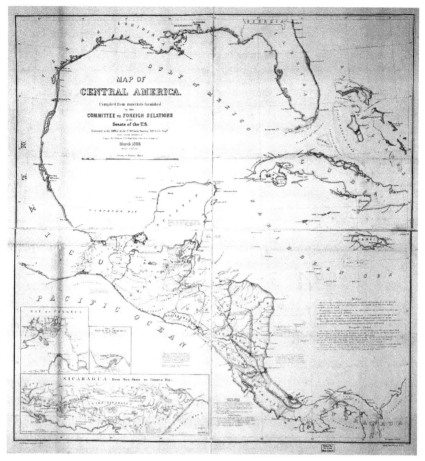

Figure 4.1. *Map of Central America: Compiled from Materials Furnished by the Committee on Foreign Relations of the Senate of the U.S.* (Washington, D.C.: U.S. Coast Survey, 1856).

proslavery and popular sovereignty wings. Economically, the "Pearl of the Antilles" continued to be of major economic import to the entire United States, constituting a major market for American goods and producing sought-after coffee, tobacco, and sugar. Finally, U.S. presidents from Jefferson to Kennedy warned of foreign influences in Cuba and the danger those forces might pose to American security should the island fall into the wrong hands or pursue its own course unchecked. Lest we forget—in April 1861 Republican secretary of state William Seward wrote to Abraham Lincoln boldly suggesting the possibility of hostilities with Spain and France. The Spanish had just annexed Santo Domingo, and the French posed a threat to Mexico. The secretary intended to rekindle Southern patriotism and hoped to persuade the seceded states to rejoin the Union. Such action might have, additionally, resulted in the annexation of Cuba or a U.S. naval base in the Caribbean. The ill-conceived scheme received an immediate and chilly response from the president. However, Seward reiterated in 1867 to the new Spanish minister with the colorful name of Fecundo Goni the view that Cuba would eventually by "means of constant gravitation . . . fall into the U.S." In the meantime, Washington would look with disfavor upon any transfer of Cuba to a European power.[25]

Buchanan had advocated the purchase of Cuba as early as the 1830s. Of course, the South would benefit from its acquisition, but arguably so would the nation. The United States opted simply to control the island in the twentieth century more indirectly through the Platt Amendment and a protectorate policy, or more recently, an embargo.[26]

Concurrently, Buchanan eyed parts of northwest Mexico—the provinces of Chihuahua and Sonora largely bordering on Arizona and New Mexico. The chaotic political situation south of the Rio Grande pitted Benito Juarez's "Constitutional Party" against a military regime led by General Miguel Miramon (whose execution with Emperor Maximilian can be seen in an 1867 painting by Eduard Manet). The disorder not only led to depredations against American lives and property in northern Mexico but prompted fears of European intervention—by the Spanish or particularly French emperor Napoleon III. Buchanan, who sympathized with the Juaristas, repeatedly asked Congress for American troops to establish a protectorate and help stabilize the situation in the north. He declared in his annual message of 1859, "as a good neighbor, shall we not extend to her a helping hand to save her? If we do not, it would not be surprising should some other nation undertake the task, and thus force us to interfere at last, under circumstances of increased difficulty." Weary of Manifest Destiny and skeptical of Buchanan's rhetoric, Congress refused the president's requests. Likewise, Congress declined to act on the McLane-Ocampo Treaty of December 1859, which granted the United States transit rights to build a railroad or canal and, in the event of civil unrest, offered Washington limited rights of intervention into Mexican domestic affairs.[27]

The president ultimately proved prophetic. In 1865, Seward demanded a French withdrawal from Mexico under the language of the Monroe Doctrine and dispatched an army of fifty thousand veterans to the border to help convince Napoleon of his point. Slavery was not the issue in Mexico as it was in Cuba. The Mexicans had abolished the institution, and Southerners were skeptical of its prospects there. Perhaps Buchanan convinced himself that his expansionist motives profited Mexicans and Americans. By advocating the principles of the Monroe Doctrine, U.S. and Mexican security, and a trans-isthmian route, he might indeed help both nations.

Nicaragua was never a target of Buchanan's expansionist notions (like Cuba, northern Mexico, or even Alaska) but formed a core element in a broader strategy to advance U.S. commercial and strategic influence in the region. The president remained concerned about the "weak and feeble states" of Central America, subject to internal strife and European influence. Neither alternative suited a United States that hoped to secure the hemisphere for republicanism, develop a trans-isthmian route to the Pacific coast, and enhance trade and settlement in the region.[28]

Filibusters jeopardized that vision through their repeated incursions into Cuba and Nicaragua. William Walker confirmed the worst nightmares of many Latinos about Yankee aggressors seeking to dominate their countries—nightmares encouraged, of course, by the Europeans. Walker's multiple invasions—1855, 1858, and 1860—were indeed launched from the United States and initially received national support. By 1858, the "grey-eyed man's" proslavery posture had cost him some backing above the Mason-Dixon Line. Regardless, President Buchanan steadfastly opposed Walker's adventurism, denouncing filibusters in his speeches and issuing a special proclamation on October 30, 1858, urging Americans to deny Walker their endorsement. Some historians remain skeptical. They cite Buchanan's criticism of Commodore Hiram Paulding, who arrested Walker on the coast of Nicaragua in 1858, as evidence of his encouragement of the famous filibuster, or at least the president's Southern sympathies.[29]

Robert May has thoroughly analyzed the incident and persuasively makes the case that the reprimand reflected issues of territorial sovereignty and not filibustering. Moreover, May contends that "there was never any doubt that the administration wanted filibustering stopped." And as for serving as a tool for Southern interests, May writes we can accuse Buchanan of many things, but "we can at least acquit him of the charge that he was a mere lackey of the slave power." While the Central Americans may have continued to regard Yankees with some suspicion, the Buchanan administration worked to halt filibustering and to negotiate treaties with

Costa Rica, Nicaragua, and Honduras. As he admonished the Senate, "The Government of the United States can never permit these [trans-isthmian] routes to be permanently interrupted, nor can it safely allow them to pass under the control of other rival nations."[30]

Alaska

Perhaps the most unknown flirtation with expansion under Buchanan involved his interest in Alaska. The Russians began exploring the region in the 1740s, and the fur trade drew permanent settlements a half-century later. After their defeat in the Crimean War in 1856, however, they became increasingly fearful of losing their North American colony to the expansionistic Americans. As the czar's officials sought to shift imperial priorities to China, St. Petersburg pondered how to divest itself peacefully of Alaska and gain some diplomatic or financial benefits in the process. The Russians knew that they could not defend Alaska against the might of an English fleet or a determined neighbor. Even so, American inquiries during the Pierce administration met with a sharp rebuff. But by 1857, attitudes shifted as Czar Alexander II's younger brother, Grand Duke Constantine, advocated the sale. He emphasized that the United States could take Alaska at will and, besides, the colony was of little practical benefit. Strong disagreement was expressed on the latter point.[31]

The Americans had already made significant inroads into the territory. U.S. fur traders had been a powerful force in the Northwest since the early 1800s. By 1838, St. Petersburg protested the activity of Yankee whalers and merchants along the Pacific Coast, demanding that Washington restrain them under the provisions of a treaty negotiated in 1824. The federal government did little to assuage the Russian demands until 1845. Secretary of State Buchanan wanted to ensure Russian neutrality in any potential conflict with Great Britain and thus agreed to issue an order restricting the activity of American vessels along the Alaska coastline.

When the Whigs regained the White House in 1849, however, they quickly reversed the policy—no wonder, given the profits involved. The 1850s was the heyday of the whaling industry, and more than five hundred New England vessels annually plied the cold waters of the northern Pacific off the Russian coast. The bowhead whales captured in the region contributed significantly to the total of over $89 million of whale products imported into the United States during the decade, far surpassing the $70.6 million garnered in the 1840s. San Francisco merchants also covetously eyed the Alaska trade and organized the American-Russian Commercial Company in 1851 for that purpose. Well organized and well funded, the company began its first imports—250 tons of ice—the following year. The amount quickly increased to over 3,000 tons per annum, supplemented by quantities of coal and fish. In turn, the firm became a major supplier of foodstuffs and finished goods to Alaska.

Neither Russian traders nor the czar was happy with these incursions, but they recognized that the rise of Yankee whaling and their own commercial shortcomings provided the opportunity for the Americans. Alexander II formally granted the trading privileges. The aggressiveness of the administrations of Zachary Taylor and Millard Fillmore, especially under the guidance of Secretary of State Daniel Webster, reflected the seriousness of the American claim to a commercial place on the Pacific coast. The cession of Alaska might be only a matter of time and circumstance.[32]

Over the course of the next four years, the drama played out as more "liberal" elements in St. Petersburg maintained the practical advantages of the sale, including improved relations with the United States. The "conservatives" wanted to assist the struggling Russian-American Company in profiting from commerce along the Pacific coast and were in no hurry to relinquish the territory. In December 1857 the discussion warmed as Russian minister Baron E. A. De Stoeckl reported a conversation with Buchanan in which the rumor of the immigration of a large number of Mormons to Alaska was discussed. The minister sought confirmation, but the president only smiled and remarked, "How to settle this question is your worry; as for us, we would be very happy to get rid of them."[33]

Such rumors only confirmed the wisdom and necessity of the sale in the mind of Grand Duke Constantine. As he admonished the czar, "there is no doubt that they [the United States] will seize our colonies, and even without much effort." The Russians were well aware of American ambitions, using terms such as "Manifest Destiny" and the "Monroe Doctrine" in their correspondence. Still, they dragged their feet, waiting for the Americans to make the first move. This occurred in the winter of 1859–60 when California senator William Gwin and Assistant Secretary of State John Appleton broached the subject with De Stoeckl. Clearly, Buchanan saw the benefits that would accrue to California and Oregon by acquiring additional empire on the Pacific and instructed his agents to inquire about Alaska in an informal fashion. If the Russians were open to the sale, the president could then proceed to discuss the matter with both the cabinet and Congress. Gwin suggested that $5 million might be suitable compensation, and while De Stoeckl remained noncommittal on the sum, he insisted that the Americans formally open negotiations.[34]

De Stoeckl's report to St. Petersburg endorsed the American offer, although the minister cautioned that it would be difficult to resolve the matter given the frenzied state of American politics and the possibility of disunion. Minister of Foreign Affairs A. M. Gorchakov, who no doubt mirrored the opinion of the czar, read the dispatch warily; he remained reluctant to sell Alaska, especially at a price he determined did not reflect the "true value" of the territory. Besides, the government did not want to ruffle the feathers of the Russian-American Company, whose privileges in the region would expire in 1862. As a result, De Stoeckl was instructed to tell the Americans that the possible sale would be placed on hold. A disappointed Gwin admitted that the tarnished Buchanan administration was unlikely to gain additional funds from Congress, and the subject was tabled. An America divided by Civil War was unprepared for further negotiations, but in 1867, Secretary of State William Seward seized the moment and the colony at the somewhat elevated cost of $7.2 million. As historian Victor Farrar has emphasized, the movement to sell Alaska in the 1850s was premature. The Russians had no pressing need to dispose of the territory, and key figures within the government were "lukewarm" to the idea. Even so, the discussions held during the Buchanan administration laid the groundwork and prompted the Russians to think more seriously of a sale—especially to the United States. The talks also reaffirm the president's openness to acquire territory and markets that might be of benefit to the nation.[35]

East Asian Commerce

Buchanan's interest in the Pacific did not stop at the waterline. During his term agents concluded agreements with both China and Japan intended to expand American trade, if not territory. Although the United States had a commercial treaty with China negotiated at Wanghia in 1844, revisions of such items as additional open ports, reduced tariffs, and religious freedom needed to be addressed. In July 1857 the president dispatched an old comrade and fellow Pennsylvanian, William B. Reed, to handle the assignment. Upon his arrival, Reed found the Chinese in yet another painful military conflict with the English and French. By June 1858 the Europeans had predictably triumphed, and the Americans shared in the benefits of a new round of Chinese concessions, including access to the desired ports, a most-favored-nation clause, and religious liberties for foreigners. In 1859 Reed brought the Treaty of Tientsin home to Washington, where the Senate and a grateful president echoed their approval. Chinese ratification took a bit longer as new American diplomat John E. Ward's refusal to kowtow to the emperor complicated the situation.[36]

To the east, Commodore Matthew Perry had "opened" Japan in 1854, but his treaty of peace and friendship did not include a commercial entente. Franklin Pierce sought to rectify that omission the following year when he dispatched merchant Townsend Harris to secure a new pact. Harris proved to be an excellent choice and along the way negotiated a treaty with Siam as well as an agreement with Japan signed in 1857. The emperor added an interesting twist, however, by requesting that several princes carry the treaty to America for the exchange of ratifications. Although their journey was delayed until February 1860, eighteen officials and their sixty servants sailed for Washington, D.C., aboard a naval steamer, the USS *Powhatan*, on a trip paid for by the U.S. government.[37]

The delegation arrived on May 15 amid great pomp, fanfare, and fascination that engulfed the wider populace as well as government officials. The ladies of capital society, decked out in their finery, exerted special efforts to see and be seen with the Oriental visitors—much to the embarrassment of the latter. Buchanan received the delegation in a packed East Room of the White House on May 18 at the commencement of the tour. One reporter noted being drowned in a sea of lace and crinoline and overwhelmed with the smell of perfume. In a brief, half-hour ceremony, the president focused on the anticipated benefits of mutual peace and commerce shared by both nations. The Japanese had brought fifteen boxes of presents for the chief executive, including several exceptional rifles and a magnificent tea set delicately inlaid with gold and pearls.

For six weeks, the Japanese were indeed treated royally, and given high-profile tours of Baltimore, Philadelphia, and New York. Each city attempted to outshine the other in an effort to impress the princes, who seemed more interested in textile factories than theater. No doubt their inability to speak any English limited their curiosity about the arts. While the Americans relentlessly carted them about to various parades, parties, dinners, and demonstrations, the royals generally handled each situation with patience and grace. The press, which reported each move of the Japanese to their readers on a daily basis, praised the visitors for their long suffering and blasted the Americans for their rudeness and incivility.

The *New York Times* likely spoke for many Americans, however, when it editorialized about the departure of the Japanese on June 30. "It may seem discourteous, but we cannot help saying we are glad they have gone. Their visit with us has not been without a certain interest to us, but we have had enough of it. . . . Their social intercourse with us has not been especially fascinating. . . . The truth is, the Japanese came to acquire knowledge, not to impart it." The *Times* sagely analyzed the intellect and ingenuity of the Japanese and predicted that they would profit from their observations of American factory operations and weapon designs. Mistrusting their intentions, the paper cautioned "We can only hope that we may not find ourselves among the earliest victims of our over-zealous and mistaken benevolence." Both the administration and the press realized that the princes had been dispatched to the United States to determine whether this part of Christendom could contribute to Japanese learning and was worthy of the island's commerce. Buchanan could only hope that he and his countrymen had passed the test. Predictably, the Civil War portended a dramatic decline in American trade with the Orient. The much-coveted export market did not pass the 1860 level of $8 million until the 1880 figure of a modest $11 million. As for Asian imports, they remained far more lucrative, bouncing back more quickly, and almost doubling from $29 million in 1860 to $55 million two decades later.[38]

Conclusion

In sum, Buchanan sought to advance established principles and goals of his party and his government: additional land and commercial opportunity for American farmers and merchants (Cuba, Mexico, and Alaska); a transit across Mexico or Central America to facilitate that trade, as well as treaties with China and Japan to promote Oriental commerce; the Monroe Doctrine to remove the existing European presence from the Western

Hemisphere and foster security and commerce in Central/South American (Paraguay) and the Caribbean; and national honor with Great Britain relating to rights of search and seizure and San Juan Island. He did so with some success. But his failures doomed the Jacksonian vision of perpetual growth and expansion for the farmer. Following the war, Americans turned inward. The Homestead Act helped settle the Great Plains, and industrialization produced the flooding of cities with immigrants from rural Iowa and rural Italy, small-town Pennsylvania and small-town Poland.[39]

Certainly, Buchanan embraced many of the elements of racism, cultural arrogance, and Anglo-Saxon superiority common to those formulating American foreign policy into the twenty-first century. Likewise, his objectives, his wider goals, were wedded to an older and more nationalist vision of Manifest Destiny and mission. He held a lonely vigil, pursuing ideas whose time had come and gone. Those ideas, however, would arise phoenix-like in the next generation, led by William Seward as the harbinger of the "New Manifest Destiny" of the 1880s. Nearly two decades ago, Frederick Moore Binder, the leading authority on Buchanan's diplomatic career, maintained that we should look beyond his failing and flailing on the domestic front and grant "justice" to his foreign policy. That time may be now.[40]

Notes

1. Daniel Walker Howe, *What Hath God Wrought* (New York: Oxford University Press, 2007).

2. Robert E. May, *Manifest Destiny's Underworld: Filibusters in Antebellum America* (Chapel Hill: University of North Carolina Press, 2002), 216.

3. Kirk H. Porter and Donald Bruce Johnson, eds., *National Party Platforms, 1840–1960* (Urbana: University of Illinois Press, 1961), 23–26, 30–31.

4. James D. Richardson, *A Compilation of the Messages and Papers of the Presidents*, vol. 5 (New York: Bureau of National Literature, 1917), 430–36.

5. J. Buchanan to Lord Clarendon, March 27, 1858, in John Bassett Moore, ed., *The Works of James Buchanan, Comprising His Speeches, State Papers, and Private Correspondence*, 12 vols. (New York: Antiquarian Press, 1960), 10:199; Roy Franklin Nichols, *The Disruption of American Democracy* (New York: MacMillan, 1948), 90; Willard Klunder, *Lewis Cass and the Politics of Moderation* (Kent, Ohio: Kent State University Press, 1996), 288–89; Elbert B. Smith, *The Presidency of James Buchanan* (Lawrence: University of Kansas Press, 1975), 68; Jean H. Baker, *James Buchanan* (New

York: Times Books, 2004), 107–8; Frederick Moore Binder, *James Buchanan and the American Empire* (Selinsgrove, Pa.: Susquehanna University Press, 1994), 222–25.

6. Binder, *Buchanan and the American Empire*, 259–61; Baker, *James Buchanan*, 111–12; E. B. Smith, *Presidency of James Buchanan*, 74; Philip S. Klein, *President James Buchanan: A Biography* (University Park: Pennsylvania State University Press, 1962), 323–24; George Ticknor Curtis, *The Life of James Buchanan*, vol. 2 (New York: Harper and Brothers, 1883), 224–26; James Buchanan, "First Annual Message to Congress," in Moore, *Works of James Buchanan*, 10:145; "Second Annual Message to Congress," ibid., 262–63; "Third Annual Message to Congress, ibid., 348–49; James Buchanan, *Mr. Buchanan's Administration on the Eve of the Rebellion* (New York: D. Appleton, 1866), 264–67. A recent thoroughgoing analysis of the Paraguayan expedition that reveals Buchanan's nationalist intentions can be found in Gene A. Smith, "A Most Unprovoked, Unwarrantable, and Dastardly Attack: James Buchanan, Paraguay, and the Water Witch Incident of 1855," *Northern Mariner* 19 (July 2009): 269–81.

7. Clarendon to Buchanan, March 13, 1857, April 15, 1858, in Moore, *Works of James Buchanan*, 10:114–15, 207–8; Buchanan to Clarendon, September 9, 1857, March 27, 1858, ibid., 122–23, 199.

8. Binder, *Buchanan and the American Empire*, 229–39; E. B. Smith, *Presidency of James Buchanan*, 69–71; Klein, *President James Buchanan*, 318–21; John M. Belohlavek, *George Mifflin Dallas: Jacksonian Patrician* (University Park: Pennsylvania State Press, 1977), 165–73; Curtis, *Life of James Buchanan*, 2:213–14; Amy Greenberg, *Manifest Manhood and the Antebellum American Empire* (New York: Cambridge University Press, 2005), 54–55; Buchanan, *Mr. Buchanan's Administration*, 260–63; "First Annual Message," in Moore, *Works of James Buchanan*, 10:142–45; "Second Annual Message," ibid., 246–49, 257–62; "Fourth Annual Message," ibid. 11:26–27.

9. Klein, *President James Buchanan*, 325; Scott Kaufman, *The Pig War: The U.S., Britain, and the Balance of Power in the Pacific Northwest, 1846–1872* (Lanham, Md.: Lexington Books, 2004), 82; Buchanan to Clarendon, November 3, 1859, in Moore, *Works of James Buchanan*, 10:336–37; "Third Annual Message," ibid., 350–52.

10. Robert Ralph Davis Jr., "James Buchanan and the Suppression of the Slave Trade, 1858–1861," *Pennsylvania History* 33 (October 1966): 448.

11. Buchanan, "Congressional Speech on the Panama Mission," April 11, 1826, in Moore, *Works of James Buchanan*, 1:202–3; "Third Annual Message," December 19, 1859, ibid., 10:345–46.

12. Robert Ralph Davis Jr., "Buchanan Espionage: A Report on Illegal Slave Trading in the South in 1859," *Journal of Southern History* 37 (May 1971): 271–72.

13. Tom H. Wells, *The Slave Ship Wanderer* (Athens: University of Georgia Press, 1967), 38, 50–51; *Harper's Weekly*, December 25, 1858, *New York Times*, April 20, 1859. Buchanan's personal involvement with the *Echo* Africans is detailed in Davis, "Suppression of the Slave Trade," 451.

14. *New York Times,* June 11, June 12, July 8, 1858. Also see Eric Calonius, *The Wanderer* (New York: St. Martin's Press, 2006).

15. *New York Times,* December 14, 17, 21, 31, 1858. One paper suggested that the *Wanderer* did not carry slaves itself but rather served as a pilot ship or a decoy for a much larger vessel. *Harper's Weekly,* December 25, 1858, January 8, 15, 1859. Sailors in the African squadron had miserable duty, serving for two years with little relief and, because of the threat of disease, little shore time. *New York Times,* May 24, 1859.

16. Wells, *Slave Ship Wanderer,* 36–39; Calonius, *The Wanderer,* 150–51; *New York Times,* January 4, 1859.

17. Calonius, *The Wanderer,* 186–220.

18. James Lockett, "The Last Ship That Brought Slaves from Africa to America: The Landing of the *Clotilde* at Mobile in the Autumn of 1859," *Western Journal of Black Studies* 22 (Fall 1998): 159–63. For a study of the fate of those who landed, see Sylviane A. Diouf, *Dreams of Africa in Alabama: The Slave Ship Clotilda and the Story of the Last Africans Brought to America* (New York, Oxford University Press, 2007).

19. *New York Times,* December 28, 1858.

20. Ibid., January 15, 1859; *Harper's Weekly,* January 29, 1859.

21. *New York Times,* December 22, 1858, May 24, 1859. The administration already evidenced a more aggressive policy, arresting the bark *Ardennes* at Jacksonville on suspicion of being a slaver. *New York Times,* December 20, 1858. The five steamers purchased for the Paraguay expedition were shifted to the Africa squadron. Davis, "Suppression of the Slave Trade," 452–54.

22. *Harper's Weekly,* March 24, 1860; Wells, *Slave Ship Wanderer,* 86–87. Account should be taken of the president's efforts in terms of the moral and humanitarian dimension of his foreign policy. Historian Davis cautions, however, that the Democrats sought political advantage, too, by demonstrating they were capable of ending the slave trade. Davis, "Suppression of the Slave Trade," 458–59.

23. Buchanan to Christopher Fallon, December 14, 1857, in Moore, *Works of James Buchanan,* 10:165; Buchanan, *Mr. Buchanan's Administration,* 258–60; Curtis, *Life of James Buchanan,* 2:222–24; Buchanan, "Second Annual Message," in Moore, *Works of James Buchanan,* 10:249–53; Buchanan, "Third Annual Message," ibid., 358–59.

24. Klein, *President James Buchanan,* 324–25; Robert E. May, *Southern Dream of Caribbean Empire* (Baton Rouge: Louisiana State University Press, 1973), 163–89; E. B. Smith, *Presidency of James Buchanan,* 77–78; Binder, *Buchanan and the American Empire,* 251–59.

25. John Bassett Moore, *The Digest of International Law* (Washington, D.C.: Government Printing Office, 1906), 456; Allan Nevins, *War for the Union: The Improvised War* (New York: Scribner, 1959), 62–64; John Taylor, *William H. Seward* (New York: Harper Collins, 1991), 152; Greenberg, *Manifest Manhood,* 68–69; W. Seward to A. Lincoln, April 1, 1861, in *The Complete Works of Abraham Lincoln,* ed. John G. Nicolay and John Hay, vol. 6 (New York: Francis D. Tandy, 1904), 234–36; Lincoln to Seward,

April 1, 1861, ibid., 236–37. The Spanish annexed the Dominican Republic from 1861 to 1865, and the French occupied Mexico from 1862 to 1866. Pressure from Seward following the Civil War was a significant factor in the withdrawal of both European powers.

26. Klein, *President James Buchanan*, 324.

27. Buchanan, "Second Annual Message," in Moore, *Works of James Buchanan*, 10:253–57; Buchanan, "Third Annual Message," ibid., 353–59; Buchanan, "Fourth Annual Message," ibid., 11:32–34; E. B. Smith, *Presidency of James Buchanan*, 75–77; Baker, *James Buchanan*, 108–9; Klunder, *Lewis Cass*, 290; Curtis, *Life of James Buchanan*, 2:215–22; Klein, *President James Buchanan*, 321–23; May, *Southern Dream of Caribbean Empire*, 154–62; Buchanan, *Mr. Buchanan's Administration*, 267–76, Binder, *Buchanan and the American Empire*, 247–51.

28. Buchanan, "First Annual Message," in Moore, *Works of James Buchanan*, 10:142; Binder, *Buchanan and the American Empire*, 263–64, addresses the attempted Alaska purchase.

29. May, *Manifest Destiny's Underworld*, 217–18; Greenberg, *Manifest Manhood*, 156–61; Baker, *James Buchanan*, 110; E. B. Smith, *Presidency of James Buchanan*, 73–74; "Mr. Buchanan's Proclamation Concerning an Expedition against Nicaragua, October 30, 1858," in Moore, *Works of James Buchanan*, 10:230–32; Binder, *Buchanan and the American Empire*, 239–45.

30. Robert E. May, "James Buchanan, the Neutrality Laws, and American Invasions of Nicaragua," in *James Buchanan and the Political Crisis of the 1850s*, ed. Michael J. Birkner (Selinsgrove, Pa.: Susquehanna University Press, 1996), 123–40; May, *Manifest Destiny's Underworld*, 124–27, 160–61, 268–69; May, *Southern Dream of Caribbean Empire*, 114–35; Robert E. May, "The Slave Power Conspiracy Revisited: United States Presidents and Filibustering, 1848–1861," in *Union and Emancipation: Essays on Politics and Race in the Civil War Era*, ed. David Blight and Brooks D. Simpson (Kent, Ohio: Kent State University Press, 1997), 11, 22–28; Buchanan "Treaty with Honduras and on Inter-oceanic Transit," to the Senate, April 5, 1860, in Moore, *Works of James Buchanan*, 10:413.

31. Nikolay N. Bolkhovitinov, "The Crimean War and the Emergence of Proposals for the Sale of Russian America, 1853–1861," *Pacific Historical Review* 59 (February 1990): 16–34.

32. Howard I. Kushner, *Conflict on the Northwest Coast: American-Russian Rivalry in the Pacific Northwest, 1790–1867* (Westport, Ct.: Greenwood Press, 1975), 92–105, 119–20. The whaling trade suffered mightily when oil was discovered in Pennsylvania in 1859 and cheaper kerosene began to replace whale oil in lamps across America.

33. Bolkhovitinov, "Crimean War," 35–36.

34. Ibid., 37–40; Kushner, *Conflict on the Northwest Coast*, 135–38.

35. Bolkhovitinov, "Crimean War," 41–49; Victor J. Farrar, *The Annexation of Russian America to the United States* (1937; New York: Russell and Russell, 1966), 1–14.

Elbert B. Smith suggests that Buchanan might have been successful if he had offered the $7.2 million to the Russians in 1859, but his commitment to obtain Alaska was much weaker than his interest in Cuba. E. G. Smith, *Presidency of James Buchanan*, 72.

36. Binder, *Buchanan and the American Empire*, 264–68. Additional concessions came within the year, including the abolition of the kowtow, when the French and British renewed their attacks on China. The United States remained neutral but profited from the European demands. Reed, a Democratic Party activist, had been state attorney general and a history professor at the University of Pennsylvania.

37. Ibid., 268–69.

38. Ibid., 269–70. *Harper's Weekly*, May 26, June 2, June 23, 1860; *New York Times*, May 10–June 30, 1860. Export and import data can be found in the U.S. Bureau of the Census, *Historical Statistics of the United States, 1789–1945* (Washington, D.C., 1949); *Foreign Trade*, 251.

39. Binder, *Buchanan and the American Empire*, 226–27.

40. Ibid., 273–76.

5

President James Buchanan

Executive Leadership and the Crisis of the Democracy

MICHAEL A. MORRISON

When James Buchanan died in June 1868, the *New-York Times* obituary scorned that he met "the crisis of secession in a timid and vacillating spirit, temporizing with both parties, and studiously avoiding the adoption of a decided policy." Following Abraham Lincoln's inauguration, the paper sniffed, he "retired to the privacy of his home in Wheatland, followed by the ill will of every section of the country." Unhappily, the Old Public Functionary's reputation fares little better today. In a C-Span presidential survey done in 2000, a panel of "experts" ranked Buchanan dead last among all presidents, as did viewers. Ever the bottom feeder, he ranked last in crisis of leadership, vision, pursuit of equal justice, and performance in historical context; he finished no higher than thirty-seventh in any category. Michael Birkner asserts that no serious scholar could "doubt that Buchanan exacerbated the sectional conflict which he claimed he intended to alleviate, or that he was out of touch with northern public opinion, and too much attuned emotionally to southern political friends and an idealized southern social system."[1]

This is not to say that all contemporaries or historians scorned the man or his many abilities. Martin Van Buren, former Democratic president and Free Soil candidate in 1848, thought Buchanan "a cautious, circumspect and sagacious man." Woodrow Wilson observed in an essay written in 1899 that "he was a man of unsullied integrity, and punctilious in the performance of what he considered to be his duty." And more recently a historian has contended that "of all the occupants of the highest office in the land there has been none who could offer better credentials upon assuming the office." But it is James Buchanan's performance as chief executive that melds the political with the personal. Wilson claimed that Buchanan was "past the prime of life, had never possessed great courage or any notable gifts of initiative, and of course suffered himself to be guided by the men whom he regarded, and had good reason to regard, as the real leaders of the Democratic Party. . . . He was weak." To the contrary, Professor Jean Baker argues that Buchanan's selection of his cabinet indicated that he was "a strong president intent on having his way, surrounded by advisors who agreed with him." His performance as president was at variance with the weak executives of the late antebellum era; Buchanan, she concludes, was a strong executive, "if an exceptionally misguided one."[2]

To consider whether Buchanan was a weakling or willful as president is one way to assess his leadership of the party. But it may be helpful and more productive to reverse the proposition and consider the state of the party—and by extension the country—during his presidency. President Buchanan can be used as a vehicle for analyzing the state of the sectionalization and fragmentation of the Democracy (and again by extension the nation) in the years immediately preceding the secession crisis and Civil War. Put in reductive terms, to move away from the "great man in history" analysis of the sectional crisis to the broader question of the many dilemmas facing the Democracy during his tenure in office might shed greater light on his presidency (and by extension yet again the nation).

Although some historians have contended that Buchanan's elevation to the White House "is a testimony to the breakdown of the American political system," I would argue that Democratic politicians (and Republicans) all conceived of their work as principled, responsible, and noble.[3] Buchanan—no less than Stephen Douglas or Robert Barnwell Rhett, politicians all—created the Civil War; they were doing what they were supposed to do. By defining and articulating a new cause—the slavery issue—they were representing the popular will through the manipulation of a popular symbol: slavery. Viewed in that light and given the importance of the sectional crisis in the late 1850s, war could only have been avoided if Buchanan, among others North and South, had taken actions that they would have regarded as ignoble, immoral, and cowardly.

The election of 1856, the battle over the Lecompton Constitution, the sectional response to the president's handling of the Panic of 1857, and the subsequent and inevitable alienation of Buchanan and Douglas after the English compromise are illustrative of these points. A closer look at the election suggests that Buchanan was not the "doughface" candidate that antislavery Northerners and historians alike assert. Reaction to his nomination was far less enthusiastic in the South and more underwhelming and problematic among free-state Democrats than historians believe. For example, a slave-state Democratic editor keened, "we regret Pierce has been thrown overboard, for we know the cause of it has been his devotion to the rights of the states, the South included."[4] However inept and ham-handed (and corrupt) his less-than-diplomatic efforts to secure Congress's approval of the Lecompton Constitution, divisions within the party over it exacerbated sectional fractures long extant in the national party and more ominously in the political culture that defined and gave substance to the Second Party System. Worse, Republican charges of widespread corruption in the administration that were themselves tied to the Lecompton struggle further linked the president to the slave power in the Northern public's mind. Finally, contemporaries and historians alike have made much of the break between Buchanan and Douglas following the internecine warfare over Lecompton and the bogus "solution" of the English bill. Yet for all their infighting, both Democrats were insensitive to the widespread moral repugnance to slavery in the North. Their tragic bond lay in their inability to recognize that by 1856 the territorial crisis had burned a swath across the political landscape and separated the nation from the ebullient nationalism of the 1840s.[5]

The Election of 1856

The South made him President. They took him for one of their own. Since his first term as a watery-legged mooncalf in the lower house of Congress he played the parasite on Southern political genius.

John Slidell in John Updike, *Buchanan Dying*

There is a wrong impression about one of the candidates. . . . There is no such person running as James Buchanan. He is dead of lockjaw. Nothing remains but a platform and a bloated mass of political putridity.

Thaddeus Stevens

His political views are summed up in the following extract from one of his speeches in Congress: "If I know myself, I am a politician neither of the West nor the East, of the North nor the South. I therefore shall forever avoid any expressions the direct tendency of which must be to create sectional jealousies, and at length disunion—

*that worst of all political calamities." That he endeavored in his future career to act
in accordance with this uncertain policy no candid mind can doubt.*

Ben. Perley Poore

Despite his assertions to the contrary in 1856, James Buchanan lusted after
the presidency. With one blue eye, the other hazel, one near-sighted, the
other far-sighted, Buchanan had eyed the nomination since at least 1844.
He had much to recommend him. He had served in the Pennsylvania legislature and then United States House of Representatives, was minister to
Russia and later to Great Britain, United States senator, and secretary of
state under James K. Polk. He believed passionately that service was not
its own reward, but rather that it should be rewarded. His devotion to
party and nation would, he hoped, be capped by a presidency. Buchanan's
ardent defense of Southern rights and reluctant endorsement of popular
sovereignty made him popular in the South. But pro-industry elements
within the Pennsylvania Democracy opposed him and somewhat vitiated
Buchanan's strength in his home state.

At the Democratic Convention in 1852, none of the candidates who
were in the field were able to secure the two-thirds vote necessary for
the party's nomination. Lewis Cass, the party standard-bearer in 1848,
faded quickly; and although Buchanan, William L. Marcy, and Senator
Stephen A. Douglas all had surges, none could obtain the nomination.
All the while, Franklin Pierce's supporters worked the floor, assuring delegates that "Young Hickory of the Granite Hills" could unite the party,
win the fall election, and would distribute patronage lavishly. On the forty-
ninth ballot, the persuasiveness of their argument and the lure of victory
and postmasterships swept the convention as delegation after delegation
hopped aboard the Pierce bandwagon. The final vote as announced by the
chair was "Cass 2, Douglas 2, Butler 1, Franklin Pierce of New Hampshire
(God bless him) 282 votes."[6]

Pierce would soon prove himself to be as inept as a president as he
was a senator or brigadier general. As president he tried to use the glue
of patronage and cabinet appointments to cement the party's cracks, but
the Democracy's fissures became even wider. Unable to resuscitate either
Democratic unity or public support, he took to the jug. His support for
Stephen Douglas's Kansas-Nebraska Act made him the darling of the
South but a scourge to the Northern wing of the party. Douglas, the

architect of the act, was similarly excoriated then and thereafter in the free states for repealing the Missouri Compromise ban on slavery extension as the price for Southern support. Worse, the act destroyed the ascendancy of the Democracy in the North. In the off-year elections following the passage of the act in 1854, the party was only able to save twenty-five of ninety-one free-state seats it had won in 1852. The effect, if not the intent, of the act was to upset the bisectional balance of power within the Democratic Party and thus weaken a powerful voice of nationalism in a period of growing sectional animosity.[7]

While the Democracy was imploding and violence in territorial Kansas was exploding, Buchanan was safely removed in Britain. Although his name was floated by friends North and South as a possible nominee in 1856, he proclaimed himself "indifferent" to the nomination. Although he expressed his gratitude for the efforts made on behalf of his possible nomination by allies in Pennsylvania, Buchanan hastened to add that "if my own wishes had been consulted, my name should never again have been mentioned in connection with that office." Then leaving his fate to the Almighty, Buchanan bravely decided to wait on Divine Intervention. He stoically observed, "If it be the will of Providence to bestow upon me the Presidency, I shall accept it as a duty, a burden, & a trial, & not otherwise. I shall take no step to obtain it."[8]

Most Southern Democrats preferred Pierce in 1856 or Douglas if the president could not be renominated. If neither could secure the nomination, they would have supported Mississippi's John A. Quitman. But all three favorites of the Southern wing of the party were strongly opposed at the North. In this context Buchanan had much to recommend him. He was as experienced as Pierce. Free from the taint of the Kansas fiasco, Buchanan was known to oppose extremists North and South. Coming to political maturity in the Age of Jackson, he continued to embrace the Democracy's commitment to self-governance and territorial expansion. Buchanan also came from a crucial Northern state. Above all he was solid. Praising Buchanan with faint damns, Henry Foote remembered him to be "a man of solid and vigorous intellect, without having the least claim, though, to be ranked as a man of genius." Although Foote professed that he could not remember Buchanan delivering a "single speech remarkable either for eloquence, for potential reasoning for valuable practical illustration" during his tenure in the Senate, he admitted him to be "a man of inflexible integrity." Viable in the North and acceptable to the South, the sixty-five-year-old Buchanan could be marketed as a Union man and the Democracy could restore its claim as the nation's true conservative party.[9]

And so he was; and so they did. Meeting in Cincinnati in June, Democratic delegates nominated the Old Public Functionary on the seventeenth ballot. The party endorsed the Nebraska legislation while maintaining a cagey ambiguity on the power of territorial legislatures to prohibit slavery. And the convention overwhelmingly adopted an aggressive, expansionist foreign policy. During the campaign, party activists declared that the nation's problems could be traced to the neglect of the Democracy's fundamental principles. Taking direct aim at the newly formed Republican Party, the *Cleveland Plain Dealer* asserted that the battle against their opponents' commitment to restriction of slavery was the same "that has ever existed between the democratic and antidemocratic parties in this country. It was the doctrine of HAMILTON and the elder ADAMS that the people were not capable of self-government, and therefore should not be trusted with power. JEFFERSON held differently; and here political parties sprang up, dividing on the principle of popular sovereignty." Moving beyond defense of traditional principles, party members went on the attack against "a Fusion, Free Soil, and Abolition conglomeration . . . which, blending all the isms and one-ideans [sic] of this free thinking or political freebooting community, promises to give us plenty of business for some time to come."[10]

For the moment, the Democratic message was upbeat and familiar. "The only party in the country at the present time which can set up a pretense of nationality is the Democratic party," the *Nashville Union* asserted. "There is nothing wonderful in this, to those who believe that no party can permanently exist save as the representatives of sound and national principles."[11] But as the canvass unfolded the fragmentation of the political system sparked a three-way race for the presidency. And national divisions over popular sovereignty intensified sectionalism not only on a national level but within the Democratic Party itself. Both boded ill for Buchanan if elected.

In the 1856 canvass, three candidates held five different nominations. John Frémont was nominated by Republicans and the nativist North American Party. Former president Millard Fillmore was the choice of Know-Nothings in the South and Whigs. And as the campaign unfolded it ominously foreshadowed the sectional presidential contest of 1860.

Figure 5.1. *The Buck Chase of 1856* (Philadelphia: John Childs, 1856). Lithograph. This cartoon depicts the 1856 presidential campaign. Buchanan, whom contemporaries often called "Old Buck," clearly wins the race. Millard Fillmore's head, placed on a collapsed and emaciated horse, laments that he entered the contest. John Frémont rides on two horses—one representing abolitionism and the other bearing the head of *New York Tribune* editor Horace Greeley. Greeley complains that Frémont has placed too much weight on his back but vows that "next time we'll head off that hard old Buck."

THE BUCK CHASE of 1856.

Despite three candidates in the field, there were essentially two presidential contests. Buchanan squared off against Frémont in the North. Yet in the slave states, the race was solely between Buchanan and Fillmore. As David Potter has rightly observed, "for the first time since the Compromise of 1850, there was widespread fear for the safety of the Union that undoubtedly influenced many voters." James Buchanan sensed the same threat in a letter sent to Nahum Capen in August. "I consider that all incidental questions are comparatively of little importance . . . when compared with grand and appalling issue of Union or Disunion. . . . In this region, the battle is fought mainly on this issue."[12]

Once Pennsylvania went Democratic in October (where much money and energy were spent), Buchanan's election was secure. That was the good news for the soon-to-be president-elect. He lost only Maryland among the slave states but carried only five in the North: Pennsylvania, New Jersey, Illinois, Indiana, and California. Frémont carried eleven free states. Put simply, Buchanan won because his dominance in the South was more pronounced than Frémont's in the North. Had Pennsylvania and either Illinois or Indiana gone for Frémont, the Republicans would have triumphed in their first presidential contest. Moreover, the sectional imbalance within the Democratic Party became more marked. Buchanan had become the first president since Andrew Jackson to carry the national contest without carrying a majority of free states as well as slave states. A Vicksburg Democrat taking measure of Buchanan's victory observed to Jefferson Davis, "We are far from being satisfied with the result of the election . . . because the northern vote shows that the *immediate* future . . . is big with peril. . . . Had Gen. Pierce been nominated, as he ought to have been, and elected, as he would have been, the triumph would have been decisive." As it now stood, he concluded, "the democracy have the office four years more, and that is all."[13]

Lecompton Crisis

> It is the imperative and indispensable duty of the government of the United States to secure to every resident inhabitant the free and independent expression of his opinion by his vote. . . . This being accomplished, nothing can be fairer than to leave the people of a Territory free from all foreign interference, to decide their own destiny for themselves, subject only to the Constitution of the United States.
>
> Inaugural Address, James Buchanan

At present I am an out sider. My advice is not coveted nor will my wishes probably be regarded. I want nothing but fair play. . . . If on the contrary the power of the administration is to be used either for plunder of ambition I shall return every blow they may give.

Stephen Douglas

Buchanan, the incoming president, has very little of the respect or the confidence of the men from the south, by whose support alone he was sustained & elected. I anticipate for him a reign that will bring him but little of either pleasure or honor.

Edmund Ruffin

When Buchanan assumed the presidency he was determined to end the "long agitation" of the slavery question in order that "the geographical parties to which it has given birth, so much dreaded by the Father of his Country, will speedily become extinct." For more than twenty years, he argued, the debate and divisions over the slavery extension issue have "been productive of no positive good to any human being, [while] it has been the prolific source of great evils to the master, the slave, and to the whole country. It has alienated and estranged the people of the sister States from each other, and has even seriously endangered the very existence of the Union." To that end, the president would settle the Kansas territorial question "upon the basis of popular sovereignty—a principle as ancient as free government itself." Once Kansas was admitted as a state, everything of a practical nature regarding slavery would have been decided. "No other question remains for adjustment," Buchanan asserted, "because all agree that, under the Constitution, slavery in the States is beyond the reach of any human power, except that of the respective States themselves wherein it exists."[14]

Because the unhappy story of the Buchanan administration is the story also of the disruption of the Democracy, most historians have tended to draw a line from the *Dred Scott* decision to the party's blowup in 1860. The decision, announced two days after Buchanan's inauguration, repudiated the power of Congress to outlaw slavery in the territories. Yet it was the struggle over the Lecompton Constitution that fatally exacerbated the sectional divisions within the Democratic Party and essentially ruined the Buchanan administration that supported it. The battle in Congress over its passage would test the abilities—as well as the limits—of Buchanan's executive leadership. The resolution of this congressional imbroglio by the

English bill sham would disappoint Southern Democrats and dissipate their already tepid support for the president. It would alienate the Douglas wing of the party from his administration and more generally slave-state Democrats. When Douglas split with the administration over Lecompton, extreme state's-rights Democrats concluded that their alliance with the Northern wing was as big a sham as the English bill. Lecompton, not *Dred Scott*, was the beginning of the end for the Democracy—and Buchanan's presidency.

President Buchanan was convinced that if Kansas were admitted as a state after every free and independent voter there had a voice and a vote in determining whether the territory would be free or slave, he would have gone a long way to removing this vexed question of slavery extension which had so long agitated the public mind and politics. Events in Kansas were already moving in that direction. At the end of the Pierce administration, the proslavery legislature in Kansas called for an election of delegates to a convention that would draft a state constitution. Buchanan, realizing that a skilled and forceful governor would be essential to the task of seeing the process through to a successful conclusion, selected Robert J. Walker to be governor of the territory. Walker had served with Buchanan in the Polk administration and was known to be a hardworking, deft politician. He was also astute. Before leaving for his post in Kansas, he received the president's approval for his inaugural address, which said, "In no contingency will Congress admit Kansas as a slave state or free state, unless a majority of the people in Kansas shall first have fairly and freely decided this question for themselves by direct vote on the adoption of the Constitution, excluding all fraud and violence."[15]

Walker set off for Kansas—an assignment he at first was reluctant to accept—determined to impose order and to secure an impartial and fair election. Instead, he alarmed proslavery settlers with what many considered as his overly familiar trafficking with free-state settlers in Kansas. Walker then proceeded to infuriate Southerners with loose talk about an "isothermal" line north of which slavery could not exist. He suggested to proslavery settlers that they explore the possibility of a slave state in the Indian territory south of Kansas, a suggestion that Southerners considered if not insane then "vile hypocrisy" and "flimsy twaddle." When he read the portion of his inaugural address regarding the process by which the territorial constitution would be ratified, Walker altogether discredited himself in the eyes of the South by seeming to dictate the terms of Kansas's admission to the Union. *"We are betrayed,"* one Southerner keened; "our victory [read: Buchanan's election] has turned to ashes on our lips, and before God I will never say well done to the traitor or his master who lives in the White House." Because many observers believed the president knew of and approved Walker's actions, he, too, came under fire. "Buchanan has his finger in the fire, for his deuced cunning," South Carolina's Lawrence Keitt wrote. "Bring in Kansas as a slave State, and the Northern Democracy goes to the devil—therefore she must come in as a free state—and at the same time the South be blinded—We have a political Mephistopheles—only a worse rascal—an ingrained knave."[16]

Howell Cobb, a close associate of the president's and secretary of the treasury in the administration, came to Buchanan's defense. In a letter to Alexander H. Stephens he claimed that the president acted in good faith in accordance with the principles in the Kansas bill and in conformity with the *Dred Scott* decision. "He did not wish Gov. Walker or any other official of the Government to use his position to effect the decision of the slavery question, one way or the other," Cobb maintained. "He was indifferent to that decision, so [long as] it was fairly and honestly made by the people of Kansas, and that was the position of every member of the cabinet."[17]

Buchanan's indifference to the outcome in Kansas, whether real or imagined by Cobb, extended to a large degree to his attitude toward slavery. As Jean Baker has persuasively contended, Buchanan had never appreciated "the determination not only of abolitionists, who wanted to end slavery, but of those northerners [many of whom were in his own party] who saw the South as an aggressor. As a leader of a party whose strength lay with the slaveholders, he discounted the moral and political anachronism that slavery was to many." As the president himself observed in his inaugural address, he considered slavery a domestic affair over which the states had complete control, and his concern for the impact of the institution was primarily how it affected Southern families. Thus as Professor Baker concludes, his "vision and inspiration for the future of the United States were increasingly at odds with most Americans, whose definitions of freedom and liberty did not include a slave republic dominated by a minority of slave owners."[18]

Buchanan's vision and inspiration for the future of Kansas soon put him at odds with Douglas and many other Northern Democrats. Free-state settlers in Kansas refused to participate in the election for delegates to the constitutional convention. Arguing that the voting procedure was a fraud, they insisted that they had been discriminated against in drawing district lines. Thus although the proslavery delegates to the convention were not representative of the free-soil majority in the state, they were formally elected. They proceeded to frame a constitution legalizing slavery. Instead of submitting the entire document to the voters, as Walker had demanded (and the president seemed to have promised), the delegates offered settlers the option of voting for a constitution "with slavery" or one "without slavery." In either case, those slaves in the territory and their descendants would remain. Put simply, Kansas would be a slave state in either case.[19]

Buchanan maintained in his first annual message in December 1857 that it was never his "intention to interfere with the decision of the people of Kansas, either for or against slavery." Despite his earlier endorsement of Walker's inaugural promise that the people of Kansas would decide for themselves whether they would form a free or slave state "by a direct vote on the adoption of the Constitution," the actions of the convention were strictly legal, and his instructions to the governor "in favor of submitting the constitution to the people, were expressed in general and qualified terms." Thus a vote on the slavery question alone conformed to an earlier pledge to "stand or fall" on the right of the people to vote on the constitution. Disclaiming any sectional or partisan advantage in Kansas's admission to the Union, Buchanan contended that the territory had occupied the public's attention too long. "It is high time this should be directed to far more important objects," he claimed. "When once admitted to the Union, whether with or without slavery, the excitement beyond her own limits will speedily pass away, and she will then, for the first time, be left, as she ought to have been long since to manage her own affairs in her own way." Free-state voters in Kansas were unmoved by the president's logic and prediction. Again charging voting fraud and convinced that partial submission was a hoax, they stayed home. To no one's surprise, the Lecompton Constitution was carried by a vote of 6,226 "with slavery" and 569 without.[20]

Douglas, the architect of the Nebraska act, already had a strained relationship with the president. Alienated by the president's patronage appointments in Illinois, he had a heated exchange with Buchanan in early December over the Lecompton issue. Buchanan reminded Douglas of the ill-fate that had befallen two senators who had broken with President

Jackson over administration policy. Douglas in turn replied, "Mr. President, I wish you to remember that General Jackson is dead." After hearing the president's annual message, Douglas led renegade Northern Democrats in a rebellion against Lecompton. In a long, heated speech, he flatly denied that submission of the slavery question alone complied with the intent or meaning of the Kansas-Nebraska Act. Worse, Douglas complained, the Lecompton swindle was a gross violation of Democratic practice; it smacked of deceit. Above all he excoriated the delegates at Lecompton and the administration for attempting to force this constitution on the people of Kansas against their will. Like Buchanan, Douglas claimed—not for the first or last time—that he did not care whether slavery "is voted down or up in Kansas." Dismissing the constitution as the product of "trickery and jiggle," he thundered that "neither the North nor the South has the right to gain sectional advantage by trickery or fraud."[21]

Buchanan's initial support of Walker and his seemingly shifting position on Kansas had already forfeited the trust and support of many Northern Democrats who were lukewarm to his presidency from its inception. One Georgian taking measure of the Walker fiasco and the president's positions on submission claimed, "Nothing short of seeing the Holy Ghost descending on old Buck in the shape of a dove patent to my eye sight could ever make me trust in him again." Apparently insensitive to how Lecompton would play out at the polls in the North, Buchanan faced more defections now from party members in the free states who had bolted with Douglas. These Democrats took great pains to detail the various swindles and irregularities swirling around the Lecompton convention. Taking issue with President Buchanan, anti-Lecompton Democrats contended that the semblance of legality should not be confused with honesty. Party members also scoffed at Buchanan's suggestion that if Kansans were unhappy with the constitution, they might amend it after statehood had been granted. (The constitution contained a provision that prohibited any amendment for a period of seven years.) More to the point and most tellingly, free-state Democratic dissidents believed that support for the constitution would revolutionize the genius of American government. That governments derived their power from the consent of the governed, Gideon Welles maintained, was "as self-evident a truth in 1857 as it was in 1776." To abandon that principle now "would be to surrender the cornerstone of our whole political system."[22]

In the face of growing opposition to his administration in the South and outright revolt by party members in the North, Buchanan pressed grimly on. He was fully prepared to stake the success of his administration and reputation on Lecompton. He had little choice. Although Buchanan could count on the Senate, where Southern Democrats provided the critical balance of power, the House was less certain. Here he needed 118 votes but could only count on 100. The president and members of his administration used persuasion, patronage, government contracts, liquor, and the incomparable charms of female pulchritude to ram Lecompton through the two houses. They had little effect, and the House turned into an armed battlefield.

Illustrative of the chaos in Congress and the divisions in the Democracy was a scrum in the House in February 1858. When Republican Galusha Grow infiltrated the Democratic camp to chat with anti-Lecompton Northerners, Lawrence Keitt, stretched out between two seats, ordered him to leave. Grow hotly replied that it was a free House and he was a free man; he went where he pleased. Keitt, who had been asleep, grabbed Grow by the throat, initiating a fistfight that involved thirty members of the House. Henry Clay's son John Brown Clay, fueled by malt and hops power, scrambled up on a desk and shrieked that members should stop fighting. The battle royal ended when Elihu Washburne of Illinois grabbed for and then knocked off William Barksdale's wig. The Mississippi representative was angry because he thought few knew he wore one but also because his hairpiece was being trampled under the feet of the combatants. In his haste to retrieve his dignity, he snatched the wig up but put it on wrong side out, "much to the amusement of the spectators." Amid howls of laughter, the fray came to an end. But by this point most congressmen suspected, if Buchanan did not, that the Senate and House were deadlocked.[23]

Despite using all the executive power at his disposal, Buchanan simply did not have the votes in the House. What he failed to see, or at least appreciate, was the damage Northern Democrats would suffer at the polls in support of Lecompton. Northern Democratic losses in off-year elections following the passage of the Kansas-Nebraska Act had been severe. Some of the losses had been recouped in the 1856 election: when Buchanan took the oath of office there were fifty-three free-state Democrats (up from twenty-five) and seventy-five slave-state Democrats. Anti-Lecompton Democrats would have to face another off-year election reminiscent of that of 1855. Buchanan simply could not overcome the principled, practical, and sectional opposition to Lecompton within his own party. Worse, he could not negate or even vitiate the personal opposition to him by slave- and free-state Democrats alike.

Buchanan finally accepted a compromise known as the English bill that resubmitted the Lecompton Constitution shorn of its extravagant request of twenty-three million acres of public land (six times the normal grant to new states). If voters insisted on the larger grant requested, then Kansas would remain a territory until its population was equal to the number required for one representative in the House. Although Douglas stood firm in opposition to this latest swindle perpetrated by the Buchanan administration, enough other anti-Lecompton delegates wavered. Finally, on April 30, the English bill cleared the Senate 31 to 22 and the House 112 to 103. In August 1858 the people of Kansas rejected the Lecompton Constitution (or strictly speaking insisted upon receiving the larger land grant) by a margin of more than ten to one. Influential and extreme elements within the party's Southern wing were disgusted. Buchanan "does not come up to my idea of a Southern Rights Administration," Alabama's William F. Samford complained. "We cannot accept the issues of this Administration and make the battle of 1860 upon them. . . . Depend on it, *defeat*—disastrous—ruinous, awaits us if we make this Administration the standard and watchword of the Democracy!"[24]

As Michael Holt has rightly noted, the Lecompton struggle was a turning point for the Democratic Party. Douglas and Buchanan would remain alienated. The president would oppose the senator both in his reelection bid in 1858 and in his campaign for the presidential nomination in 1860. The Lecompton fight, precipitated in large measure by the president, permanently estranged Southern Democrats from Douglas and popular sovereignty. In 1854, the passage of the Kansas-Nebraska Act was costly to the Pierce administration. Yet it passed. Tellingly, in 1858, in spite of Buchanan's best—or worst—efforts, the administration failed to carry Lecompton. And in the first years of his administration the disruption within the Democracy became more—not less—pronounced. Of the fifty-three free-state seats at the beginning of the Lecompton struggle, only thirty-two were left after the off-year elections following the English "compromise." Of the thirty-two, twelve had opposed Lecompton. When Congress met in 1859, the House had sixty-nine Southern Democrats, nineteen party regulars from the North, and twelve anti-Lecompton Democrats. Although Buchanan believed his party to be the last bastion against a sectionalized Union, by the late 1850s his handling of Lecompton had intensified and reified the rift within his own party, which demolished what remained of its sectional balance. As Jean Baker succinctly observes, "he ensured his nightmare: the election of a Republican president in 1860."[25]

Panic, Plunder, and Patronage

It is the duty of the government, by all proper means within its power, to aid in alleviating the sufferings of the people occasioned by the suspension of the banks, and to provide against a recurrence of the same calamity. Unfortunately, in either case it can do little.

First Annual Message, James Buchanan

I am inclined to think that this is the most corrupt Administration we have ever had.

Benjamin French

I fear there is no hope of an amicable adjustment of the Kansas Question. It has become apparent that the administration is more anxious for my destruction than they are the harmony & unity of the Democratic Party. You have doubtless seen that they are removing all of my friends from office & requiring pledges of hostility to me from all persons appointed to office. . . . I am determined to stand firmly by my position. . . . If the party is divided by this course it will not be my fault.

Stephen Douglas to Samuel Treat, February 1858

Lecompton was surely the turning point, and a fatal one at that, of the Buchanan administration. But three other events of his presidency provided the impetus for, though they did not ensure, the election of a Republican president in 1860. The Panic of 1857 revealed how deeply Buchanan was steeped in the economics of Andrew Jackson. Worse, his free-trade, hard-money, anti-bank economic agenda, which had evolved and hardened since the 1830s, linked him ever more closely in the northern public mind with the South—and by extension the Slave Power. The Covode Committee investigation into corruption in the post offices, customhouses, and navy yards, as well as the administration's use of money and patronage during the Lecompton struggle, discredited the administration and made corruption a centerpiece in the Republican campaign in 1860. Finally, the patronage war waged by the president and his supporters against Douglas and anti-Lecompton Democrats contributed to the irreconcilable difference between the party's sectional wings that precluded any chance for a unified front against the Republicans in 1860. A brief look at the manner in which these three issues, separately and together, made possible (though not inevitable) a Republican victory will illuminate both Buchanan's executive leadership and his relation to the national party as it lurched to the denouement of the 1860 election.

The Ohio Life Insurance and Trust Company, the most respected institution in the state, failed in August 1857, suspending specie payment. The suspension, which "acted like a clap of thunder in a clear sky" and startled investors and financiers like a "cannon shot," triggered a national fiscal panic that led to the bankruptcy of thousands of businesses and individuals alike. The British investors' withdrawal of their funds from unsound American banks, the fall of grain prices owing to the Crimean War, and the collapse of land speculation in the West were factors in the crisis. Most western railroads failed, and the notes of state banks became worthless overnight. By fall major cities had angry, displaced workers demanding "bread or blood." In September the Bank of Philadelphia closed its doors. The following month, Amos A. Lawrence wrote, "Conceive of the rate of interest here being fifty per cent, and for large sums! Our manufacturing interest is for the present completely broken down and discredited." In Virginia, R. K. Crallé groaned, "Money is a mere name. No one can safely sell anything except for specie—and there is no specie to be had."[26]

President Buchanan's reaction was like that of many citizens and financiers alike: disbelief and bewilderment. "In the midst of unsurpassed plenty in all the productions of agriculture, and in all the elements of national wealth," he told the nation in his first annual message, "we find our manufacturers suspended, our public works retarded, our private enterprises of different kinds abandoned, and thousands of useful laborers thrown out of employment and reduced to want." Initially unsettled by the onset of the panic, the president quickly identified the cause. Although past financial crises could be "attributed to a variety of co-operating causes," not so the current panic. "It is apparent that our existing misfortunes have proceeded solely from our extravagant and vicious system of paper currency and bank credits, exciting the people to wild speculations and gambling in stocks."

Believing that the states, not the federal government, had the responsibility and power to address and redress the causes and consequences of the financial crisis, Buchanan coldly asserted that the government "could do but little" in alleviating the suffering of the people. Buchanan's and Democrats' solution to the panic followed inexorably from this classical Jacksonian analysis of it: stiffer specie ratios, a bankruptcy law for corporations, creation of independent state treasuries, curtailment of the creation of paper money, and the occasional call for the abolition of banks.[27]

Cold comfort that. Buchanan's callous reaction to this severe economic downturn disheartened the suffering and appalled financial leaders throughout the nation. Gloucester fishermen and New Bedford whalers were idled, their ships tied up. Half of the twenty-five thousand clothing establishment workers in Cincinnati lost their jobs. Lumberjacks in Wisconsin and Michigan, discharged with a day's wages, were near starvation. Mayor Fernando Wood's message to the Common Council, calling for public works projects to sustain the unemployed, decried the reality that multitudes "labor without income while surrounded by thousands in selfishness and splendor." The state election in 1858 in Pennsylvania, in which Republicans took twenty-one congressional districts with the Democrats taking four, was seen as a stinging rebuke to the president and his handling of the panic. The *Richmond Whig* contended, "Never, never has any public man encountered so stern and withering a rebuke as has Mr. Buchanan in the result of the election in Pennsylvania on Tuesday." Other editors contended that the election was a "rout," a "revolution," and a "complete repudiation of the administration." For his part the president wrote that after learning of the returns he spent the evening with friends making "a merry time of it, laughing among other things over our crushing defeat. It is so great that it is almost absurd."[28]

Although the economy began to improve significantly within two years, Buchanan's reputation and faux good humor did not recover with it. Worse, Southern Democrats' opposition to the expansion of free territories and to free-handed federal spending, and their support for fiscal retrenchment, increased the specter of a slave power. And looming behind this slave power stood a president who, as a historian of Buchanan's presidency notes, "prepared to veto any such measures that might accidentally clear Congress." The effect, if not intent, of Southern opposition to a protective tariff and a homestead bill (which Buchanan vetoed in 1860) was to impel the proponents of dynamic economic growth into a coalition with political antislavery activists. And, as David Potter contends, the logical vehicle for that coalition nationally, as it was in Pennsylvania, was the Republican Party. "The tyranny and despotism of the slave-led powers at Washington have been emphatically condemned, and their Kansas policy repudiated," a Harrisburg Republican editor proclaimed, "and with equal emphasis has the American policy of Protection to Home Industry been sustained and vindicated." Put simply, the panic and the administration's handling—or mishandling—of it had allowed the Republicans to exploit and take advantage of economic issues, which in turn increased both the party's base and its alienation from, and hostility to, the South.[29]

A second incident that neatly dovetailed with Buchanan's indecisive reaction to the financial crisis was a House investigation begun in 1859 (in the same session as debate over the homestead bill) into the corruption of the administration. Headed by "Honest John" Covode of Pennsylvania, the committee probed the pressures, as well as the political and financial plums, that the president and his administration brought to bear to ensure the passage of the Lecompton Constitution. Covode, a Republican, had taken offense when the president suggested that Republicans had carried the 1858 Pennsylvania election with money, and Covode was eager to settle that score. Intent on providing his party with more evidence of administration corruption—and by extension that of the entire Democratic Party—Covode proposed an open-ended, wide-ranging investigation of the administration's powers of persuasion. When the president sent a protest complaining, House Republicans exploded in laughter and sent it to the House Judiciary Committee, which was headed by an anti-Lecompton Democrat.[30]

After the committee took eight hundred pages of testimony, its report, released in June 1860, provided ample evidence of fiscal laxity and outright corruption. Offers of foreign appointments and money were made to Democrats from New Jersey, Ohio, and Pennsylvania as an inducement to support the Lecompton Constitution. A Pennsylvania Democrat was promised whatever he wanted. All declined, and one shouted he was not in the market (this comment prompted Horace Greeley to quip that "if the President were not already as bankrupt as the Treasury, he would yet win"). A Democratic representative from Pennsylvania who wavered in his support for the English bill sided with the administration after his brother received a contract to supply the army with three hundred mules at a profit of fifty-five dollars each. Cornelius Wendell, who received printing contracts to subsidize Democratic newspapers, testified that he had agreed to print the *American State Papers* for twenty thousand dollars. The government, however, agreed to pay the contractors (Gales and Seaton) fifty thousand. The list of questionable practices and outright corrupt bargains seemed endless.[31]

Not only did the report make the administration look corrupt, it became part of the warp and weft of the Republican charge that the Slave Power, working through the Democratic Party, had endangered the survival of republican government. Put in reductive terms, Buchanan, dancing to the tune of the Slave Power, endangered the Republic, had contempt for the public will, and used and abused the powers of the presidency to corrupt Congress. Nonetheless, the president proclaimed, "I have passed triumphantly through this ordeal. My vindication is complete." Perhaps. To be sure, none of the findings in the report were grounds for impeachment. And Buchanan could rightly claim the report leveled no criminal charges against him. Yet released five months before the 1860 election, the report made Democratic corruption a significant and powerful element of the Republican campaign. Even Democrats were disheartened by the report. One Virginian noted that the Constitution had guaranteed "a republican form of government, and that is as much an exclusion of democracy as it is of a monarchy." What the Covode report proved too plainly was that the administration "now distribute[s] alms amongst the people to buy their votes."[32]

The third episode that paved the way for a Republican triumph in 1860 was the internecine warfare within the Democratic Party and especially the war made by Buchanan on Douglas and other anti-Lecompton Democrats. While the Republicans were fashioning a message (aided inadvertently and in no small measure by Buchanan) that looked to broaden the party base, Democrats expended an equal amount of energy narrowing theirs and attacking one another. From 1858 to the nominating conventions and election of 1860, the sectional wings of the Democracy continued to fire salvos at each other, forgetting William Marcy's observation of a decade earlier that "politicians have the abstract right to commit suicide if they only kill themselves—They have no right thereby to injure their friends."[33]

President-elect Buchanan came to the presidency determined to revitalize and reunite the party structure. Committed to "selective rotation"—or the rule of rotation—in office in order to "arrest if possible, the agitation of the slavery question at the North & the destruction of sectional parties," President Buchanan was determined that "in all appointments to office I shall endeavor to select the best & most efficient individuals to aid me." To that end, he sought to build on demonstrated strengths of the party at the state and local level rather than past political friendships. Lecompton, Douglas's bolt, and the opposition of free-state anti-Lecompton Democrats to the administration altered permanently and fatally for the Democracy that measured approach. By the time Douglas returned home in 1858 after defying the president first over Lecompton then the English bill, the feud between himself and the president was irreconcilable. The division among the rank and file in Illinois, owing as much to patronage practices as to principled differences over Lecompton, resulted in two Democratic tickets in Illinois state elections that year. Bowed but not yet beaten, Douglas claimed the administration was determined to "crush every public man who dissents from their policy of forcing a constitution on the people of Kansas against their will."[34]

Administration officials told Douglas supporters throughout the North that they had a choice: support the administration or lose their jobs. In Illinois, supporters of Douglas—the state mail agent, the Chicago postmaster, the federal marshal for the northern portion of the state—were cashiered and replaced by administration—and pro-Lecompton—appointees. Isaac Cook, the new postmaster, had been dismissed from the same position in 1857 owing the department eighteen thousand dollars. He now headed the splinter faction opposed to Douglas. Illinois Republicans basked in the glow of the pyrotechnics. More to the point, they hoped to profit by the animosity between the president and the senator. William Herndon, Abraham Lincoln's law partner and confidant, hoped that Republicans would make the split in the Democracy "wider and deeper, hotter and more impassible. Political hatred, deep-seated opposition is what is so much desired, and if we can do this between the worshippers of Buchanan and Douglas we will effect it.... I am this day ready to go further

FORCING SLAVERY DOWN THE THROAT OF A FREESOILER

Figure 5.2. *Forcing Slavery down the Throat of a Freesoiler* (Philadelphia: J. L. Magee, 1856). Lithograph. Reminiscent of Jonathan Swift's *Gulliver's Travels*, Stephen Douglas, Franklin Pierce, James Buchanan, and Lewis Cass restrain a free-state set-tler in Kansas, depicted as Gulliver, and force slavery and the Democratic platform upon him. Meanwhile, the background shows violence erupting in Kansas.

than I have ever gone, if the nigger drivers force Kansas on this free People. I am ready to go *any length for self defense*, though that length should *end in war* bloody and to the hilt. . . . I hate power and I hate and dread the nigger power."[35]

Although anti-Lecompton Democrats and the administration had already found themselves in heated opposition during the Lecompton struggle, the subsequent hostility between them proved fatal to the party for two interrelated reasons. First, it reinforced and made permanent the sectional division within the Democracy. Second, the Northern wing of the Party, decimated in the off-year elections, became patronage-centered in those states where it ceased to be competitive at the state level. Suscep-tible and responsive to the agenda of the Buchanan administration, these state organizations were implacably hostile to Douglas and his presiden-tial aspirations. In effect, by 1860 there were two Democratic parties. The popularly based Northern wing supported Douglas. The other one was

Southern (but with patronage allies in the North), whose strength or political center of gravity was in Congress. As David Potter astutely observed, the split issued in large measure from the incompatibility of Buchanan and Douglas. The president was stubborn, defensive-minded, and shrewd; the senator, energetic, imaginative, and impetuous. Buchanan opted for safety and the status quo, while Douglas took risks and was too much the innovator. On the eve of the Charleston convention, the crisis of the Democracy was at hand.[36]

Coda

> *They were all there, Miss Hetty, as real to me as you are this minute—little Cobb fair to bursting to speak his piece, like a student certain to please his teacher, and Judge Black as dour and grim and rumpled in his clothes as a Glasgow chimney sweep, and old Cass struggling to stay awake with his wig slipping sideways, and poor John Floyd yellow as a ghost stretched out on the divan in his dressing gown too sick himself to stand; they were all wanting something from me Miss Hetty. They were demanding I perform some task. I couldn't for the life of me make out what it was. They were frightened, Miss Hetty, every man of them. And I stood above them majestic and serene as one of those pinioned eagles that used to roam the lawn.*

John Updike, Buchanan Dying

It may be, as one historian has contended, that when James Buchanan took the office in 1857 amid the bitter war in Kansas he "was the hope of the nation—the one man who would make no reckless, impulsive mistake." Yet by the spring of 1859, Edmund Ruffin observed that "there never has been a president, when parties existed, who was so plainly denounced & spoken of so contemptuously, in almost every peculiar act as Buchanan." And in December of that year, Robert Toombs ruefully concluded that "Old Buck is determined to rule or ruin us. I think he means to continue his own dynasty or destroy the party, and the times are at least favorable to his accomplishing the latter result and the country with it."[37]

And it may also be, as Henry Foote remembered, that although exceedingly truthful and confiding, Buchanan "selected often as the special counsels men of very small mental caliber . . . who had recommended themselves to his regard men mainly by their adroitness in the arts of adulation, to the influence of which arts he was indeed most lamentably open." How telling, then, Professor Baker's observation that Buchanan's "best opportunity for keeping the Union intact was to maintain the status quo; his best friends in this project were, ironically, southerners." But equally ironic is that many Southerners, especially those fire-eaters, became disillusioned with Buchanan's leadership. As one Alabamian noted, many slave-state Democrats had believed in 1856 that the South would be advantaged by Buchanan's election. Especially appealing were visions of an expanding empire for slavery. "Kansas, Cuba, South America all loomed up as inviting southern expansion, outlet and development," he wrote in 1858. "The *dream* has been sadly dissipated; the galling *reality* is too recent and current for the South to listen to the miserable party mongering and party expediencies of the Cabinet and Washington *Union*."[38]

One might argue that James Buchanan's growing unpopularity in the free states did not arise from his insensitivity to a growing moral repugnance of slavery—a repugnance that spread beyond and transcended the abolitionist movement.[39] Supporters and opponents of the Kansas-Nebraska Act and the Lecompton Constitution were similarly indifferent. Rather, Buchanan's failure resulted from his inability to recognize—good Jacksonian Democrat that he was—that the territorial crisis that followed the Mexican cession had separated the nation from the ebullient nationalism of the mid-1840s when he was President James K. Polk's secretary of state and oversaw the expansion of the Union to the shores of the Pacific. What Buchanan did not—or could not—realize is that by his presidency the slavery extension issue had become for Americans of the 1850s what the conflict over the Second Bank of the United States had been for Jacksonians in the 1830s: a way of identifying and rooting out subversive elements in American politics. But whereas Jackson's attack on the bank divided the nation along partisan lines, the fault lines of the territorial issue were sectional.

As late as his third annual message in December 1859, the Old Public Functionary continued to urge extremists North and South "to cultivate the ancient feelings of mutual forbearance and good will toward each other, and strive to allay the demonstrated spirit of sectional hatred and strife now alive in the land." Delivered almost two months to the day after John Brown's raid at Harpers Ferry, Buchanan's speech confidently asserted that the effect—though certainly not the intent—of the attack would cause Americans "to pause and reflect upon the possible peril to their cherished institutions, [and be] the means, under Providence, of allaying the existing excitement." The president who noted with pride that his service to the nation commenced in the last generation confidently predicted that like the bitter divisions that grew out of the bank war in the 1830s, the current sectional excitement would become "volcanoes burnt out, and on the lava and ashes and squalid scoria of old eruptions [would] grow the peaceful olive, the cheering vine, and the sustaining corn."[40] By the end of his term in office, Buchanan's misplaced optimism would become the nation's tragedy. More is the pity.

> *I was President, Miss Hetty, and all the Union lay visible beneath me. The North with its smoking mills, the soft green Southland as yet unscarred by the war, the West with its deserts and mountains, the Mormon lake, the shining Pacific beyond. Beneath me lived a vast humming, which became a murmurous cry, a subdued and multitudinous petition for mercy; while above me a profound silence obtained, a silence as crystalline and absolute as a ladle of water from my corner spring. . . . Now tell me, dear all-knowing Hetty, what might my dream signify?*
>
> John Updike, *Buchanan Dying*

Notes

1. *New-York Times* obituary cited in Fergus M. Bordewich, "Digging into a Historic Rivalry," *Smithsonian*, February 2004, 102; C-Span poll cited in Allen F. Cole, "Asserting His Authority: James Buchanan's Failed Vindication," *Pennsylvania History* 70 (Winter 2003): 81; Michael J. Birkner, "Looking Up from the Basement: New Biographies of Franklin Pierce and James Buchanan," *Pennsylvania History* 72 (Autumn 2005): 541. In the 2009 CNN poll, Buchanan again finished dead last, nosing out Andrew Johnson and Franklin Pierce for that distinction. However, Buchanan did somewhat better in the midst of Bill Clinton's presidency. In a poll taken in 1996 by Arthur M. Schlesinger Jr., "the ineffectual Franklin Pierce and the rigidly dogmatic Herbert Hoover tie with Grant as the best among the Failures. Next down the list comes Nixon." However, Buchanan, like Andrew Johnson, received more Failure votes than they did in Schlesinger Sr.'s poll; once again, Buchanan's "irresolution," which "encouraged the secession of the Confederate states," damned his reputation. And in a backhand swipe, Schlesinger scorns that Buchanan, along with Johnson, Hoover, and Nixon, "damaged the republic a good deal more than did the hapless Grant and the feckless Harding." Schlesinger, "Rating the Presidents: Washington to Clinton," *Political Science Quarterly* 112 (Summer 1997): 185.

2. Martin Van Buren, *The Autobiography of Martin Van Buren*, ed. John C. Fitzpatrick, *Annual Report of the American Historical Association for the Year 1918*, 2 vols. (Washington, D.C., 1920), 2:496; Woodrow Wilson, "States Rights (1850–1860): An Historical Essay," in *The Papers of Woodrow Wilson*, ed. Arthur Link et al., 69 vols.

(Princeton: Princeton University Press, 1966–1994), 11:338; Robert A. Brent, "Failure of Executive and Legislative Leadership during the Decades of the 1850s," *Southern Quarterly* 9 (October 1970): 57; Wilson, "States Rights," 338; Jean H. Baker, *James Buchanan* (New York: Times Books, 2004), 79, 78. In the spirit of fairness and transparency, I should note that Van Buren noted that the OPF's positive traits were "amply endowed with those clear perceptions of self interest and of duties connected with it that are most inseparable from the Scotch character." For a stimulating and thought-provoking discussion of Buchanan's presidency and legacy, see Michael J. Birkner, Don Fehrenbacher, Kenneth M. Stampp, Robert Johannsen, and Elbert Smith (discussants), "The Presidency of James Buchanan: A Reassessment," in *James Buchanan and the Political Crisis of the 1850s*, ed. Michael J. Birkner (Selinsgrove, Pa.: Susquehanna University Press, 1996), 171–202. For a comparative assessment of Buchanan and Lincoln, see William E. Gienapp, "'No Bed of Roses': James Buchanan, Abraham Lincoln, and Presidential Leadership in the Civil War Era," ibid., 93–122.

3. Brent, "Failure of Executive and Legislative Leadership," 57.

4. Democratic editor quoted in J. Mills Thornton III, *Politics and Power in a Slave Society: Alabama, 1800–1860* (Baton Rouge: Louisiana State University Press, 1978), 370.

5. Professor Baker has put it succinctly, imaginatively, and with sardonic wit: "With his tilted head, protruding stomach, proportionally diminutive lower body, and heavily lidded eyes, one sometimes shut, he resembled an erect, two-footed tyrannosaur. Antislavery northerners believed his principles to be antiquated. Unlike most American men of his age and station, who favored black bow ties, Buchanan customarily wore a white high collar with a white handkerchief that overflowed onto the lapels of his morning coat. His clothes, identical to those of public men two generations earlier, were another reflection of his old-fashioned tastes." Baker, *James Buchanan*, 46–47.

6. Roy Franklin Nichols, *Franklin Pierce: Young Hickory of the Granite Hills* (1931; rev. ed., Philadelphia: University of Pennsylvania Press, 1958), 197–204; Larry Gara, *The Presidency of Franklin Pierce* (Lawrence: University Press of Kansas, 1991), 17–34 (quotation at 34). See also the sympathetic two-volume biography by Peter A. Wallner, *Franklin Pierce* (Concord, N.H.: Plaidswede Publishing Company, 2004, 2007).

7. David M. Potter, *The Impending Crisis, 1848–1861* (New York: Harper and Row, 1976), 174–75.

8. Buchanan to Harriet Lane, January 25, 1856, Buchanan to Bigler, February 12, 1856, in John Bassett Moore, ed., *The Works of James Buchanan, Comprising His Speeches, State Papers, and Private Correspondence*, 12 vols. (Philadelphia: J. B. Lippincott, 1908–11), 10:21, 45. Despite his distance—geographical and political—from Washington, Buchanan was still capable of making mischief for the Democracy and adding to poor Pierce's woes. He was one of the authors of the Ostend Manifesto, which advocated the purchase of Cuba from Spain. If Spain should not acquiesce then "we shall be justified in wresting it from Spain if we possess the power." As David

Potter has pointed out, the Ostend Manifesto, along with the Kansas-Nebraska Act, "were the two great calamities of Franklin Pierce's presidency." The former discredited Manifest Destiny, while the latter brought into disrepute popular sovereignty. As president, Buchanan would persist in supporting spread-eagle expansion and self-government in Kansas. Potter, *Impending Crisis*, 192.

9. Henry S. Foote, *Casket of Reminiscences* (Washington, D.C.: Chronicle Publishing Company, 1874), 111–12. On Buchanan's wealth of experience and conservatism see Brent, "Failure of Executive and Legislative Leadership," 58; Pearl T. Ponce, "Pledges and Principles: Buchanan, Walker, and Kansas in 1857, *Kansas History* 27 (Spring–Summer 2004): 86; Frederic S. Klein, "James Buchanan: Man on a Tightrope," *American History Illustrated* 1 (May 1966): 13; and Philip Shriver Klein, *President James Buchanan* (University Park: Pennsylvania State University Press, 1962), 248–60.

10. Quotations from Michael A. Morrison, *Slavery and the American West: The Eclipse of Manifest Destiny and the Coming of the Civil War* (Chapel Hill: University of North Carolina Press, 1997), 178, 179.

11. Ibid., 180.

12. Potter, *Impending Crisis*, 262 (first quotation), 264 (Buchanan quotation). The 1860 presidential canvass also became two separate contests. Stephen Douglas, the Union Democrat, would face Abraham Lincoln in the North, while John Breckinridge, the nominee of the Constitutional Democrats, would square off against John Bell, the Constitutional Union Party's choice for president. Lincoln won every single Northern state; although he lost New Jersey's popular vote, he nevertheless won four of its seven electoral votes. Douglas only carried Missouri (and narrowly at that over Bell); Breckinridge took eleven Southern states; and Bell took Virginia, Kentucky, and Tennessee.

13. Ibid., 264–65; Morrison, *Slavery and the American West*, 185–86; Michael J. Birkner, "The Election of 1856," in *American Presidential Campaigns and Elections*, ed. William G. Shade and Ballard C. Campbell, 3 vols. (New York, 2001), 1:376–77; Horatio J. Harris to Davis, December 3, 1856, in Jefferson Davis, *The Papers of Jefferson Davis*, 11 vols. (Baton Rouge, 1971–2004), 6:97. James Buchanan could also read an electoral map; he warned Virginia's John Y. Mason that if his election "should be accomplished by the votes of the Southern States United with Pennsylvania & New Jersey alone, it might be the beginning of the end." Buchanan quoted in Morrison, *Slavery and the American West*, 185. Michael Holt argues that "the Democrats were a likelier destination than the Republicans for National Whigs if they were allowed to float free" and that "prominent Whig defectors gave Democrats a powerful weapon, especially in the slave states where Whigs had once been competitive." In the South, however, "most rank-and-file Whigs, whatever they thought of Know Nothingism, appeared to have voted for Fillmore." Holt, *The Rise and Fall of the American Whig Party: Jacksonian Politics and the Onset of the Civil War* (New York, 1999), 970, 979. See also Michael F. Holt, "Another Look at the Election of 1856," in Birkner, *James Buchanan and the Political Crisis of the 1850s*, 37–67.

14. Buchanan, "Inaugural Address, March 4, 1847," in Moore, *Works of James Buchanan*, 10:108, 107–8. One historian has maintained that Buchanan was "in deep denial" when he took the oath of office and that his inaugural "reflected an almost pathological complacency." Bordewich, "Digging into a Historic Rivalry," 100.

15. Quoted in Potter, *Impending Crisis*, 299.

16. "Vile hypocrisy" quoted ibid., 301; Thomas W. Thomas to Alexander H. Stephens, June 15, 1857, in Ulrich B. Phillips, ed., "The Correspondence of Robert Toombs, Alexander H. Stephens, and Howell Cobb," *Annual Report of the American Historical Association for the Year 1911*, 2 vols. (Washington, D.C., 1913), 400–401; Keitt quoted in Morrison, *Slavery and the American West*, 196.

17. Cobb to Stephens, June 18, 1857, in Phillips, "Correspondence of Toombs, Stephens, and Cobb," 402.

18. Baker, *James Buchanan*, 47, 150.

19. The best account of the shenanigans that led to the Lecompton disaster is Nicole Etcheson, *Bleeding Kansas: Contested Liberty in the Civil War Era* (Lawrence: University of Kansas Press, 2004), 139–67. See also Kenneth M. Stampp, *America in 1857: A Nation on the Brink* (New York: Oxford University Press, 1990), 266–94.

20. "First Annual Message, December 8, 1857," in Moore, *Works of James Buchanan*, 10:149, 151; Walker quoted in Potter, *Impending Crisis*, 299; Morrison, *Slavery and the American West*, 197; P. S. Klein, *President James Buchanan*, 301, 304–5. Frederick Stanton, who had replaced the Walker as acting governor, persuaded the free-state legislature of Kansas (which had been elected in October 1856) to adopt a law submitting the entire constitution to the voters for outright acceptance or rejection. It did. On January 4, 1858, the vote was 10,226 against the entire Lecompton Constitution, 138 for it with slavery, and 24 for it without. Potter, *Impending Crisis*, 318.

21. Douglas's Jackson rejoinder quoted in Potter, *Impending Crisis*, 316; Douglas's views on Lecompton quoted in Morrison, *Slavery and the American West*, 198. The rift between the president and Douglas stretched back to the 1852 Democratic convention, when Douglas supporters dismissed Buchanan as an "old Fogie." Buchanan was not one to forget a slight. When Douglas withdrew his candidacy in 1856 in favor of Buchanan, he expected to have some influence in the selection of the cabinet. His hopes for influence with the new administration were further inflated after he campaigned tirelessly for Buchanan in Illinois during the 1856 canvass. Douglas soon discovered that Indiana senator Jesse Bright had the president-elect's ear when it came to patronage in, and cabinet representation from, the Old Northwest. For his part, the president distrusted Douglas (as he did Bright) for his seemingly naked ambition for the presidency. And the two were never close. The battle over Lecompton simply made overt tensions and hostilities between Douglas and Buchanan that had long simmered beneath the surface of national politics. Robert W. Johannsen, *Stephen A. Douglas* (New York: Oxford University Press, 1973), 550–51; P. S. Klein, *President James Buchanan*, 266–67, 282–84; Roy Franklin Nichols, *The Disruption of American Democracy* (1948; rpt. New York, 1962), 98–101.

22. Thomas W. Thomas to Stephens, February 7, 1858, in Phillips, "Correspondence of Toombs, Stephens, and Cobb," 430; Welles quoted in Morrison, *Slavery and the American West*, 200. See also William W. Freehling, *The Road to Disunion*, vol. 2, *Secessionists Triumphant* (New York: Oxford University Press, 2007), 135–37.

23. Potter, *Impending Crisis*, 318–19; Nichols, *Disruption of American Democracy*, 165, 170; Mark W. Summers, *The Plundering Generation: Corruption and the Crisis of the Union, 1849–1861* (New York: Oxford University Press, 1987), 251–54.

24. Samford quoted in Thornton, *Politics and Power*, 368–69; Potter, *Impending Crisis*, 324; Morrison, *Slavery and the American West*, 205–6; Etcheson, *Bleeding Kansas*, 168–89; Freehling, *Road to Disunion*, 140–44.

25. Michael F. Holt, *The Political Crisis of the 1850s* (New York: Wiley, 1978), 205; Potter, *Impending Crisis*, 320, 326; Baker, *James Buchanan*, 106. A defender of Buchanan's policy regarding Lecompton has made the argument, not very persuasively, that Buchanan had full confidence in the public will (which had no limits—despite his specific recommendation on the Lecompton vote) and believed that, after admitted as a slave state, Kansas would amend its constitution and be both free and Democratic. Put in other terms, Buchanan tacitly acknowledged that a Democratic Kansas would also be a free Kansas. David E. Meerse, "Buchanan's Patronage Policy: An Attempt to Achieve Political Strength," *Pennsylvania History* 40 (January 1973): 37–52.

26. "Clap of thunder" and "cannon shot" quoted in James L. Huston, *The Panic of 1857 and the Coming of the Civil War* (Baton Rouge: Louisiana State University Press, 1987), 14; "bread and blood" quoted in Elbert B. Smith, *The Presidency of James Buchanan* (Lawrence: University of Kansas Press, 1975), 55; Lawrence and Crallé quoted in Allan Nevins, *The Emergence of Lincoln*, vol. 1, *Douglas, Buchanan, and Party Chaos, 1857–1859* (New York: Scribner, 1950), 191.

27. Moore, *Works of James Buchanan*, 10:129, 130, 133; Huston, *Panic of 1857*, 42. Buchanan's attitude toward banks had evolved since the controversy emerging from Jackson's opposition to re-chartering the Second Bank of the United States in 1832. Like many other Pennsylvanians then, he was "rather inclined to be friendly to the re-charter of the Bank of the United States." But any support for re-charter would have put him at odds with Jackson (not a man to be crossed) and likely frustrated his ambition to become a United States senator. Thus with sober second thoughts Buchanan tactfully wrote to the president that he "should vote for no bill for that purpose liable to the objections of that which passed both Houses of Congress." Once the bank war was afoot in earnest, his support of Jackson and opposition to the Bank of the United States had hardened. "The Bank are [sic] entirely mistaken in supposing that the pressure which they have occasioned will operate in their favor," he claimed. "Directly the contrary is the truth. The more they make their power felt, the more alive the people will become to the dangers which threaten them from a continuance of that institution." Buchanan to Jackson, October 1–13, 1832, and Buchanan to Jackson, January 18, 1834, in Moore, *Works of James Buchanan*, 2:241, 398.

28. Wood quoted in Nevins, *Emergence of Lincoln*, 1:194–95; *Richmond Whig* quoted in Huston, *Panic of 1857*, 166; Buchanan to Harriet Lane, October 15, 1858, in Moore, *Works of James Buchanan*, 10:229. James Huston has contended that Buchanan and other Democrats were eager to make banks and banking practices a national issue, hoping to garner political capital out of it in 1858 as Jackson had in 1832. But by the off-year elections, banks had resumed specie payments and the issue disappeared before it could produce electoral profits. Huston, *Panic of 1857*, 57–58. Meerse has contended that the state-by-state results were not the debacle that historians suppose; rather, the 1858 elections reveal a party that "had remarkable vitality" and show that contemporaries "saw neither the congressional elections of 1858 as a great struggle over Kansas nor the results as an epic defeat for a repudiated party, its past national policies, or its President." David E. Meerse, "The Northern Democratic Party and the Elections of 1858," *Civil War History* 19 (June 1973): 136–37.

29. Smith, *Presidency of James Buchanan*, 56–57; Potter, *Impending Crisis*, 392; Harrisburg editor quoted in Huston, *Panic of 1857*, 168. The vote on the homestead bill is suggestive of how sectionalism infused economic debate. Of the 115 ayes in the House, 114 were cast by free-state representatives; 64 of the 65 nays came from slave-state members.

30. Summers, *Plundering Generation*, 257. In a subsequent protest, Buchanan asserted that the committee "was more tyrannical than the Star Chamber" and that its proceedings initiated "a reign of terror." "Star Chamber" in Allan Nevins, *The Emergence of Lincoln*, vol. 2, *Prologue to Civil War, 1859–1861* (New York: Scribner, 1950), 197; "reign of terror" in P. S. Klein, *President James Buchanan*, 340. "Honest John" was an active participant in the Grow-Keitt melee, swinging a heavy spittoon to warn off any potential attackers.

31. Summers, *Plundering Generation*, 252–53, 257–58 (Greeley quotation at 253); the whole sordid mess can be examined in its interminable entirety in *House Reports*, 36th Cong., 1st sess., No. 648 (Serial Set 1071). During the Lecompton battle one Illinois defaulter was summoned to Washington and given the Hobson's choice of "five years in the penitentiary . . . for taking public money, or an office and a declaration in behalf of Lecompton." The poor soul chose the office, which led one astute wag to comment how unpopular the constitution must be that it took at least five years in the penitentiary to make it worth supporting. Summers, *Plundering Generation*, 252.

32. Smith, *Presidency of James Buchanan*, 98–99; Potter, *Impending Crisis*, 392; Summers, *Plundering Generation*, 257–60; Virginian quoted in Nichols, *Disruption of American Democracy*, 330. Cornelius Wendell, one of the star witnesses before the committee, proved to have a convenient memory—one that was particularly sharp on details when being questioned by Republicans but proved faulty and then blank when cross-examined by Democrats. Summers, *Plundering Generation*, 257–58.

33. Marcy quoted in Morrison, *Slavery and the American West*, 119.

34. Meerse, "Buchanan's Patronage Policy," 56, 42–43 (first quotation); Douglas

quoted in Richard Allen Heckman, "Out-of-State Influences and the Lincoln-Douglas Campaign of 1858," *Journal of the Illinois State Historical Society* 59 (Spring 1966):
31. Meerse contends that patronage fueled the feud between Douglas and Buchanan
in 1858 but that the two had sought accommodation on Illinois appointments in 1857
down to their break over Lecompton. David E. Meerse, "Origins of the Buchanan-
Douglas Feud Reconsidered," *Journal of the Illinois State Historical Society* 67 (June
1974): 154–74.

35. Herndon quoted in Nichols, *Disruption of American Democracy*, 218; Summers,
Plundering Generation, 252.

36. Potter, *Impending Crisis*, 393–94.

37. F. S. Klein, "James Buchanan," 14; Edmund Ruffin, *The Diary of Edmund Ruffin*,
ed. William K. Scarborough, 3 vols. (Baton Rouge, 1972–89), 1:299 (entry for April
25, 1859); Toombs to Thomas W. Thomas, December 4, 1859, in Phillips, "Correspondence of Toombs, Stephens, and Cobb," 450.

38. Foote, *Casket of Reminiscences*, 113; Baker, *James Buchanan*, 117; Alabamian
quoted in Thornton, *Politics and Power*, 369.

39. Some historians have maintained that Buchanan's inability to recognize and
appreciate the strength of antislavery sentiment was not only congenital but was exacerbated by his absence from the country from 1854, when the Nebraska bill was
passed, until his return in 1857. Ponce, "Pledges and Principles," 90. It should be
noted that Buchanan, "motivated primarily by humanitarian and moralistic beliefs,"
did conduct a vigorous campaign against the slave trade. Robert R. Davis Jr., "James
Buchanan and the Suppression of the Slave Trade," *Pennsylvania History* 33 (October
1966): 454–59 (quotation at 458); Frederick Moore Binder, *James Buchanan and the
American Empire* (Selinsgrove, Penn.: Susquehanna University Press, 1994), 261–62;
John M. Belohlavek, "In Defense of Doughface Diplomacy: A Reevaluation of the
Foreign Policy of James Buchanan," in this volume, esp. 116–19.

40. Buchanan, "Third Annual Message, December 19, 1859," in Moore, *Works of
James Buchanan*, 10:340, 341, 340.

6

The South Has Been Wronged

James Buchanan and the Secession Crisis

JEAN H. BAKER

This essay considers President James Buchanan's words and actions during the secession crisis, specifically the period from Abraham Lincoln's election on November 6, 1860, until Lincoln's inauguration on March 4, 1861. During these final four months of Buchanan's presidency, seven Southern states left the Union and in February 1861 created the Confederate States of America. In some instances Buchanan's refusal to take action is the critical component in this story. First, however, Buchanan's words, uttered a few weeks after Lincoln's election, when Buchanan delivered his annual address to Congress on December 3, 1860, serve as a proper beginning point.

Buchanan's Theory of Secession

In this address the president considered the constitutionality of secession. Indeed, in what we now call the State of the Union speech, which in the nineteenth century was read to an often-somnolent audience of congressmen by a clerk, Buchanan began with the topic and exerted some energy reviewing the possibility that Southern states would leave the Union. He had consulted with his attorney general, Pennsylvanian Jeremiah Black, about what he called "the discontent" in the Republic. At the time South Carolina seemed likely to secede, having already set up a secession procedure of elected delegates and a special convention in case the Republican candidate, Abraham Lincoln, won the November election. Most importantly for Buchanan, federal officers had already begun resigning their commissions by December.

Figure 6.1. East King Street, Lancaster, Pennsylvania, c. 1850. Buchanan's law office was located on the second floor of the building in the center of the photograph. Courtesy of LancasterHistory.org.

Considering what was obviously a significant threat to the Union, Buchanan had developed some interrogatories for his cabinet officer Black to answer. All five dealt with the relationship between the state and federal government in the looming crisis and the power of the executive in relation to the legislative branch of the national government. But the last two of Buchanan's questions to Black were crucial: "What are the legal means at my disposal for executing those laws of the United States which are usually administered through the courts and their officers? Can a military force be used for any purpose whatever under the Militia Acts of 1795 and 1807, within the limits of a state where there are no judges, marshals or other civil officers?"[1] Black's answers were tautological and unhelpful, but they did not foreclose legal actions by the president. For example, the attorney general advised the president that the Militia Act of 1807 authorized the use of military force in cases "where it was lawful." The chief executive must make the judgment as to the legality.

Still, the president knew the reasons why he—a sixty-eight-year-old chief executive who wanted nothing more than peace so that he might concentrate on his specialty of foreign affairs—must deal with these issues. Accordingly, in the sectionalized climate of the period he had no compunction about condemning the North. He attributed the unrest to "the long-continued and intemperate interference of the Northern people with the question of slavery in the southern states for over twenty-five years," which had produced two sections aligned against each other. "I have long foreseen and forewarned my countrymen of the danger."[2]

In fact, according to Buchanan, who was here employing the Southerners' own representation of the sectional crisis, the violent agitation had even produced a "malign influence" on Southern slaves. As a result, "many a matron throughout the South retires at night in dread of what may befall herself and her children before the morning." The Republic might survive disagreements over slavery in the territories, but not this lack of security "at the family altar" as slaves continued to be contaminated by "vague notions of freedom." Using the same rhetoric as that used in Southern secession conventions, Buchanan concluded that "the people of the North . . . have no more right to interfere [with slavery, which Buchanan called a "domestic institution"] than with similar institutions in Russia or in Brazil." Of course, at this particular time Lincoln agreed with him on this last point.

In this conviction Buchanan trumpeted the views of his Southern cabinet officers, though he needed no persuasion, perhaps only reinforcement, having long opposed abolitionism and having never separated the views of those who would summarily end slavery—like William Lloyd Garrison and John Brown—from those who merely wished to contain it by preventing its spread into the territories. It is worth noting that Buchanan, in his selection of a cabinet when he came to office in 1857, tilted toward the South from the beginning. Four members of seven in the first Buchanan cabinet (Howell Cobb of Georgia, Aaron Brown of Tennessee, John Floyd of Virginia, and Jacob Thompson of Mississippi) were slaveholders from the future Confederacy, and two of the three Northerners—Jeremiah

Black of Pennsylvania and Isaac Toucey of Connecticut—were Southern sympathizers, labeled in the national court of public opinion as Northern doughfaces willing to mold themselves into Southern supporters.

Only Michigan's Lewis Cass represented the interests of most of the Democratic Party's Northern supporters, and Cass, who had been the losing Democratic Party candidate in 1848, was an exhausted, perhaps even sclerotic, seventy-five-year-old. By any measure the future Confederacy and its slaveholding interests were initially overrepresented among a group in which there was more turnover and replacement than in any single-administration presidential cabinet before or since.

By the fall of 1860, Americans, like Buchanan, were well aware that the earlier bluff of Southern states to leave the Union (as in the spasmodic efforts in the 1830s and 1850s) might actually occur if Lincoln were elected. During the hot, dry summer of 1860 there had been rumors of slave uprisings, as well as talk, in newspapers and conventions like that in Georgia, "for the states of the South . . . to concentrate their energies and power in a simple form of Republican government."[3] There was growing opinion, especially in the Lower South's cotton-producing states, that slaveholding states must never submit to the "abolitionist" Lincoln, though the incoming president stood adamantly on a promise not to interfere with slavery in the Southern states and only to prevent its expansion into the territories.

Responding to the mounting crisis, in his annual address Buchanan conscientiously spoke to the issue, offering his view of the illegality of secession. While it resulted from the "violent agitation by northerners," secession was not a constitutional remedy. Here the president was referencing John Brown's raid of the year before and the personal liberty laws in Northern states such as Pennsylvania and Wisconsin that hampered the return of fugitive slaves as required by the 1850 Fugitive Slave Act. In his own self-image Buchanan was a fervent constitutionalist, saying often that he was for nothing if not "the Constitution and the Union." And the Constitution did not allow secession. But such a philosophical commitment to the central document of American history engendered his stubborn view that he knew precisely what was constitutional, though the United States Constitution, then and now, does not interpret itself.

In any case, the departure of Southern states, according to Buchanan in his annual address, would render the Union into "a mere voluntary association" and make it a "rope of sand," to be dissolved at any whim. And while the U.S. Constitution did not explicitly deny secession (nor did the later Confederate Constitution, written in Montgomery, Alabama, in 1861), still a perpetual Union was implicit in the placing of the powers of the sword and purse within the authority of Congress and the president—that is, in Articles I and II. No instrument of government ever implanted, wrote Buchanan, "in its bosom the seeds of its own destruction." Of course there was a right of resistance to oppression; indeed, the course of history and especially of the American republic revealed times when secession was a proper remediation in response to oppression. But secession, according to Buchanan, was also revolution, and Lincoln's election did not justify such action. Buchanan thus counseled the South, "Let us wait for the overt act."

But what could—what should—he as the chief executive of the United States and, most significantly, the commander in chief of the army, navy, and militia, do about secession, which surely was an overt act? Of course, as chief executive it was his duty at all times to defend and protect public property. But if a state seceded, what could he do? His answer was—nothing. Buchanan believed—and unfortunately said so—that since all the federal officers in South Carolina had resigned, he had no power to call out the militia to enforce orders, to disperse dissidents, and to force them to obey the laws of the nation. Technically, a federal officer in South Carolina must raise the alarm and ask for assistance, insisted Buchanan in this strained interpretation. Thus "the Executive has no authority to decide what shall be the relations between the Federal Government and South Carolina," where before and immediately after Lincoln's election federal officers had begun resigning, like birds flying away from their roosts at the beckoning of a morning's ripe cornfield.

Because there was neither a federal marshal nor a district judge to execute any order and call for federal intervention, Buchanan could only hope that Congress would change the militia law. Doing so would permit him to call out the nation's forces. He also called for amending the U.S. Constitution to protect slavery in the territories so that he could placate the South and keep the peace. But he had no influence, much less authority, over Congress. In any case, the president could not use what he considered illegal means to carry out legal tasks. Whatever prevention or redress there might be rested with Congress. In another of his pro-Southern interpretations, Buchanan held that Congress possessed no right to "make war against a state."

There remained the problem of the federal installations, those under-manned pentagonal fortifications designed to protect the United States from possible foreign invaders. Many were located off southern coasts. In an incorrect prediction that would haunt his presidency, Buchanan insisted that there would not be any attempt to forcefully expel the United States from its property—that is from forts, customhouses, garrisons, and armories.

The Effect of Buchanan's Views

Certainly Buchanan's views indicated to the North, even to Democrats like Stephen Douglas (not to mention Republicans who were now the majority party), just how sectionally partisan their president was and just how far he would go to appease the South. The *Springfield Daily Journal* caught the paradox: "Mr. Buchanan, while denying the right of secession and asserting the necessity of enforcing the laws sought excuse for evading the performance of his duty in such a case by showing that it could not be done without coercion and making war on a state. This, he argued, he had no constitutional right to do. A state [according to Buchanan] could not be the object of the war powers of the executive. . . . This is an unfortunate and illogical conclusion—executing the laws is not coercion," concluded the editors.[4]

With his usual wit and acumen, William Henry Seward, a senator from New York and soon to be Lincoln's secretary of state, summarized Buchanan's position: "He shows conclusively that it is the duty of the President to execute the laws unless somebody opposes him and that no state has a right to go out of the Union unless it wants to."[5]

The error was far more serious: Buchanan had given the South a blank check on which they soon wrote the name of nearly every federal installation in the Lower South. While he may have hoped that his doughface reputation would give his views on maintaining the Union standing in the South, in fact rebellious Southerners now intimated that any challenge to their departure would lead to a bloody civil war unless Buchanan kept the peace by handing over government property. The president was hoisted on his own petard—a hostage to radical pro-Southernism through his words and later his inaction.

Of course, at the time radical Southerners detested Buchanan's interpretation of the right of secession. He had disappointed his cabinet officers, and his favorite member, Secretary of the Treasury Howell Cobb of Georgia, promptly resigned. Others in this original prosecessionist cabinet remained, realizing how beneficial to the cause they might be as insiders willing to pass on crucial information about the president's intentions. In the constitutional arguments used by Southerners like Cobb and Mississippi senator Jefferson Davis, under the Articles of Confederation, states had never surrendered the sovereignty they attained during the American Revolution. They carried this standing forward into the U.S. Constitution, which the Preamble to the Constitution, with its famous claim "We the People," did not neutralize. Moreover secession was justified by the Declaration of Independence: as the justifiably rebellious Americans to the British, so the Southerners to the Americans. And too, the Tenth Amendment—by which all powers not given to the federal government were reserved to the states—implied that the federal government had no right to coerce any state.[6]

Meanwhile, Northerners, not just Republicans, thought differently and were horrified that Buchanan had surrendered his role in shaping the crisis. Seemingly, their president was no nationalist but rather a sectionalist who had taken sides. In despair, even residents in the border slave states believed that Buchanan was required by his oath of office to protect and defend the law. Quoting the federal constitution, one Marylander wrote, "'He is Commander-in-Chief of the Army and Navy.'... He needs, therefore no statute law to enable him ... to defend the assault on the nation's life."[7]

The Jacksonian Precedent

Americans remembered Andrew Jackson and his stern treatment of an earlier controversy with South Carolina when Jackson had vigorously rejected South Carolina's ordinance nullifying the 1832 federal tariff. In this controversy Jackson warned South Carolina that states had no right to invalidate any federal law; he encouraged Congress to pass the Force Bill mobilizing the army, even as he began readying the navy at Norfolk along with three units of artillery to counter South Carolina's actions. He also established communication with Unionists in the state, sending his own agents to collect tariffs and maintain the presence of the federal government. Buchanan did none of these things.

In case Buchanan did not remember this precedent, Winfield Scott, who at the time of the nullification crisis was the commander of federal forces in Charleston harbor, reminded the president in a letter written on December 15, 1860, before the secession of South Carolina. According to Scott,

> Long *prior* to the *force bill*, (March 2, 1833,) and *prior* to the issue of his proclamation, and in part *prior* to the ordinance of nullification, President Jackson, under the act of March 3, 1807, "authorizing the employment of the land and naval forces," caused reinforcements to be sent to Fort Moultrie, and a sloop of war, (the Natchez,) with two revenue cutters, to be sent to Charleston, in order, 1, to prevent the seizure of that fort by the nullifiers, and 2, to enforce the execution of the revenue laws.... President Jackson familiarly said at that time "that ... he was not making war on South Carolina; but if South Carolina attacked them, it would be South Carolina that made war on the United States."[8]

Even Buchanan's fellow Democrats from the North were, like his great rival, Illinois senator Stephen Douglas, disgusted with the president. They believed the Militia Acts of 1795 and 1807 authorized the president's calling out of the militia whenever the laws of the United States could not be sustained by normal police action. All government, said Douglas, is coercion. "I go in for asserting this principle at every hazard. Rather a million men should fall on the battlefields than that this government lose one single state."[9]

By laying out this do-nothing position in his annual address, Buchanan, at the very least, abandoned any strategic advantage he might have otherwise won (later, in his exculpatory memoir, he laid the blame on Congress, which had refused to pass legislation for the recovery of the forts).[10] Buchanan's position is even more puzzling given his experience as a diplomat in Russia and in England, as secretary of state in James Polk's administration, and as one who understood the importance of negotiating from strength without relinquishing one's minimal position. For example, as a minister to the Court of St. James in Franklin Pierce's administration,

Buchanan had skillfully bargained over controversial issues such as the British presence in Belize and Nicaragua.[11]

Buchanan's Pro-Southern Sympathies

The explanations for Buchanan's views during the secession crisis surely lie with his Southern sympathies. He had taken sides for the South against the Union and would continue to do so during the 119 days separating Lincoln's election from his inauguration. Some Southerners—Mississippi Henry Foote was one—believed Buchanan was "morbidly solicitous of public reproach and wanted to please everybody."[12] But it was not everyone he sought to please with his activist pro-Southern, antiunion agenda that he would maintain with one exception throughout this crisis; it was only his Southern friends.

By the winter months of December and January, Southerners had taken advantage of Buchanan's hands-off policy and had begun what he predicted would never happen—their assaults on federal property, not just in South Carolina but throughout the South. Buchanan did not try to block the takeovers of Fort Moultrie and Castle Pinckney in Charleston harbor; nor did he comment on the surrender by a naval officer of the revenue cutter *Aiken*. He said nothing when, on January 3, 1861, Georgia troops captured Fort Pulaski, and nothing about the successful assaults by Louisiana militia forces on Forts Jackson, St. Phillips, and Pike or the seizure of the New Orleans or Baton Rouge customhouses. Nor did he respond a few days later when Florida militia seized the Pensacola navy yard along with Fort Barrancas and Fort McRae, or in February when secessionists seized the Little Rock arsenal in Arkansas. Perhaps most egregiously, he said nothing when a general of the U.S. Army, David Twiggs, simply surrendered his military units without any struggle to a local militia before Texas had even seceded. Most of these aggressive actions were prompted by the false statements and threatening propaganda, fostered by Southern governors, that the United States was about to send federal reinforcements.

For example, Governor Joseph Brown of Georgia ordered a local colonel in charge of 125 state volunteers to seize Fort Pulaski and to retain it until the Georgia convention "decided" on secession. In most cases there was no opposition from federal forces, and nearly all of these actions occurred extralegally, even before the states had seceded. The results would be devastating when the Civil War came. According to William Freehling, "some 75,000 stands of arms had been confiscated from U.S. forts and arsenals" in December and January.[13] By any rendering, through his inactivity the president of the United States had become an activist, allowing arms to be delivered into the hands of the future enemies of the United States.

Although General Winfield Scott had twice recommended to the president the immediate garrisoning of these forts to deter any attempt to take them over and to make any effort "by surprise or coup de main ridiculous," Buchanan had not agreed. Indeed, Scott, in an addendum to his "Views" written in October 1860, responded to the argument that there were no available troops by locating five specific regiments that could immediately be deployed.

Later, Buchanan wrote that he thought Scott's plan "strange and inconsistent." And the president defended his inaction because "there were no available troops within reach which could have been sent to these fortifications," despite what General Scott indicated. "To have attempted a military operation on a scale so extensive by any means within the President's power would have been simply absurd." Moreover, wrote Buchanan in his memoir, Scott's charge that he was under the influence of his secessionist secretary of war, Virginian John Floyd, was false: "All my cabinet must bear me witness that I was the President myself, responsible for all the acts of my administration."[14]

In his next spiral away from a nonpartisan effort at preserving the Union, the president agreed to send Secretary of the Interior Jacob Thompson of Mississippi as an agent to discuss the affairs of the nation with leaders in North Carolina. This authorization deserves some scrutiny, because Thompson was ardently prosecessionist and undertook the mission when he was still an official of the United States government. Buchanan knew Thompson's views from those endless Tuesday-afternoon meetings of the cabinet. What, it could reasonably be asked, was Buchanan's intention? Logically, it seemed that he was sending Thompson to encourage North Carolina to follow the path taken in December by South Carolina. In fact, two influential Southerners—Lawrence Keitt and William L. Yancey—believed that the president had changed his mind and now supported the legality of secession.[15]

Thompson's mission did not go unnoticed, as more and more Americans now saw that the president had adopted the interests of secession. This belief was reinforced when the *Washington Constitution*, an administration organ supported by presidential patronage, printed editorials favoring secession. Only in January did the president finally remove his executive patronage and shut down the paper. As one despairing Illinoisan wrote Lincoln, "Buchanan is today truly a traitor as was Benedict Arnold."[16]

There was an exception to the president's handling of the growing crisis, and this occurred in January, after members of Buchanan's cabinet resigned to be replaced by cabinet officers representing Unionist views. (In an indication of Northern opinion, Secretary of State Cass had resigned in December because he thought that the forts in Charleston harbor should be better defended.) Speaking to his attorney general, Buchanan, just days before the installations were taken over, inexplicably told Black, his closest adviser during this period, that "if those forts in Charleston were taken over by South Carolina in consequence of our neglect to put them in defensible condition it were better for you and me both to be thrown into the Potomac with millstones about our necks."[17] But of course he had practically ensured that they would be taken over. Still there was an escape clause in his calculation: now he could not place them in defensible condition in late December, as he might have been able to do so in October or November.

The Crisis at Fort Sumter

Meanwhile, as is often the case in the unpredictable crises that presidents face, events hastened the reconfiguration of decisions. In late December a defining moment for Buchanan arrived: on Christmas night Major Anderson moved his entire command of less than a hundred soldiers to the more easily defended Fort Sumter, in the middle of Charleston harbor. Southerners—and particularly the Southern commissioners now in Washington—believed that this was a violation of guarantees given by the president—a gentleman's agreement, as it were. No matter what his commander had done, they argued, Buchanan must order the nation's troops back to the land-based Fort Moultrie, now threatened by the armed forces of the independent state of South Carolina. For a time Buchanan agreed, insisting he had not given Anderson any such orders, until Scott produced the orders, signed by the secretary of war and approved by the president, that gave the commander discretionary power to move his force to the most defensible installation in Charleston harbor. And that clearly was Fort Sumter.

As his weakening Unionism collided with his much stronger pro-Southernism, even Buchanan knew it was treason to surrender a military post in these circumstances. No matter what had occurred elsewhere, Fort Sumter had become a national symbol. Yet, even in this knowledge of what constituted treason, the president at first agreed and decided to order Anderson back to Fort Moultrie, a death sentence given the ease with which the local militia could take over that land-based installation. In return, South Carolina must pledge that it would not molest the forts and the South Carolina commissioners, currently in Washington, must meet with Congress. This latter recommendation gave seditious diplomatic standing to an insurrectionary group. And by way of further ingratiating the South Carolinians, Buchanan for a time falsely insisted that Anderson had exceeded his orders.[18]

But more nationalist opinions now prevailed in Washington and in his cabinet, and Buchanan was dissuaded from what would have become the most egregious appeasement of the future Confederacy during his administration. Edwin Stanton, now attorney general when Black became secretary of state, held that to order Anderson back to Moultrie was treason. Black concurred: "No man can stand with you," he said in a statement that suggests just how far Buchanan had tipped toward the South. In any case the president briefly stiffened, encouraged—or not—by rising nationalism in the North and by the Unionist members of his reformulated cabinet who in most accounts of the episode threatened to resign. Yet it was not the president but Black who rewrote Buchanan's official document, suggesting the continuing intransigence of a president who could not bear to disappoint his Southern friends and who believed that the South had been wronged. Instead, Black's forceful response denied the right of South Carolina to take over federal property.

Now too late to forestall the process of secession that rippled through the Lower South like a tidal wave in January and February, preceded by the surrender of federal installation after federal installation, Buchanan supported what General Scott and most of his cabinet had been demanding for months: he would reinforce Fort Sumter. Perhaps Buchanan was concerned with his place in history, his resolve stiffened by shifts in northern public opinion; perhaps he believed that the South had gone too far, and

Figure 6.2. Firing on the *Star of the West*. *Harper's Weekly*, January 26, 1861.

on this point he would soon refuse to deal with the Southern commissioners who had been urging him to surrender Fort Sumter; perhaps he envisioned a different future for his nation than a divided union; perhaps, as William Freehling has written, this was simply a case of Buchanan's "errant decisiveness." Regardless, the president's own explanation came in a letter to Joseph Holt, the former secretary of war, after Buchanan had left office. Denying any change in his position, the former president wrote that he had always believed that if Anderson needed reinforcements "every effort would be made to supply them."[19]

In any case, under presidential orders on January 5, 1861, the *Star of the West*, carrying 250 men and supplies belowdecks, slipped from its anchorage in New York and headed south on the very day that Anderson informed Scott he felt secure and did not need reinforcements. Immediately Buchanan countermanded the order, but it was too late. Of course, given the efficient spy ring of Buchanan appointees in Washington, Southerners were well aware that the vessel was en route. Throughout this crisis Buchanan was very lax about any efforts at secrecy. Indeed, as soon as he learned of the reinforcements, Thompson resigned his cabinet office and headed south to inform his Southern friends. Forewarned, when the vessel entered Charleston harbor, the South Carolina batteries fired from

Morris Island and Fort Moultrie, and though the *Star of the West* dipped its flag several times, hoping for covering fire, there was no response from Anderson, as he had no orders to return fire. With no supporting fire from Anderson, the *Star of the West* steamed out of Charleston harbor, mission unaccomplished.

Sometimes we get caught up in the details of the secession crisis and forget just what was occurring. The United States was simply defensively reinforcing and resupplying a federal fort. It was not attacking South Carolina. On the other hand, the national flag had been fired on, which legitimately required a forceful response. Buchanan did nothing, although he did send a special message to Congress on January 8, urging it to do so.[20]

In this message the president continued to maintain that the North must acknowledge "the serious grievances" that the South suffered, though he acknowledged that its seizure of property had "been purely aggressive" and not justified by any actions by the federal government. The president still held to his negligent fiction that, even in the most serious crisis his nation ever confronted, "my province is to execute and not to make the laws."

It was Congress alone that held the authority to respond to South Carolina's firing on the flag: "it belongs to Congress *exclusively* to repeal, modify, or to enlarge their provisions to meet these exigencies. . . . I possess no dispensing power." Of course, even in this critical moment Buchanan insisted that the Union must be preserved by only explicitly constitutional means. And if Congress would not act, Buchanan proposed that the question be "transferred from political assemblies to the ballot box," where the American people would find a solution.[21] With this suggestion for the holding of a national convention just months after a national election, Buchanan displayed his perpetual magnification of the South and his specific misreading of the election of 1860 when the Republicans—whom he considered abolitionists all—had won the presidency and retained their plurality in the House of Representatives.[22]

Yet Southerners—soon to be Confederates—considered the *Star* incident "the first act of positive hostility," and the episode precipitated a string of state secessions by Mississippi, Florida, Georgia, Texas, Louisiana, and Alabama. In fact, coercion by the South on the United States had begun, and the Union, so neglected in the president's sensibilities, reacted. In New Haven an editor wrote that "This is not secession; it is not dissolution; it is rebellion and aggressive war." Other editorials in the North warned the president that the *Star* "must return to Charleston and land her troops at Fort Sumter or your administration will be disgraced through all coming time."[23]

Buchanan had no intention of redressing the humiliation at Fort Sumter, and a period of calm ensued, during which the president refused to give permission to his commanders to land troops at Fort Pickens off the Florida coast in the Gulf of Mexico. And Anderson did not need any reinforcements for the time being. Meanwhile, Buchanan supported the actions of the Committee of Thirteen composed of senatorial leaders such as John Crittenden of Kentucky, William Henry Seward of New York, and Robert Toombs of Georgia. The plan presented to the Senate by the respected Crittenden in the so-called Crittenden Compromise was to enact irrevocable constitutional amendments. The most significant one would prohibit interference with slavery in national territory above the latitude of 36°30' and guarantee slavery south of the line. Others would deny congressional authority over the interstate slave trade and compensate, from the U.S. Treasury, slaveowners unable to recover their slave property.

A Failed Presidency

Republicans refused to support such a pro-Southern agenda, and the compromise died on the floor of the Senate. But Buchanan, blinkered by his prejudices, never understood why Congress did not pass the Crittenden proposals, believing that it was only radical Republicans, not the majority of the Union, who had refused to placate the South. Indeed, in all the proposals presented during this period, the North gave away much and gained nothing. Buchanan also reached out to Lincoln during this period, though the incoming president wisely decided to avoid any collaboration with Buchanan. By this time Republicans, including Lincoln, had had enough of James Buchanan.

Then in February naval officers, stung by the failure of the *Star of the West* and well aware that Anderson would need supplies at some point, concocted another plan for reinforcing Fort Sumter. Navy captain Gustavus Fox gained the approval of General Scott and others for his proposal of a convoy that included launches to land troops and supplies. But Buchanan declined: he believed, after the *Star of the West* incident, that he had effected some sort of truce with the emerging Confederate States of

America. Now the president intended to do nothing more than keep the peace until his successor arrived in early March. Finally, on March 4, Buchanan's 119 days of collaboration with the South ended.

Yet even in the days before Lincoln took the oath of office, Buchanan hesitated about the need for troops in Washington to protect the transfer of power to the Republicans on Inauguration Day. Such a military presence in the capital might upset the Southerners still in the city, he complained. But by this time Scott, no longer mindful of the president, went ahead anyway. So partisan had Buchanan been that, when these troops appeared in Washington, some Republicans worried that the president might attempt a pro-Southern coup. In fact, the ancient general stationed himself in a carriage on a hill overlooking the Capitol, scanning the horizon for any efforts to disrupt the inauguration. When Buchanan and Lincoln rode to the Capitol, Washington was well defended. On the ride back, Buchanan famously turned to Lincoln and said, "If you are as happy in entering the White House as I shall feel on returning to Wheatland [his residence in Lancaster, Pennsylvania] you are a happy man."[24]

Finally, what must we say about Buchanan's performance during the 119 days of the secession crisis when, in the Irish poet William Butler Yeats's words, "Things fall apart; the centre cannot hold"? Was the president's appeasement of the South—for it was surely that—the result of his indecisiveness or his age or his lack of power as a lame duck president or even an episode of his "errant decisiveness"? There is evidence for all these positions.

My own view, however, is that Buchanan was an activist president but activist in the interests of what became the Confederate States of America. There is evidence for this in his earlier presidential actions. After all, earlier he had instigated and supported the *Dred Scott* decision; he had done his best to ensure that Kansas, against public wishes and especially the democratic desires of the population of that territory, would become a slave state; he had irredeemably alienated the northern wing of the Democratic Party, as he pushed his Southern agenda and especially the Lecompton Constitution, and he had continued to echo the South's angry complaints against the North.

During the secession crisis his partiality often appeared not in what he did but in what he did not do. Yet James Buchanan was not feeble or a weakling, nor was he controlled by his cabinet. Indeed, even during the throes of the crisis he wrote, "all our troubles have not cost me an hours' sleep or of meal's victuals, though I trust I have a just sense of my high responsibility."[25]

But surely his favoritism bordered on disloyalty, for he was an officer—the chief executive officer—pledged to protect and defend *all* the United States. Even in his memoirs he explained the causes of the war as "the result of the long active persistent hostility of northern abolitionists."[26] Defending his policies as similar to those of Lincoln, he avoided the two administrations' differences in timing and context. And the policy errors during Buchanan's administration made the Confederacy more powerful than it might have been. Lincoln faced a government that was as wealthy and well fortified as most European nations.

In the pantheon of failed presidencies, Buchanan is worth observing for what his mistakes tell us. He was that most dangerous of chief executives: a stubborn mistaken ideologue whose principles held no room for compromise. Before he was president and was a mere professor of political science, Woodrow Wilson laid out the ingredients of successful leadership in a democracy. Leadership, he wrote, requires fairness and interpretation; a leader must "creep into the confidence of those you would lead. . . . Leadership is *interpretation*. . . . A leader must read the common thought and test and calculate the preparation of the nation for the next step in the progress of politics."[27] Ultimately, Buchanan had failed to interpret the United States during the secession crisis.

Notes

1. Quoted in Philip S. Klein, *President James Buchanan: A Biography* (University Park: Pennsylvania State University Press, 1962), 359.

2. James D. Richardson, *A Compilation of the Messages and Papers of the Presidents, 1789–1897*, 10 vols. (Washington, D.C.: Government Printing Office, 1897), 5:626. All subsequent quotations from the annual message are from the same source, 626–38.

3. William Freehling and Craig Simpson, eds., *Secession Debated: Georgia's Showdown in 1860* (New York: Oxford University Press, 1992), xv.

4. *Springfield (Mass.) Daily Journal*, December 22, 1861.

5. Frederick Seward, *The Life of William Henry Seward*, 2 vols. (New York: Harpers, 1900), 2:3.

6. Secessionists' speeches are included in Freehling and Simpson, *Secession Debated*. This volume includes Robert Toombs's "Give me the sword" speech.

7. Anna Ella Carroll, *Reply to the Speech of Hon. J. C. Breckinridge*, cited in Jon L. Wakelyn, *Southern Unionist Pamphlets and the Civil War* (Columbia: University of Missouri Press, 1999), 19, 23–24.

8. General Winfield Scott to James Buchanan, December 15, 1860, in *State Secrets for the People: The Private Letters of Lieut.-General Scott, and the Reply on Ex-President Buchanan* (New York: Hamilton, Johnson and Farrelli, 1862), 4–5.

9. P. S. Klein, *President James Buchanan*, 364.

10. James Buchanan, *Mr. Buchanan's Administration on the Eve of the Rebellion* (1866; Freeport, N.Y.: Books for Libraries, 1970), 158–59.

11. See John Belohlavek's essay in this volume.

12. Henry Foote, *A Casket of Reminiscences* (Washington, D.C.: Chronicle Publishing, 1874), 113–14.

13. William Freehling, *The Road to Disunion: Secessionists Triumphant* (New York: Oxford University Press, 2007), 482, 486–87.

14. Buchanan, *Mr. Buchanan's Administration*, 99–100; James Buchanan to the editors of the *National Intelligencer*, October 28, 1862, in *Private Letters of Lieut.-General Scott*, 12.

15. Elbert B. Smith, *The Presidency of James Buchanan* (Lawrence: University of Kansas Press, 1975), 146–47.

16. C. S. Henry to Abraham Lincoln, December 23, 1860, Abraham Lincoln Presidential Papers, microfilm edition.

17. Quoted in P. S. Klein, *President James Buchanan*, 358.

18. Philip Gerald Auchambaugh, *James Buchanan and His Cabinet on the Eve of Secession* (1926; Boston: Canner Press, 1965), 161–65.

19. Freehling, *Road to Disunion*, 178, 488.

20. John Bassett Moore, ed., *The Works of James Buchanan, Comprising His Speeches, State Papers, and Private Correspondence*, 12 vols. (1910; New York: Antiquarian Press Reprint, 1960), 11:94–99.

21. Ibid., 96–97, emphasis added.

22. Michael F. Holt, *The Political Crisis of the 1850s* (New York: Wiley, 1978), 202.

23. Quoted in Maury Klein, *Days of Defiance: Sumter, Secession and the Coming of the Civil War* (New York; Vintage Press, 1999), 203–4.

24. P. S. Klein, *President James Buchanan*, 402.

25. Smith, *Presidency of James Buchanan*, 144–45.

26. Buchanan, *Mr. Buchanan's Administration*, iv.

27. Arthur S. Link, ed., *The Papers of Woodrow Wilson*, 69 vols. (Princeton: Princeton University Press, 1969), 6:659. For a more detailed exposition of this interpretation see Jean H. Baker, *James Buchanan* (New York: Times Books, 2004).

7

"In the Midst of a Great Revolution"

The Northern Response to the Secession Crisis

WILLIAM G. SHADE

In the judgment of the wife of California Democratic senator William M. Gwin, James Buchanan was "a better man than the world gives him credit for."[1] Buchanan is often given low marks by historians for his handling of secession, with the implication that had he acted differently there would have been no Civil War. My intention is not to frivolously elevate the fifteenth president but rather to reexamine his views on secession by comparing them not only with Abraham Lincoln's but also with those of several other prominent Northern leaders. Buchanan's position represented a much larger segment of Northern public opinion than most historians have previously argued. His actions—or actions he might have taken— during the secession crisis probably could not have changed the course of history.

To reorient our understanding of this subject, I would like to portray sectional differences in mid-nineteenth-century America in a more complex way.[2] We must think of a more fragmented antebellum world, and one that cannot simply be divided between the North and the South. I would like to place Buchanan in the context of what is increasingly called the Lower North, although he had close and intimate connections with the Lower South. Similarly, Lincoln was born in a Border South slave state, and the part of Illinois in which he lived was definitely Lower North, populated largely by migrants from the Upper South.[3] In short, there was not a single Northern response to secession, but many, depending upon geography and partisan orientation. But also it must be remembered that Northerners in late 1860 and early 1861 were also focused on other, sometimes totally unrelated, issues.

In this context it will be useful to discuss how some leading Northerners, such as the then president James Buchanan and the president-elect Abraham Lincoln, perceived the situation. In the process I will discuss the views of the most popular Northern Democrat, Illinois senator Stephen Douglas; Lincoln's chief rival for the Republican nomination and secretary of state, New York senator William Seward; and another Pennsylvanian from the Lower North, Thaddeus Stevens, who represented the radical wing of the Republican Party. As irony would have it, Stevens was President Buchanan's congressman. The secession crisis was played out on the political stage, and this group of politicians includes a good representation of the Northern responses to secession. The following will concentrate on the period from Lincoln's election on November 6, 1860, to his April 15, 1861, call for troops to put down the "insurrection" two days after the bombardment of Fort Sumter.[4]

Initial Responses

First, however, I must lay out a timeline of the crisis, since it was ever changing. Of course, there were twists and turns as the practical questions evolved and as men changed their minds or modified their positions. This is true of two leading Republicans, Charles Francis Adams of Massachusetts and John Sherman from northern Ohio. Like most New England Republicans, Adams had been committed to preventing slavery's expansion. He opposed negotiations, but as a member of the House Committee of Thirty-Three he proposed the admission of New Mexico, which did have a slave code and a handful of slaves, thus nominally adding a new slave state. He believed, however, that slavery could not thrive in the area and soon would be ended there. Tactically he also hoped to divide the Southern members of the committee.[5]

But there were other oddities as well. In January 1861, Fernando Wood, the mayor of New York City, which was closely tied to the Lower South for its prosperity, suggested that the city secede.[6] Many of those "Butternut" Democrats in the western end of the Lower North (southern Indiana and Illinois) who talked about joining the Confederacy or forming a Northern confederacy later became "Copperheads" during the Civil War and posed a threat to Lincoln's reelection in 1864. The most famous of these men, Clement L. Vallandigham, first opposed secession, but accepted it and vigorously opposed "coercion." He blamed the Republicans for the crisis. In a letter to his wife, Vallandigham wrote, "I see no hope for peace much less adjustment of difficulties. Every day proves still more clearly that it is the fixed purpose of the Republican party not only to refuse all compromise, but to force a *civil war*."[7]

In general, most Southerners accepted the legitimacy of secession, although they were divided into distinctly different groups: "Immediatists," who called for immediate unilateral secession of their states; "Cooperationists," who advocated secession only in cooperation with other states; and "Conditional Unionists," who were willing to accept certain compromises on the part of the Republicans but in the end joined the rebellion.[8] Most Northerners opposed secession in theory, but the North was divided by region, by party, and by factions within the parties. The radical secessionists were calling the shots, and the Northerners, along with a good number of Southerners, especially in the Upper South, were divided about how to respond. The focus of the issues and the arguments shifted from month to month, sometimes day to day. As so often in such revolutionary situations, the radicals with a plan outmaneuvered the moderates and conservatives who had none.

Secession had been discussed for many years in the rather muddled debate about "state rights," or "state's rights," or "states' rights," that was at the center of the constitutional and political debate from 1789 to 1861. There were those who gathered at the Nashville Convention in 1850 and wanted to act upon the idea a decade before Lincoln's election led to the Civil War.[9] The new president's response to the firing on Fort Sumter provoked the secession of the Upper South states of Virginia, Tennessee, Arkansas, and North Carolina in April and May 1861. The Border South states—those that not only retained slavery but also abutted the North—trembled but did not secede.

Secession

As soon as they knew of Lincoln's election, South Carolina legislators called a convention to meet in December in the state capital to consider secession. On December 20 the convention unanimously passed the ordinance of secession, which dissolved the relationship between the Palmetto State and "the other States under the name of the United States of America."[10] Several days later the convention issued its "Declaration of Immediate Causes," which argued that the state's action was in response to the election of a president "whose opinions and purposes are hostile to Slavery" and who would "inaugurate a new policy, hostile to the South, and destructive to its peace and safety."[11]

Essentially, South Carolina's secessionists defended their actions in terms of a theory of the nature of the Union that described it as a "compact" of sovereign states that in ratifying the Constitution gave up certain explicitly defined ("enumerated") powers to the federal government, which acted only as their agent in dealing with the other states and foreign nations.[12] This part of their sovereignty was given up in the conventions that ratified the Constitution, and each could withdraw that consent in a similar convention at any time that they believed their "domestic institutions"—white Southerners' euphemism for slavery—were threatened. The secessionists believed that the election of a candidate of a sectional party that challenged their property rights in the territories represented such a threat to their lives and liberties.

In relatively quick order the states in the Deep South seceded in January and February 1861. Almost as quickly, their representatives met in Montgomery, Alabama. The Montgomery Convention became a provisional government with a new constitution essentially based on the Constitution of the United States with certain changes to protect slavery and to emphasize the rights of the states.[13] The members of the convention talked about raising an army of 100,000 troops—a larger force than the standing army of the United States. On February 9, Jefferson Davis, the former secretary of war of the United States and former Democratic U.S. senator from Mississippi, was elected president of the Confederate States of America, and former congressman Alexander H. Stephens of Georgia—ironically, a former Whig ally and correspondent of Lincoln, but also a supporter of Democrats Franklin Pierce and James Buchanan—was chosen vice-president.

As each seceded state became a part of the new government, and in some cases even before the states actually seceded, local militia seized the federal forts, arsenals, and their vast store of arms within their state's jurisdiction. Officers of the American military, often educated at public expense, were fast becoming officers in the new nation's army and navy. The best known of these was Robert E. Lee, who had been offered command of the Union armies before resigning his commission and becoming the leader of the Confederate forces. Formerly loyal civil servants of the federal government in the seceded states resigned their posts, making it nearly impossible to enforce federal law in these states.

Buchanan's Response

The United States was involved in a "Great Revolution" in which the rebels had a unique position in the military and government and thus had access to the very inter-workings of those trying to resist their actions. This was most clearly seen in the Buchanan administration.[14] The president had long-term connections with the South, and in 1856 he gained the electoral votes of every slave state except Maryland. In the fight over the Lecompton Constitution for the new state of Kansas, he took the Southern position on the nature of popular sovereignty in contrast to the views of Stephen Douglas and some other Northern Democrats. As the secession crisis began to consume his administration, Buchanan's cabinet remained dominated by powerful Southerners, some of whom were his close friends. Most important were Secretary of the Treasury Howell Cobb of Georgia and Secretary of the Interior Jacob Thompson of Mississippi. But Buchanan's cabinet also included Secretary of War John B. Floyd, a Virginian, whose scandalous behavior was about to be revealed as the secession crisis hit. Assistant Secretary of State William H. Trescot, who constantly briefed the president, was little more than an agent of the secessionists.

Buchanan was on friendly terms with some of the most powerful slave-state senators, including Jefferson Davis of Mississippi, who (at least for a time, before going with his state and becoming the president of the Confederacy) remained in the Senate and discussed the situation in South Carolina with Buchanan. For Buchanan it must have been difficult to reject the counsel of Southerners whom he had worked with and trusted for years. The president believed he was following the example of Andrew Jackson, who, in spite of all his bluster, formally needed legislation from Congress to act during the nullification crisis. Jackson believed deeply in the rights of the states and was himself a large slaveholder and Southerner. He hated the abolitionists and opposed both their use of the mails and their petition campaign during his administrations.[15]

In the end Buchanan had to reorganize the cabinet, get rid of his

Figure 7.1. James Buchanan and his cabinet, c. 1859. From left: Secretary of the Interior Jacob Thompson; Secretary of State Lewis Cass; Secretary of War John B. Floyd; President James Buchanan; Secretary of the Treasury Howell Cobb; Secretary of the Navy Isaac Toucey; Postmaster General Joseph Holt; and Attorney General Jeremiah S. Black. Library of Congress.

Southern friends, and rely on Northerners, particularly Attorney General (later secretary of state) Jeremiah Black of Pennsylvania. Black served as the president's closest adviser when Buchanan composed his annual message given on December 3, 1860.[16] The situation Buchanan faced was unprecedented. It is not clear that anyone outside the inner circle of the extreme secessionists understood what was going on, and perhaps even they did not. Clearly, Buchanan did not want a war, and certainly not one started on his watch. In this position he reflected the opinion of a majority of Americans. But perhaps he should have been more aggressively searching for peaceful solutions. The problem is that it is not easy to see, even in hindsight, what solution or compromise might have succeeded, given secessionist demands.

As a Democrat, Buchanan had supported the "Manifest Destiny" of the United States to expand and had a particular interest in annexing Cuba. But also he believed in states' rights and strict construction of the Constitution.[17] With the help of Black, he took a relatively tough stand on secession in his speech to Congress. As he said, "the Federal Government is [not] a mere voluntary association of states to be dissolved at the pleasure of any one of the contracting parties." "It was intended to be perpetual." Secession was a "revolution against an established government, and not a voluntary secession from it by virtue of an inherent constitutional right."[18] He insisted that the government must enforce the laws and maintain control of federal property. Actually, from his inaugural address on he talked about the problem of "revolutions"—in the territories of Utah and Kansas—that his presidency had faced and liked to think he stood up to the challenge.[19]

Buchanan undercut his tough response in two ways, both of which revealed his long Democratic Party associations and sympathy for the South. On the one hand he blamed the crisis on Northern abolitionists, whom he associated with the Republican Party and Lincoln. He began his discussion with reference to "The long-continued and intemperate interference of the Northern people with the question of slavery in the Southern States" and maintained that Northerners had no more right to discuss slavery in the South "than to interfere with similar institutions in Russia or in Brazil."[20] He repeated the element of the proslavery argument which suggested that these actions of abolitionists and Republicans threatened women and families in the South with servile uprising, rape, and slaughter.

A separate problem is Buchanan's appeal to strict construction. The executive was bound to "take care that the laws be faithfully executed." He simply did not believe that he could "by force of arms . . . compel a state to remain in the Union."[21] Although Buchanan mentioned Jackson's response to the nullification crisis, he turned the matter over to Congress. He was not sure that constitutionally even Congress could "coerce a state into submission." Essentially, he called upon Congress to reach a compromise in which the Constitution might be amended or revised.

"Congress possesses many means of preserving it [the Union] by conciliation, but the sword was not placed in their hand to preserve it by force."[22] Buchanan favored amending the Constitution to protect slavery in the territories and called on the Northern states to remove their personal liberty laws that interfered with the enforcement of the Fugitive Slave Law. He probably was looking for something like the compromise proposed by Kentucky senator John Crittenden, who suggested a return to the Missouri Compromise "solution."[23]

Figure 7.2. *Little Bo Peep and Her Foolish Sheep* (New York: Thomas W. Strong, 1861). Wood engraving. The girl shepherd mourns as seven of her sheep separate from the flock. Her old sheepdog, labeled "Hickory" (Andrew Jackson), lies dead in the foreground, while her new sheepdog, "Buck" (Buchanan) flees from the wolves. Bo Peep exclaims, "Sic 'em Buck! sic 'em! I wish poor old Hickory was alive. He'd bring 'em back in no time." Meanwhile, one wolf says to the others (wearing crowns and representing European monarchies), "If we can only get them separated from the flock, we can pick their bones at our leisure."

Enter Stephen Douglas

As the secession movement spread, Congress came back into session to deal with Buchanan's request that it frame a compromise to settle the sectional issue once and for all. While historians have accused Buchanan of passing the buck, there was nothing irrational about asking Congress to settle the question. When Congress attempted to face the matter, the country's focus shifted from the president to Illinois senator Stephen A. Douglas. Douglas's views on secession represented a much larger segment of the North than only those of his constituents in the western part of the Lower North. He had been born in New England, had been the candidate of the regular Democratic Party in the 1860 presidential election, and remained the leader of the Northern Democratic Party at the time.[24]

Douglas, like Buchanan, had been a friend of the South in national politics and had campaigned in the South during the election. He had married a Southerner and, by odd chance, when her father died, became a slaveholder, although it was only a matter of law rather than practice (other Lower North politicians, such as Indiana senator Jessie Bright, owned plantations in slave states). Douglas's view on slavery in the territories was best stated by his opponent in their famous 1858 debates with Lincoln, who said that his opponent did not care if the territories voted it up or down.[25] His position was known as "popular sovereignty," which meant applying the democratic principle to the issue rather than mandating slavery, as the Southern radicals wanted, or excluding the institution from the territories—the major principle of the Republican Party. He believed, "Nothing will do any good which does not take the slavery question out of Congress forever."[26]

Yet in a major speech given in New Orleans on November 13, 1860, Douglas called on Southerners to have patience. He declared, "No man in America regrets the election of Mr. Lincoln more than I do." But he echoed Buchanan in saying that the election of a Republican was no reason for revolutionary action, "no reasonable ground for dissolving the Federal Union." Bitter about his own defeat, Douglas suggested a Southern conspiracy was afoot to elect Lincoln in order to claim the legal right to secede. Calmly he explained why Lincoln's election would have no effect on slavery or the rights of Southerners, since the Democrats controlled both houses of Congress and the Supreme Court. "The President will be utterly powerless for evil, if he should have the disposition to do wrong."[27] At the same time, he wrote a colleague, "We can never acknowledge the right of a State to secede and cut us off from the Ocean and the world, without our consent."[28] While the reference here was to the idea that the Confederacy might control the Mississippi River to the detriment to the economic interests of the entire Midwest, essentially Douglas—like Lincoln—believed that the secession movement was a small conspiracy led by men with no reason or right to act. Thus he believed a compromise was possible that would meet the demands of most Southerners and bring the seceded states back into the Union.

Douglas had played a major role in passing the compromise measures in 1850 and what he perceived to be a compromise in 1854—the Kansas-Nebraska Act. He now hoped to author, or at least support, a compromise of the crisis of 1860–61. The old Congress that met for its second session in December created two committees—called, because of the number of their members, the Committee of Thirty-Three in the House of Representatives and the Committee of Thirteen in the Senate—to address the crucial issues and respond to the president's message. Douglas joined with Crittenden in support of his compromise. While Crittenden was an old Border State Whig, his policies, championed by Douglas, became the general position of the Northern Democrats.

These proposals were not exactly new and had the fine hand of the compromisers, Clay and Douglas, written all over them. Thus even some conservative congressional Republicans, at least briefly, considered supporting them in the interest of saving the Union. It was not clear exactly how these proposals would be combined in amendments to the Constitution, but Crittenden's compromise, and most variants of it, included the following provisions: a reestablishment of the 36°30' line from the Missouri Compromise of 1820, prohibiting slavery above that parallel and extending the imaginary line to the Pacific; a prohibition on the abolition of slavery in the District of Columbia and in any forts, facilities, or federal properties in the boundaries of slave states; safeguarding the interstate slave trade; and upholding the Fugitive Slave Law by rescinding any state laws interfering with its enforcement.

The reference to territories "hereafter acquired" in one compromise proposal caused Republicans to imagine an extension of "the Slave Power" to future acquisitions, such as Cuba and parts of Central America, and led them to oppose the measures on principle. They opposed the bill in committee and defeated it on the Senate floor. They also rejected the idea of a national referendum on some combination of these measures. The Republicans were aided in their efforts by the abstention of radical Southern Democrats, some of whom had indicated that they might vote for this measure if the Republicans would accept it. Another effort, which came under the imprimatur of an old Whig congressman from Ohio, Thomas Corwin, to bypass the territorial phase and bring New Mexico in immediately as a state also gained no traction. Congress had failed Buchanan's hopes for a compromise.

During this "lame duck" session of Congress, the Virginia Assembly called upon the states to send representatives to a convention in Washington to try to seek a compromise solution to the growing crisis. The "Old

Gentlemen's Convention," as it was called, was a total failure.[29] Neither the states of the Upper North nor those from the Lower South sent delegates. It was presided over by former president John Tyler, who would later be elected to the Confederate Congress. The delegates, including those from the Lower North, mulled over proposals related to the Crittenden compromise but entertained no new ideas. They sent their suggestions to Congress, where they were dismissed, as all other compromises had been.

Fort Sumter

In the meantime, the situation in Charleston harbor had changed and forced upon the beleaguered president new considerations and an attempt at diplomacy to avert the crisis. General Winfield Scott, the antiquated Mexican War general and failed politician, was in charge of the American army. He blew hot and cold throughout the crisis on reinforcing the federal forts, but he seemed generally in favor of reinforcing them. By January, retaining custody of the federal forts and arsenals had become a new problem for Buchanan.

Early in this affair Scott had replaced the officer in charge of the three forts in Charleston with a career solder of Southern birth, Major Robert Anderson. Anderson with three forts had fewer than one hundred troops. One of the forts was held by an old man (a civilian) and his family. The now famous Fort Sumter was an impressive structure in the middle of the harbor, but it was unmanned and still under construction. Anderson's troops were in Fort Moultrie, whose guns faced out into the harbor to protect Charleston from foreign invasion and was nearly defenseless from a land attack by the South Carolina rebels.

Thus, on December 26, aware of the threats to his command, Anderson quite reasonably moved his troops, under cover of darkness, to the far more defensible Fort Sumter. He had orders to protect his troops, and Northerners treated Anderson as a hero. However, the South Carolinians interpreted his seemingly rational action as a violation of an honored pledge from the president.

Buchanan wished to maintain those federal properties while he could and continued to believe that secession sentiment would die down. Scott was in favor of resupplying Sumter. Against the wishes of his Southern advisers, the president agreed. Although Buchanan's decision was discussed in a cabinet meeting in which a crucial decision was made to send supplies, Interior Secretary Thompson seemed not, or chose not, to be listening. He was then kept out of the loop and finally resigned, but everyone in Washington and South Carolina knew about his "secret" mission to the secessionists. There were no secrets, only leaks, in Washington in 1861.

Unfortunately, no one informed Major Anderson that relief was coming. When the unarmed *Star of the West*, a cargo vessel, which had to be rented (!) by the U.S. government, loaded with solders and supplies, and flying the American flag, was fired upon on January 9, Sumter's guns did not respond to help. The ship turned and retreated. This was not the hapless president's fault. He had tried to resupply Sumter. There had been the usual confusion of orders, and even an earlier failed attempt to actually call the ship back. But Buchanan had sent a ship to relieve Sumter, and it was fired upon. In some respects the Civil War had begun.

The New President

As Congress failed to find a compromise, the president failed in his diplomacy, and the secession movement rolled on from state to state. Northerners began to take secession more seriously but continued to believe that only a minority of Southerners supported it. The focus of the Northern response now became the new Republican president-elect.[30] There was no war, but the Lower South was seceding and the Upper South was in question. In the North, concerned citizens wondered just how powerful Unionist sentiment in the South was. Soon it would be the Republican Lincoln's turn to confront the crisis. Would he do so differently than had his Democratic opponents?

While everyone in power in South Carolina had instant information or misinformation about the federal government's policies, which were not clear to the members of the government, most Northerners did not have a good idea of what was happening. How well could these newfangled "correspondents" actually have access to the right people or, more importantly, the "right people" related to the "real people"?[31]

Like Douglas and Buchanan, most Northern politicians did not grasp the gravity of the situation. They probably never understood what slavery meant to the real "Southrons." In part it was the Southerners' fault. Many of them discussed proslavery in a rather bombastic way that is still difficult to grasp, because the same people would deny their commitment to their peculiar institution.[32] Surely this rhetoric confused not only the most symbolic of doughfaces of the day, "Old Buck" and the "Little Giant," but also the tall, awkward, and seemingly unqualified new Republican president, nicknamed by his campaign as "The Rail Splitter."

Ideologically, Lincoln was an old Whig representing the best of that forgotten party and particularly interested in economic questions while being both an antislavery democrat and a mild racist. For a self-educated man, he was an accomplished writer, probably because his stepmother had forced him to pore through the King James Version of the Bible. Henry Clay was his hero. While Lincoln was a man of principle, he first and foremost thought about those compromises that were necessary to democratic politics. But in 1860 and 1861 practically no one knew much about him, although he had been on the public stage for thirty years.

The person in Washington who had known Lincoln the longest, as they were once both young lawyers in Springfield, was Stephen Douglas. While they clearly were not close in 1860, they were on speaking terms. Buchanan and Douglas tried to feel out Lincoln and sent emissaries to Springfield, as did several Republicans. Even the foremost members of the Republican Party did not really know him—Lincoln and Seward had never met; nor had he met his vice-president, Hannibal Hamlin. At the time candidates did not go to the nominating conventions, or at least these particulars did not. Dealing with Lincoln's views in relation to theirs, and his handling of the party, is one of the most interesting parts of the crisis story.

The country was falling apart, and no one knew when civil war might break out. Buchanan had given up, and Lincoln was consumed with patronage. His time was taken up, and his office and home were so overwhelmed with office seekers that eventually he had to seek out a hidden room over a store that belonged to one of his wife's relatives to compose his inaugural address. As the consummate politician, his innermost thoughts focused on his prospective cabinet.[33] The people around him wrote extensively about patronage; his papers are full of memoranda on this matter, and he wrote at least one letter to get a friend a government job.[34]

We now understand why Lincoln endured this as part of "creating a government." The "in-experienced" lawyer from Springfield knew exactly what he was doing. He was not courting a "team of rivals" as much as attempting to deal with the factions in his party to form a government that he could work with. In 1860, only a few years after its birth, the Republican Party was still a fragile coalition. Lincoln knew that responding to the secession crisis, which at first he did not think so important, would involve creating a government that would pull his party together, to govern. His largest problem involved his dealing with Pennsylvania and that most interesting and scandal-ridden senator, Simon Cameron.[35] Lincoln's cabinet-making process revolved around a clear sense of the geography of the Republican Party. There had to be a seat for Pennsylvania. The majority of his mail favored Cameron, although some of Lincoln's friends opposed Cameron. In the end he first extended an offer, then rescinded it, and then briefly put Cameron in the cabinet, as secretary of war, and later exiled him as ambassador to Russia.

While hindsight tells us that Lincoln was on his way to greatness, the views he held in early 1861 were not very different from those of Buchanan and Douglas. His strategy was to say little and to tell people to read his speeches. His correspondence relating to the growing secession movement focused on the idea that Republicans could compromise but not give up the Chicago Platform.[36]

The issue was fairly simple; Lincoln would not compromise on the question of slavery in the territories. Although he said nothing publicly, he was in constant contact with congressional Republicans through his close associates, like Illinois senator Lyman Trumbull, who had defeated him as the Republican candidate for the Senate four years earlier. The president-elect emphasized in his correspondence with Republicans in Congress that there was to be no expansion of slavery. He told his followers not to accept extension of the Missouri Compromise line and to stick to the Chicago Platform. And they must not accept the proviso "hereafter acquired" in any agreement. To do so would be give in to the Slave Power and force him and the Republican Party to relinquish the main policies for which they stood. Lincoln clearly thought his voters wanted to see the Chicago Platform maintained and that retreating from its provisions was to ignore the voice of the people. In his private correspondence, and in the speeches he gave in February 1861 while traveling to Washington, Lincoln the president-elect continued steadfast on halting slavery's expansion.[37]

The draft of his inaugural that Lincoln wrote in Springfield was a bit more radical than the speech he gave in Washington. A close Illinois friend, Orville H. Browning, contributed suggestions. A man Lincoln hardly knew but whom he understood was going to be important to his presidency and the future of the country, William Seward, suggested significant revisions.[38] Together they toned it down, particularly removing the idea of taking back all the forts illegally seized by secessionist militia and mobs. Seward suggested that Lincoln change the aggressive final paragraph in which he placed the issue of civil war in the hands of his "dissatisfied fellow country men." The draft included the famous sentence that reappeared in the final version: "You have no oath registered in Heaven to destroy the government, while *I* shall have the most solemn one to 'preserve, protect, and defend' it." But the original spoke of defending the Union and challenged the secessionists: "Shall it be peace, or a sword?"[39]

In the end, Lincoln chose to accept Seward's advice and they together produced the greatest peroration of any American political speech: "We are not enemies but friends. We must not be enemies. Though passion may have strained, it must not break our bonds of affection. The mystic chords of memory, stretching from every battle-field, and patriot grave, to every living heart and hearthstone, all over this broad land, will swell the chorus of the Union, when again touched as surely they will be, by the better angels of our nature."[40]

In the final version delivered on March 4, Lincoln assumed a conciliatory tone. He had essentially gone as far as a Republican could have gone and hoped to assure the moderate South that it had little to fear from his administration. Like his constituents, and like both Buchanan and Douglas, he argued that secession was illegitimate and amounted to anarchy. The Union was "perpetual." Secession was revolution. In a later speech on the origins of the Civil War he more explicitly made clear how much he believed that secession violated the basic principles of American democracy.[41] If he was more vigorous than Buchanan, it was in his declaration—Buchanan only hinted at it—that his government would "hold, occupy and possess" federal property and collect customs even if it involved using ships at sea.

Lincoln explained in his inaugural and in other speeches that the Republicans would draw the line at extending slavery to the territories but would support a constitutional amendment guaranteeing slavery where it existed. They would also work to enforce the Fugitive Slave Act and call on the Northern states to eliminate their personal liberty laws. These measures constituted the Republican view of compromise, and Congress later passed a thirteenth amendment protecting slavery, although it was never ratified. But the question shifted to coercion and just what that meant. How far might the government go in defending federal property without initiating a war?

The real issue facing Lincoln and his new appointment as secretary of state, Seward, was what to do with the issue before them.[42] Lincoln may be best known for the story that he once told a woman that he hoped that God was on his side, but he had to have Kentucky. The whole question involved the Upper South. Seward wanted to nip this revolution in the bud and have what he called "voluntary reconstruction" when the secessionists came to their senses. If he and Lincoln could hold the trust of the Upper South, the radicals would have no significant support.

Lincoln attempted to get a Southern politician, John Gilmer of North Carolina, into his cabinet, but that effort failed. Even if it had succeeded, things might still have followed the murky path that they did. The main problem with the Seward plan was that there were too few hard-core Unionists in the Upper South. We all know that in desperation the new secretary of state suggested that a foreign involvement might get everyone together and begin the process of "voluntary reconstruction."[43] Posterity has laughed, but he was just attempting a variant of what Buchanan had tried.

The Radical Republican View

The cases I have presented reflected what various segments of the Northern people thought about secession. We should consider another element, however. One of the reasons why the various compromise measures failed in Congress was the constant opposition of the "stiff-backed" Republicans whose position on secession, coercion, and slavery was more radical than Lincoln's.

Although this faction of the party came generally from the Upper North, and particularly New England, Buchanan's neighbor and congressman, Thaddeus Stevens, is a perfect example of the rather sizable group of radical Republicans.[44] Stevens is best remembered as the "scourge of the South" during the Civil War and the early years of Reconstruction, but before being elected to the Thirty-Sixth Congress as a Republican in 1858 he had a long political career in Pennsylvania, first as an Anti-Mason and then as a Whig. He served two terms in Congress in the 1840s, where he knew Lincoln, and was sufficiently well known in national political circles to be floated in 1860 as a possible member of Lincoln's cabinet. His career as a Lower North politician reminds us to be careful about regional generalizations. But then Stevens was born and educated in New England, although his political career was played out in southern Pennsylvania—the quintessential Lower North.

Stevens's speeches have often been described as "vituperative," and his hostility to the Slave Power seems to have been boundless. In his major speech on secession, given in Congress on January 29, 1861, Stevens pulled few punches.[45] At this point he believed that no form of compromise could be reached. "[W]hen I see these States in open and declared rebellion against the Union, seizing upon her public forts and arsenals, and robbing her of millions of the public property; when I see the batteries of seceding States blockading the highway of the nation [the Mississippi River], and their armies in battle array against the flag of the Union; when I see, sir our flag insulted, and that insult submitted to I have no hope that concession, humiliation and compromise, can have any effect whatever."[46]

Congress, he believed, could do nothing to retard or accelerate "the headlong career of treason and rebellion."[47] This was because the seceded states did not want to compromise. He put forth several examples, the most striking of which was South Carolina's refusal to accept Virginia's plea to consider constitutional amendments that would lead to the state's return to the Union. Rather, the general assembly of South Carolina declared "that the separation of South Carolina from the Federal Union *is final*, and she has no further interest in the Constitution of the United States."[48]

Turning to the president's message, Stevens considered it mixed. Buchanan was correct in denouncing secession but totally wrong in ascribing secession to the long effort of the "antislavery party of the North" to interfere "with slavery in the States." Here and elsewhere, Stevens challenged the president—whom he referred to as the longtime "slave of slavery"—and his Southern colleagues in the House to point to some action by "the freemen of the North" that justified their claim. However, Stevens was more concerned about how Buchanan could denounce secession and then say that there was "no power in the Government to prevent or punish it."[49] In contrast to the advocates of the compact theory of the Union, he, like Lincoln, argued that the Constitution created a perpetual Union of the people and that any attempt of a single state to destroy it involved revolution and treason. In the course of his argument, which often doubled back on itself, Stevens was interrupted by Southern representatives citing incidents in the North such as the Christiana Riot.[50]

Unlike any of the other Northerners I have mentioned, Stevens was not trying to pacify the South or win the support of Southern Unionists. Not only did he defend the North against Southern charges, but he also attacked the Southern treatment of Northerners and white Southerners who did not conform. He knew how to push the buttons of the Slave Power, suggesting that the North was an area where the rule of law was respected, even in relation to the Fugitive Slave Law. The South was not only lawless, but refused to respect the common "rights of conscience and freedom of speech." Stevens added, "for twenty years past it has been unsafe for northern men to travel or settle in the South, unless they would avow their belief that slavery was a good institution." Consequently, "the South, at this moment, is a hideous despotism, so far as northern citizens are concerned."[51]

Stevens did not shrink from specific examples that caused further debate in and out of Congress. He taunted "the Kingdom of South Carolina"[52] and described the "social inequality" of free whites laboring under the foot of "lordly nobility."[53] When "the American people dared to disobey the commands of slavery" in electing Lincoln in 1860, slaveholders proclaimed this a "just cause of secession and a civil war." "The truth is, all these things are mere pretenses. The restless spirits of the South desire to have a slave empire, and they use these things as excuses."[54]

When it came to coercion, Stevens also went a bit—but only a bit—beyond what other Republicans were saying. He believed that the government would be justified in using force to punish those guilty of treason and that no state laws could protect those partaking of treasonable acts. But even he wanted no bloodbath. He was in favor of cutting off the mails and using American naval power to deprive the Kingdom of South Carolina of its revenue. (He had earlier suggested that the ports of seceding states be closed completely, depriving them of revenue and trade.) He drew a picture of a country "with a flag recognized by no civilized nation: with no vessel entering ports, except now and then in a low black schooner scudding in from the river Congo; with no ally or sympathizer except the King of Dahomey."[55]

Throughout the remainder of the crisis, Stevens, like his fellow Northerners in Congress, considered other matters. For example, he defended the Morrill Tariff—Stevens had the economic views of an old Whig like Lincoln—in an exchange of letters with his friend Salmon P. Chase, Lincoln's incoming secretary of the treasury.[56] During the war Stevens often criticized the administration he served, but he also played crucial roles in the passage of several pieces of economic legislation and in continuing to push the country in the direction of abolishing slavery.

And the War Came

Obviously, the Sumter situation turned into a big problem related to the question of secession. Lincoln had tried to defend federal property, but another of the many administrative "confusions" limited his alternative of making a stand on Fort Pickens. Thus he decided to send only supplies to Anderson, whom he knew was running out. While in a pacifistic moment Lincoln informed the South Carolina governor, Francis W. Pickens, that a ship would soon attempt reprovisioning Fort Sumter and there would be no troops on board, Lincoln knew something untoward would likely happen.

In Montgomery, Jefferson Davis and his government instructed General P.G.T. Beauregard, who had been an officer in the Army of the United States and commandant of West Point, to reduce the fort if Major Anderson would not surrender. In the early morning of April 12, a crazed Virginian, Edmund Ruffin, who had waited all his life for this moment, was allowed to set the first fuse. In less than two days Anderson was forced to surrender. Lincoln must have known that war was inevitable, but he carefully remained on the defensive. The Confederacy fired the first shot. Two days later he called "forth the militia of the several States of the Union, to the aggregate number of seventy-five thousand, in order to suppress said combinations, and to cause the laws to be duly executed." Still he was talking about maintaining the honor of the Union and "the perpetuity of popular government" by retaking "the forts, places, and property which had been seized."[57] Lincoln's call for troops was not a call for the war that followed.

But as Kenneth Stampp famously quoted Lincoln, "And the War Came." Most Northerners believed there would be no real war. They all knew who started it and why they were fighting it. In time almost as many Americans died in the Civil War as died in all other American wars put together. For most Northerners the war initially had little to do with freeing the slaves. Except for a small group of abolitionists, white Northerners were generally racists and uncaring about the existence of slavery in the South. They agreed with Lincoln, however, in that their initial response to Fort Sumter was not about slaves but about preserving the Union. Lincoln responded to an editorial by Horace Greeley saying that the federal government should let the Confederate states "go in peace," by saying:

> I would save the Union. I would save it in the shortest way under the constitution. . . . If there be those who would save the Union unless they could at the same time save Slavery, I do not agree with them. If there be those would not save the Union unless they could at the same time *destroy* Slavery, I do not agree with them. My paramount object in this struggle *is* to save the Union and it is not either to save or destroy Slavery. If I could save the Union without freeing *any* slave, I would do it; and if I could save it by freeing some and leaving others alone, I would do that. What I do about Slavery and the colored race, I do because I believe it helps to save this Union.[58]

Undoubtedly, Buchanan and Democrats like Douglas would have agreed with Lincoln. In fact, Douglas met with Lincoln on April 14 and issued a statement to the press that while he opposed "the administration on all its political issues, he was prepared to sustain the President in the exercise of all his constitutional functions to preserve the Union."[59] We think so highly of Lincoln not because of his indecisive behavior during the secession crisis, when he acted only a bit more consistently and aggressively than Buchanan, but because he grew into the presidential office as the situation worsened and the poor young man with modest militia experience became "tried by War."[60] While Buchanan was both more thoughtful and more flexible than most people think, it is impossible that he could have, like his Lower Northern counterpart Lincoln, grown so fast on the crucial issues of slavery and race. Buchanan could not have outrun the secession-ists. Lincoln did not, nor could he have prevented the war.

Notes

1. Quoted in Philip S. Klein, *President James Buchanan: A Biography* (University Park: Pennsylvania State University Press, 1962), 390. Briefer and less sympathetic views are provided in Elbert B. Smith, *The Presidency of James Buchanan* (Lawrence: University Press of Kansas, 1975), and Jean H. Baker, *James Buchanan* (New York: Times Books, 2004). In constructing a timeline of events below I have generally fol-lowed these accounts.

2. On this point see the collective work of William W. Freehling, most particularly *The South vs. the South: How Anti-Confederate Southerners Shaped the Course of the Civil War* (New York: Oxford University Press, 2001) and *The Road to Disunion*, vol. 2, *Secessionists Triumphant, 1854–1861* (New York: Oxford University Press, 2007).

3. While historians such as Freehling, Robert Wiebe, and David Hackett Fischer have been drawing a more complex picture for years, there is no agreed-upon termi-nology. I would follow Freehling's description of a Lower South, Upper South, and Border South, but would split Virginia to include some of the northwestern counties in the Border South. In addition to these designations, I would add a Lower North, Upper North, and, perhaps, New England as separate sections, although there were real divisions within New England. I also would differ from Freehling by dividing the states of Illinois, Indiana, Ohio, Pennsylvania, and New Jersey along a line running in the first three states along the National Road; this line could be extended east, in a slightly elevated fashion, through Pennsylvania and New Jersey. This is of course a historian's game, but one that tries to *remind* readers how complicated settlement pat-terns and accompanying attitudes were in antebellum America.

4. "Proclamation Calling Militia and Convening Congress," in *The Collected Works of Abraham Lincoln*, ed. Roy P. Basler (New Brunswick, N.J.: Rutgers University Press, 1953), 4:331–33. Since I wrote the initial version of this article, Harold Holzer, *Lincoln President-Elect: Abraham Lincoln and the Great Secession Winter 1860–1861* (New York: Simon and Schuster, 2008), has appeared, offering a day-by-day discus-sion of Lincoln's activities and thoughts. Also, Russell McClintock, *Lincoln and the Decision for War: the Northern Response to Secession* (Chapel Hill: University of North Carolina Press, 2008), has constructed a month-by-month analysis of the crisis.

5. See Martin B. Duberman, *Chares Francis Adams, 1807–1866* (Boston: Houghton Mifflin, 1961), 223–57.

6. "Mayor Fernando Wood's Recommendation for the Secession of New York City, January 6, 1861," in *Documents of American History*, ed. Henry Steele Commager, 5th ed. (New York: Appleton-Century-Crofts, 1949), 374–76.

7. Quoted in Frank L. Klement, *The Limits of Dissent: Clement L. Vallandigham and the Civil War* (Lexington: University Press of Kentucky, 1970), 51. See also Wood Gray, *The Hidden Civil War: The Story of the Copperheads* (New York Viking Press 1964); Frank L. Klement, *The Copperheads in the Middle West* (Chicago: University of Chicago Press, 1960); Jennifer L. Weber, *Copperheads* (New York: Oxford University Press, 2006); David E. Long, "Copperhead Conspiracy Adverted," in *American Presidential Campaigns and Elections*, ed. William G. Shade and Ballard C. Campbell, 3 vols. (New York: M. E. Sharpe, 2003), 2:414–15; and Ronald P. Formisano and William G. Shade, "The Idea of Agrarian Radicalism," *Mid-America* 52 (January 1970): 3–30.

8. The best book on this is Freehling, *The Road to Disunion*, but see also Ralph A. Wooster, *The Secession Conventions of the South* (Princeton: Princeton University Press 1962). Eric H. Walther, *The Fire Eaters* (Baton Rouge: Louisiana State University Press, 1992), concentrates on the most radical secessionists. Richard Current's *Lincoln's Loyalists: Union Soldiers from the Confederacy* (New York: Oxford University Press, 1992) reminds us that many white Southerners did not accept secession and over 100,000 served in the Union army.

9. See Avery O. Craven, *The Growth of Southern Nationalism, 1848–1861* (Baton Rouge: Louisiana State University Press, 1953); Thelma Jennings, *The Nashville Convention: the Southern Movement for Unity, 1848–1851* (Knoxville: University of Tennessee Press, 1980); and Elizabeth R. Varon, *Disunion! The Coming of the American Civil War, 1789–1859* (Chapel Hill: University of North Carolina Press, 2008).

10. Commager, *Documents of American History*, 372.

11. Ibid., 374. William L. Barney, *The Road to Secession: A New Perspective on the Old South* (New York: Praeger, 1972), is a brief, readable book designed for classroom use.

12. Harold M. Hyman and William M. Wiecek, *Equal Justice Under the Law: Constitutional Development, 1835–1875* (New York: Harper & Row, 1982), surveys the subject of constitutional debates at the time. See also Richard B. Morris, *The Forging of the Union, 1781–1789* (New York: Harper & Row, 1987), and Joseph M. Lynch, *Negotiating the Constitution: The Earliest Debates over Original Intent* (Ithaca: Cornell University Press, 1999).

13. Commager, *Documents of American History*, 376–84. Emory M. Thomas, *The Confederate Nation, 1861–1865* (New York: Harper & Row, 1979), is a useful brief history of the subject.

14. Klein, *President James Buchanan*, offers the most detailed and sympathetic scholarly evaluation. More critical is Baker, *James Buchanan*, and her essay in this volume. Buchanan did write his own defense, *Mr. Buchanan's Administration on the Eve of the Rebellion: A History of Four Years before the War* (New York: D. Appleton, 1866.)

15. Merrill D. Peterson, *Olive Branch and Sword: The Compromise of 1833* (Baton Rouge: Louisiana State University Press, 1982), and Richard E. Ellis, *The Union at*

Risk: Jacksonian Democracy, States' Rights and the Nullification Crisis (New York: Oxford University Press, 1987).

16. "Fourth Annual Message," in *A Compilation of the Messages and Papers of the Presidents, 1789–1897*, ed. James D. Richardson (Washington, D.C.: Published by Authority of Congress, 1900), 5:626–53.

17. The seeming contradiction of Manifest Destiny being based in Democratic conceptions of states' rights—rather than nationalism—is best explained in the work of Frederick Merk, particularly *Manifest Destiny and Mission in American History: A Reinterpretation* (New York: Knopf, 1963).

18. "Fourth Annual Message," 630, 632.

19. Ibid., 430–36. The public documents in Richardson can be complemented by those in *The Works of James Buchanan, Comprising His Speeches, State Papers, and Private Correspondence*, ed. John Bassett Moore, 12 vols. (Philadelphia: Historical Society of Pennsylvania, 1908–11). The material relevant to the secession winter is generally in volume 11.

20. Richardson, *Messages and Papers*, 5:626–27. One has to understand that Buchanan's contemporaries sometimes referred to the United States, as James K. Polk put it, as an "Empire of Independent Republics," rather than a nation.

21. "Fourth Annual Message," 634–35.

22. Ibid., 635–36.

23. Commager, *Documents of American History*, 369–71. See also Albert J. Kirwan, *John J. Crittenden: The Struggle for Union* (Lexington: University of Kentucky Press, 1962).

24. In 1860 Douglas was the only candidate who received popular votes in all the states. He did well throughout the North and would have done even better if Connecticut and Pennsylvania Democrats had not supported Breckinridge. For Douglas see Robert W. Johannsen, *Stephen A. Douglas* (New York: Oxford University Press, 1973); James L. Huston, *Stephen A. Douglas and the Dilemmas of Democratic Equality* (Latham, Md.: Rowman & Littlefield, 2007) is an excellent brief biography.

25. The Lincoln-Douglas debates are abridged in Commager, *Documents of American History*, 347–58. Robert W. Johannsen, ed., *The Lincoln-Douglas Debates of 1858* (New York: Oxford University Press, 1965), is a modern scholarly edition of the entire set of debates.

26. "To August Belmont, Dec. 25, 1860," in *The Letters of Stephen A. Douglas*, ed. Robert W. Johannsen (Urbana: University of Illinois Press, 1961), 505. Regarding Buchanan and Douglas's differences on popular sovereignty, see Nichole Etcheson's essay in this volume.

27. "To Ninety-six New Orleans Citizens," ibid., 499–503.

28. "To Charles H. Lanphier, December 25, 1860," ibid., 504–5.

29. Robert G. Gunderson, *Old Gentleman's Convention* (Lexington: University of Kentucky Press 1961).

30. Lincoln's course from the election can best be followed in David Herbert Donald, *Lincoln* (New York: Simon & Schuster, 1995), and in the fourth volume of Basler, *Collected Works*.

31. While we know that there was an emergent national press and that New York papers had correspondents in Charleston, it is hard to know what most people thought. It is difficult for historians to admit that perhaps huge numbers were unaware of the crisis facing them.

32. Jefferson Davis's message of April 29, 1861 (see Commager, *Documents of American History*, 407–10), exhibited a deep commitment to slavery and to the proslavery argument; Davis later argued that the defense of states' rights was the reason behind secession. There are many biographies of Davis; the latest and the best is William J. Cooper Jr., *Jefferson Davis, American* (New York: Knopf, 2000).

33. Doris Kearns Goodwin, *Team of Rivals: The Political Genius of Abraham Lincoln* (New York: Simon & Schuster, 2005).

34. Basler, *Collected Works*, 4:151, 168, 182, and 184 serve as examples in his published papers.

35. See Lee F. Crippen, *Simon Cameron: Ante-bellum Years* (Oxford, Ohio: Mississippi Valley Press, 1942), and Erwin Stanley Bradley, *Simon Cameron: Lincoln's Secretary of War* (Philadelphia: University of Pennsylvania Press, 1966).

36. See Kirk H. Porter and Donald Bruce Johnson, eds., *National Party Platforms* (Urbana: University of Illinois Press, 1966), 31–33.

37. Basler, *Collected Works*, 4:149–246.

38. Ibid., 248–71. Lincoln had read the former presidents' inaugurals and thought about them as well as listening to a collection of rather odd correspondence while composing his speech.

39. Ibid., 261.

40. Ibid., 271.

41. "Message to Congress in Special Session, July 4, 1861," ibid., 421–41.

42. Glyndon G. Van Deusen, *William Henry Seward* (New York: Oxford University Press, 1967), is the best biography. See also Daniel Crofts, "Secession Winter: William Henry Seward and the Decision for War," *New York History* 65 (1984): 228–56 and "The Union Party of 1861 and the Secession Crisis," *Perspectives in American History* 12 (1977–78): 327–76, as well as *Reluctant Confederates: Upper South Unionists in the Secession Crisis* (Chapel Hill: University of North Carolina Press, 1989). See also the correspondence between Seward and Lincoln in volume 4 of Basler, *Collected Works*.

43. Commager, *Documents of American History*, 392.

44. On Stevens see Fawn Brodie, *Thaddeus Stevens: Scourge of the South* (New York: Norton, 1959); Richard N. Current, *Old Thad Stevens: A Story of Ambition* (Madison: University of Wisconsin Press, 1942); and Hans L. Trefousse, *Thaddeus Stevens: Nineteenth-Century Egalitarian* (Chapel Hill: University of North Carolina Press, 1997).

45. "'State of the Union,' January 29, 1861, in Congress," in *The Selected Papers of Thaddeus Stevens*, vol. 1, *January 1814–March 1865*, ed. Beverly Wilson Palmer and Holly Byers Ochoa (Pittsburgh: University of Pittsburgh Press, 1997), 180–97.

46. Ibid., 180–81

47. Ibid., 182.

48. Quoted in ibid.

49. Ibid., 183.

50. Ibid., 186–90.

51. Ibid., 189.

52. Quoted in "From Benjamin F. Morgan," Palmer and Ochoa, *Selected Papers*, 204. The entire letter (201–6) is an attack on Stevens' portrayal of the South.

53. "State of the Union," 191.

54. Ibid., 190.

55. Ibid., 194. King Gelele of Dahomey was a notorious slave trader.

56. "Remarks on the Tariff, February 25, 1861, in Congress," "To [Salmon P.] Chase," "From [Salmon] P. Chase," and "To [Salmon] P. Chase," in Palmer and Ochoa, *Selected Papers*, 207–9, 177, 178, and 200.

57. Basler, *Collected Works*, 332.

58. See Lincoln's August 22, 1862, response to Horace Greeley's "Prayer of Twenty Million," which took the position of a small number of Northern radicals that the states should be allowed "to go in peace": "To Horace Greeley," in Basler, *Collected Works*, 5:388–89.

59. Johannsen, *Letters of Stephen A. Douglas*, 509.

60. James M. McPherson, *Tried by War: Abraham Lincoln as Commander in Chief* (New York: Penguin, 2008).

8

Joseph Holt, James Buchanan, and the Secession Crisis

DANIEL W. CROFTS

Nothing is likely to rehabilitate President James Buchanan's reputation. At best, we recall an inept chief who dithered ineffectually while blindly allowing disloyal underlings to betray his trust and imperil the very integrity of the nation. A more scathing version sees the president himself as a knowing ally of those who conspired to gain Confederate independence. As Doris Kearns Goodwin observed, Buchanan "deliberately chose men for his cabinet who thought as he did and, with the agreement of those around him, did nothing to prevent the secession of the Confederate states."[1]

Goodwin's dismissal has a long history. Republican newspapers and spokesmen said the same thing a century and a half ago. Like all too much of what we think we know about the political crisis that led to war, the conventional wisdom regarding Buchanan is shaped by the providential nationalism that pervaded the postwar North, which is to say, the postwar Republican North. If Abraham Lincoln was the martyr who saved the Union and abolished slavery, then his predecessor must have been the polar opposite—either a dupe or a traitor.

The conventional wisdom includes an unmistakable set of villains. Three Southern members of his cabinet did much to stigmatize Buchanan's presidency as a tainted failure. Secretary of the Treasury Howell Cobb of Georgia, Secretary of the Interior Jacob Thompson of Mississippi, and Secretary of War John B. Floyd of Virginia all became secessionists. They made common cause with Southern leaders in the U.S. Senate, most notably Jefferson Davis, who soon departed to lead the Confederate States of America. Although Cobb, Thompson, and Floyd all resigned from the cabinet in December and early January, they stayed long enough to weaken the Union cause and give Confederate architects a chance to start building.[2]

A conventional wisdom that is replete with bad guys must also have virtuous counterparts wearing white hats. Three Northern Union Democrats get credit for demanding that Buchanan resist the secessionists. Pennsylvania's Jeremiah Black, the attorney general, was appointed secretary of state as the crisis intensified in December. He persuaded Buchanan to name Ohio's Edwin M. Stanton to the vacated attorney general slot. Black and Stanton soon were reinforced by a new secretary of the treasury, New York's John A. Dix. The good guys could not reverse the fatal drift toward disunion. But they did at least end the pattern of surrendering federal installations in the Deep South. In particular, they stiffened the heretofore spineless Buchanan to hold Fort Sumter, the ticking time bomb in the harbor of Charleston, South Carolina.[3]

This essay will attempt a reconsideration. While any conventional wisdom contains elements of truth, it also tends to obscure what actually happened. The focus here will be on the one member of Buchanan's cabinet whose role did not fit the North-South dichotomy. Postmaster General Joseph Holt of Kentucky, who replaced Floyd as secretary of war at a pivotal juncture, followed a course that differed dramatically from that of his three Southern colleagues. Holt started as an anxious moderate and ended as an outspoken, unconditional Unionist. This has earned him a white hat from the custodians of conventional wisdom.

But if Holt gets a white hat—and he certainly deserves it; after all, being a pro-Union Southerner was much tougher than being a pro-Union Northerner—then an intriguing anomaly develops. Holt's course closely paralleled that of his oft-criticized chief. The two worked shoulder to shoulder during the last two-plus months of Buchanan's presidency. They stood ready to defend Sumter against secessionist assault. In March, however, they both hoped that Sumter might be evacuated to preserve the peace and keep the Upper South on the Union side. But once the war began, Holt and Buchanan each saw that Lincoln had no choice but to fight and they both fully supported the Union war effort. The affinity between Holt and Buchanan will be the central idea that holds this essay together—and that affinity is hard to square with conventional put-downs of Buchanan.

Figure 8.1. Joseph Holt, James Buchanan's postmaster general, secretary of war, and Abraham Lincoln's judge advocate general. Painting (c. 1889) by Louis P. Spinner, completed about five years before Holt's death, and based on earlier photographs. Courtesy of the Army Art Collection, U.S. Army Center of Military History, Washington, D.C.

Let me briefly anticipate. Before turning to Holt, we must first learn how the crisis arose. We shall do this by looking at the three secessionists-to-be in Buchanan's cabinet. Next we shall examine Holt's distinctive perspective on the crisis in November and December, opposed to secession but uncertain how to challenge it. Third, we shall see that Holt and Buchanan were ready to use force if necessary to protect Sumter between January and March. They hoped, however, that war might yet be averted and that the Upper South's allegiance to the Union might be made more unconditional. Finally, we shall recognize the broadly parallel outlook that Holt and Buchanan shared after the war started.

The Secessionist Trio

Howell Cobb, Jacob Thompson, and John B. Floyd must be seen as characteristic Southern Democrats. "They were for the Union as long as they could rule it," historian Roy Franklin Nichols tersely noted. "But if they could not? As yet they were not ready to face that reality."[4] Yes, the three certainly did become secessionists, and they soon played roles in the Confederate government or military. But they could not have told you in advance what was going to happen or what they were going to do. Southern Democrats ignited the conflagration, but they seemed surprised when a huge fire resulted.

Georgia's Howell Cobb, the most talented of Buchanan's inner circle, made it a point to spend time at the White House. The affable Cobb had reasons for befriending his reticent bachelor chief. It was widely understood that Cobb aspired to succeed Buchanan. As a mainstream Southern insider who cultivated a reputation as a sectional moderate, Cobb saw himself as the candidate who could diminish the Democratic Party's grievous North-South strains, while at the same time minimizing any possible bid for power by the South's former Whigs, or Southern Opposition.[5]

In contesting for the great prize, however, Cobb needed to appease Southern-rights malcontents. They could veto any Democrat not to their liking—and they had long suspected that Cobb was not to be trusted. By late 1859 and early 1860, the only way to establish one's Southern bona fides was to give lip service to the argument that the South must have a congressionally certified right to take slaves to the territories. Although Cobb knew that the territories were an annoying sideshow, he and other Southerners with presidential aspirations had to toe the new mark. But Northern Democrats proved unwilling to give ground to the South, either with regard to the platform or the choice of a candidate. Their base of support was eroding, and they could not carry "another ounce of Southern weight." Cobb and other Southern aspirants found themselves obliged to support the Southern bolters, who split the Democratic Party. Cobb hoped to lead the separate Southern ticket, but Democratic managers thought it more expedient to choose a candidate from the Upper South—Kentucky's John C. Breckinridge, Buchanan's vice-president.[6]

Throughout the presidential campaign, Breckinridge and most of his supporters denied that they plotted disunion. Quite the contrary, they insisted. Only they stood squarely in favor of the Constitution as interpreted by the Supreme Court in the *Dred Scott* decision. A vote for Breckinridge thus was a vote for a Union in which all states would enjoy equal rights, and he was the only genuinely national candidate. On that basis, Buchanan himself endorsed the Breckinridge ticket.[7]

But the mood in the Deep South was ominous. October's state elections in the North indicated that Abraham Lincoln, the candidate of the Republican Party, was likely to become the next president. Asserting that free labor was more productive than slave labor, Republicans deemed the South a drag on national progress. Some Republicans—though not Lincoln—sneered at the slave system as a vast brothel and accused white Southerners of moral degeneracy. Because Lincoln was not even on the ballot in most slave states, rumors abounded that he plotted to revolutionize the South. Cobb, while out stumping for Breckinridge, found the heretofore pro-Union uplands of north Georgia "in a perfect blaze." He suddenly realized that "the people of Georgia will not stand the election of Lincoln." Cobb, still smarting at having lost the presidential nomination, coveted a U.S. Senate seat. His ambitions presupposed that the South would remain in the Union. In a desperate effort to avert disaster, Cobb rushed to New York City. He tried to persuade influential business and political elites there to support a joint electoral ticket that would unite Lincoln's three opponents on a "fusion" ticket. Conservatives of differing party backgrounds had joined hands to block Republicans in 1856. They could do it again.[8]

But 1860 was not 1856. "Fusion" failed. Republicans persuaded themselves that the South was bluffing and that the time had come to call the bluff. The election results confronted Cobb and other leading Southern Democrats with an impossible dilemma. Their home states were being swept by a mass panic that threatened to break the ties binding state and nation. This was not the outcome they hoped for or expected, however much they bore responsibility for it. Most unwisely, Cobb and other influential Breckinridge backers had conjured up "ominous and exaggerated scenes of the South's future under Republicanism" even though he "did not honestly believe Lincoln threatened southern interests."[9]

The uproar in Georgia and the rest of the Deep South following the election proved even more intense than Cobb had expected. Initially hopeful that secession could be sidetracked until after Lincoln's inauguration,

Cobb decided during November to stand with the immediatists. On December 6 he issued a remarkable public letter to the people of Georgia, filled with extravagant distortions. It contended that the Republican Party was committed to "immediate and unconditional abolition in every State" and that Lincoln soon would begin to build up a party in the South to promote "this insidious warfare upon our family firesides and altars." Cobb pooh-poohed Buchanan's hopes for a Union-saving compromise and announced that "equality and safety in the Union are at an end." Immediately after issuing his polemic, Cobb resigned from the cabinet.[10]

Cobb had long presumed that the Union would hold together, and that he would wield power in Washington. His conversion to secession was sudden, opportunistic, and personally wrenching. Cobb mourned that "the ordeal through which I am now passing is the most trying of my life." He knew that his actions were undermining the man whom he regarded as "the truest friend to the South that ever sat in the Presidential chair." But when Buchanan insisted in his annual message on December 3 that no state had a right to secede, Cobb knew that he could not remain.[11]

Jacob Thompson, Buchanan's secretary of the interior, also came from the Deep South. Though born in North Carolina, he had moved to and made his fortune in Mississippi. He and Cobb viewed matters similarly—from a Southern perspective, to be sure—but with confidence that the status quo would hold, through which the South dominated the Democratic Party, and the party ruled the nation. Cobb and Thompson appear to have shared more affinity with Buchanan than other members of the cabinet. The relationship had a sociable aspect. Mary Ann Cobb and Kate Thompson were intimate friends. The "vivacious" young Mrs. Thompson, in particular, could charm the crusty old bachelor in the White House.[12]

Thompson and Cobb collaborated during the presidential campaign. They traveled together to New York City in October to try to breathe life into the "fusion" movement. But once the election took place and Lincoln emerged victorious, Thompson, like Cobb, found it impossible to maintain his national allegiance. Extremism was even more rife in Mississippi than in Georgia. Thompson first persuaded Buchanan, however, to include in his annual message the troublesome idea that the federal government lacked the power to coerce a state to remain in the Union. This needless assertion invited misunderstanding, because Buchanan also insisted that a state had no right to secede and that individuals (as distinct from states) could be compelled to obey the Constitution and national law.[13] Unlike Cobb, Thompson chose to remain in the cabinet even after the president delivered his annual message, and Buchanan made no effort to remove him.

Two of Thompson's actions soon exposed Buchanan to sharp censure. First, Thompson secured Buchanan's permission to visit his original home state of North Carolina—as a representative from the state of Mississippi. His purpose was to promote secession, though he pretended that a proposed concert of Southern states might yet become a vehicle for preserving the Union.[14] Second, shortly after Thompson's return from North Carolina, the Fort Sumter crisis burst into prominence. The Mississippian found himself marginalized as Buchanan and his reconstituted cabinet rejected demands by the South Carolina commissioners to abandon the outpost. Buchanan instead prepared to send reinforcements to the beleaguered fort. Thompson wired a warning to South Carolina officials. Only at that point did he finally resign from the cabinet.[15]

Buchanan's third secessionist-in-waiting, Secretary of War John B. Floyd, was a former governor of Virginia. Unfortunately, Floyd lacked the administrative skills to function at an executive level. He repeatedly embarrassed the administration by allowing favored insiders to profit from their dealings with the War Department. Just as the secession crisis erupted, news broke that friends of Floyd's had taken advantage of his trust to engineer a massive swindle. Appalled at Floyd's "apparent complicity with this fraudulent transaction," Buchanan asked him to resign, something he should have done long before. Floyd nonetheless dragged his feet, fearing that his resignation would be seen as an admission of his own guilt. His problems were compounded when other news reports accused him of moving weapons to Southern arsenals, where they might be captured by secessionists. Floyd thereupon became a lightning rod for patriotic outrage in many Northern newspapers. As of late December when Fort Sumter vaulted to attention, however, he remained in the cabinet. He joined with a delegation of Southern senators in pressing Buchanan to evacuate Sumter. Only when Buchanan rejected their entreaties did Floyd take advantage of the opportunity to resign in protest—ostensibly for principle rather than in disgrace.[16]

Floyd followed the predictable Southern-rights trajectory—supporting the territorial slave code, Breckinridge (a kinsman), and soon secession. He was blind to indications that Virginia and the Upper South initially were disinclined to secede. The Deep South had become the focus of attention in November and December. Floyd and other leading Virginia Democrats such as U.S. senator R.M.T. Hunter presumed incorrectly that pro-secession enthusiasm would sweep with equal strength through all the slave states. They soon found themselves dangerously out of step with their home state. By early February, a coalition of conditional and unconditional Unionists routed the Democratic machine that had controlled Virginia for decades.[17]

In sum, we may conclude that Cobb, Thompson, and Floyd each thought that state and national loyalty could be reconciled—and that a Southern-dominated Democratic Party could continue to exercise national power. They and many others painted a lurid account of how the Republican Party would instigate social revolution. Lincoln's victory hoisted them on their own petard. Mass panic in the Deep South meant that they had to go with the secession current. A situation that few if any had anticipated became the dreadful new reality. Even though it cannot fairly be said that Cobb, Thompson, and Floyd were disloyal conspirators who planned in advance to destroy the Union, it certainly can be said that they blundered into a situation that inflicted terrible hardships and suffering on the people of their home states and the entire nation.

Joseph Holt—Finding His Footing

Let us turn now to Joseph Holt. His home base was Kentucky, but he had extensive connections to the Deep South, where secession sentiment was most intense. From the mid-1830s until the early 1840s, Holt had been a prominent lawyer and politician in Mississippi. A younger brother to whom he was close, Robert S. Holt, remained active on the Mississippi bar. Holt also had ties by marriage to Governor Robert Wickliffe of Louisiana and Senator David L. Yulee of Florida. Since early adulthood, Holt had been an unswerving Democrat. His political allegiances were entirely conventional.[18]

Buchanan appointed Holt the commissioner of patents in September 1857. In early 1859 he was elevated to head the Post Office, with a mandate to cut back on expenses. A "hardheaded, stern administrator," Holt eliminated or consolidated small-scale post offices and mail routes. In so doing, however, he antagonized many elected officials, for whom post office appointments provided essential patronage lubricants. He became an "excellent Postmaster General," Buchanan later recognized, but his "silent and ungracious manner" often offended those "with whom he transacted business." The taciturn Holt could be "severe in his judgments of men" and a ferocious polemicist who was "terrible in denunciation." In short, Holt was a man of high standards and great integrity. But his prickly temperament set him apart from most of his colleagues. By elevating Holt to head the War Department in the midst of the Sumter impasse, Buchanan plainly selected someone whom he knew to be tough and uncompromising.[19]

The crisis of the Union took place at a dismal juncture in Holt's personal life. Widowed in 1846 by the death of his first wife, the former Mary Harrison, Holt married Margaret Wickliffe four years later, in 1850.[20] Surviving correspondence suggests that the pair shared closer ties of warmth and affection than the usual. "Maggie" apparently had fragile health. She spent time away from Washington with kin in the South, and Holt pined for the time when she would be "well enough to brighten again our lovely home by your presence." Her responses suggest that the bond was both mutual and passionate. "Oh!" she once exclaimed, "if I could only have the precious blessing *now* to put my arms around your neck to lay my cheek to yours and tell you as in days gone by how 'very much' I love you." The "loving and devoted" husband's fond chitchat to his "precious darling" ended abruptly in mid-1860.[21] Maggie died, and Holt never again remarried. Before long he came to be regarded as a dour and solitary widower.

Holt's emergence as an unconditional Unionist did not take place overnight. Writing on November 30, he privately blamed the crisis on the North's ministers, press, and "unscrupulous politicians." They had planted the insidious idea that one could be "faithful to God" only by disobeying the Constitution. He blasted the "infamous" personal liberty laws enacted by several Northern state legislatures, which purported to provide violators of the Fugitive Slave Act with greater legal safeguards. Holt condemned these laws as "a shameless violation of the Federal Constitution, in a point vital to the material interests of the South, and yet more vital to her honor." Were the free states promptly to repeal such laws and "and offer the same repose and safety to Southern homes and property enjoyed by those of the North, the impending tragedy *may* yet be averted, but not otherwise."[22]

Holt was not the only one to complain about Northern meddling and personal liberty laws. Buchanan's annual message to Congress, issued just a few days later on December 3, insisted at length that the South was the injured party. The president thus gave official imprimatur to ideas that closely paralleled Holt's letter of November 30. To defuse the crisis, Buchanan recommended a constitutional amendment that, among other things, would have invalidated state-level tampering with the Fugitive Slave Act.[23]

Holt's letter of November 30 ignored the nub of the dilemma—that the Lower South refused to accept the results of the recent presidential election. Instead, Holt attempted to breathe life into a tangential matter, the supposed unwillingness of several Northern states to respect the Fugitive Slave Act. As secessionists attempted to rationalize their actions, they seized upon personal liberty laws as evidence that the free states had trampled Southern rights under the Constitution. The issue suddenly became Exhibit "A" among secessionist grievances in November and December. Would-be mediators instinctively fastened on it, misled into thinking that it offered a key to defusing the crisis.[24]

Holt's understanding of the situation reflected private exchanges with his brother in Mississippi, Robert S. Holt. The latter condemned Lincoln's election as "a declaration by the northern people" that they intended to "emancipate the Slaves of the South." Convinced that "poison, knives and pistols" had been distributed to slaves throughout "the planting states" by abolitionist agents, Robert Holt declared that Mississippi was "almost unanimously in favor of an immediate withdrawal from the Union" and the establishment of "a government of our own." If the federal government acted wisely, it would not interpose. Were it to do so, however, "the bloodiest conflict in modern annals" would result.

Robert Holt, who concurred "fully" with Mississippi sentiment, feared that his brother was so strongly attached to the Union that his "sympathies may not be altogether with the South." He hoped rumors that Joseph Holt might either be neutral or "against us" were untrue. "I know your heart is altogether Southern," Robert pleaded, "and that you cannot but abhor the fanatics and assassins by whom our rights and firesides are invaded." Were he to side against his home region, it "would strike your Southern friends like a cold dagger in their bosoms."[25]

Joseph Holt promptly replied, to hope that secession might yet be averted and to implore his brother "to exert his influence in allaying the phrenzy." But Robert scoffed at Joseph's naive "devotion to the Union." People in the North were "marked by dishonesty, injustice, rapacity, and an infernal greed," Robert fumed. Between them and the South there was "nothing in common." The only possible outcome was "complete separation" and "immediate secession." Throughout the "planting states" there was "scarcely a show of opposition to it." Moreover, he continued, "it is a movement not of the leaders, but of the masses whom the leaders could not control if they would. The conviction is strong and universal, and I share it fully, that submission by the South is now death." He closed with the hope that "when the separation shall occur I hope to see you in our midst—in the midst of the only people with whom I think you would be willing to live."[26]

A few weeks later, on December 8—still barely a month after Lincoln's election—Robert adamantly insisted that secession was irreversible. "Since I wrote you last the revolutionary sentiment here has rapidly grown in intensity," he reported. He specifically spurned the palliative that his brother had advocated—it would be "utter futility" to attempt to persuade the free states to repeal their personal liberty laws. The "fullest retraction" of every "obnoxious" state law "would not in the slightest degree affect the determination of the Southern people." They would never accept any "compromise or adjustment." While crediting his brother's "highest and most patriotic motives" in trying to save the Union, Robert pleaded again with him to honor his ties to the South.[27]

The grim news from Mississippi plainly weighed on Joseph Holt. In a private letter written at the end of November, and subsequently widely reprinted, Holt alluded specifically to the message from his brother, a cotton planter and lawyer who never had any connection with politics and who was normally "calm and conservative," but who now saw secession as the only possible remedy for a situation in which mothers "lay down at night, trembling, beside their children, and wives cling to their husbands as they leave their homes in the morning." Holt stated that his brother "truthfully expresses the Southern mind, which at this moment glows as a furnace in its hatred of the North." Did the Northern preacher or antislavery agitators ever think, Holt wondered, "of the Southern homes he has robbed of sleep, and of the helpless women and children he has exposed to all the nameless horrors of servile insurrection?"[28]

In two crucial respects, however, Holt's letter of November 30 differed from the thinking of other Upper South anti-secessionists. First, Holt doubted whether the crisis could be resolved without bloodshed. While ostensibly advocating Northern concessions—the repeal of personal liberty laws—he had little hope that a compromise could be effected. A source he knew and trusted had assured him that secession was irreversible. Holt consequently judged that the movement had "passed beyond the reach of human control." South Carolina was determined to leave the Union. During the following weeks and months other slave states would follow, Holt mourned, and even "the Border States, now so devoted to the Union, will linger a little while, but they will soon unite their fortunes with their Southern sisters."[29] Holt thus considered the Union broken, with war the likely consequence. Most other anti-secessionists still hoped to peacefully reverse the disunion movement, with the wish the father of the thought. Second, Holt said nothing about his own ultimate allegiance. Unlike the typical Upper South Unionist, Holt never hinted that state allegiance might supersede his national allegiance, or that he would side with his state if it came to war. These two notable deviations from the norm provided the foundation for Holt's rapid emergence as a Southern heretic during the next fateful weeks.[30]

South Carolina quickly became the center of attention in December. The Palmetto State, throwing all caution to the winds, stampeded toward secession. On December 20 the South Carolina convention proclaimed the state's independence. Like-minded secessionists elsewhere in the Deep South, initially open to the idea that a number of disaffected states should act in concert or perhaps even wait to withdraw until Lincoln's inauguration in early March, decided to follow South Carolina's audacious example. During December and January, state legislatures across the Lower South hastily authorized elections for state conventions. These gatherings promptly severed all ties to the Union.[31]

Assertions of Southern independence triggered confrontations between the seceding states and the federal government. Who was entitled to control U.S. post offices, customhouses, arsenals, and fortifications? The difficulty first flared in South Carolina. On December 26, Major Robert Anderson—also from Kentucky—decided to move his small contingent of federal soldiers in Charleston Harbor from Fort Moultrie, an indefensible sandspit, to Fort Sumter, an artificial island a mile offshore.

Major Anderson's surreptitious move to Sumter captured the national spotlight. It raised the dread possibility that secession might lead to war. For many in the North, Anderson suddenly personified the cause of American nationality. He had stood by the flag and defied the secessionists. In so doing, Anderson presented Buchanan with a quandary. Desperate to prevent war, the president hoped to avoid provoking South Carolina hotheads. His "first prompting" would have been to remove Anderson from Sumter.[32] But the groundswell of Northern acclaim for Anderson showed that Buchanan would pay a high price indeed if he yielded to South Carolina.

For five days, from December 27 to 31, Buchanan and his cabinet struggled with the Sumter dilemma. Three commissioners from South Carolina demanded Anderson's withdrawal and waited impatiently. Thompson and Floyd predicted that continued federal occupation of Sumter would lead to civil war and insisted that Buchanan surrender the outpost. But Black, Stanton, and Holt insisted that the president dare not give more ground to secessionists. A terse message from Black to Holt reported that Buchanan had given Black "the paper he had written and requested me to make such changes as I desired. I shall propose a radical alteration of the whole document; and have some reason to believe that my view of the subject may be adopted."[33] Buchanan finally decided to spurn the South Carolina commissioners. He promised to defend Sumter "against hostile attacks, from whatever quarter they may come."[34] Buchanan then ordered the War and Navy Departments to begin secret preparations to reinforce Anderson. And on New Year's Day he placed Holt in charge of the War Department. Floyd's and Thompson's position in the cabinet became untenable once Buchanan sided with Holt and the Northerners. As we have seen, Floyd flamboyantly resigned. Soon too Thompson was out, not to be replaced. And Dix arrived to take charge of the fast-hemorrhaging Treasury.[35]

Holt and Buchanan: Prepared to Fight but Hoping for Peace

From January into March, Holt stood at the eye of the storm. Anderson's communications to Winfield Scott, general in chief of the army, were routed through the War Department. Peace hung by a thread and war threatened to erupt at any moment in Charleston harbor, where both Union and Confederate forces remained on hair-trigger alert. The situation there held both Buchanan and his successor hostage. Even though the fort had no strategic value, it became a symbol of the federal government's refusal to accept secession. In the end, Lincoln chose to risk war rather than surrender the symbol. But this gets us ahead of the story. Let us return to early January.

Holt's new post in the War Department won him wide acclaim, at least in the North. His predecessor, Floyd, left office under a cloud of suspected malfeasance and secession sympathies. By contrast, Holt was hailed as an exemplary Southerner, for whom national loyalties were paramount.[36] But Holt's new stature did nothing to appease his Mississippi brother. Robert Holt warned that Buchanan was "fast shifting into coercion" and that coercion meant "war upon the South, upon your Country, your friends, [and] your kindred." It was "simply madness" to go to war. The South could not be conquered "until she has been made a desert, and her last defender has been put under the sod." In Robert Holt's view, Buchanan either had "gone over to the Black Republicans" or had "lost his reason." He could not believe that his brother was "advising and sustaining the President in his war policy."[37]

Writing more in sorrow than anger, Robert Holt contended that officials in Washington misunderstood developments in the South. They were disposed to treat "a great popular revolution" as if it were a "village mob." In so doing, they failed to recognize that "all measures of hostility and coercion adopted only accelerates the movement and intensifies the feelings which prompted it." And they were deluded into thinking that the seceded states would reverse their course: "Let me assure you that no delusion was ever more vain. I am in the midst of these people, converse with them, read their papers, and share fully in their feelings, opinions and purposes, and I assure you in all soberness and truth that the restoration of the Union is impossible, that the fixed and almost unanimous purpose of our people is never again to be united under a common government with the free States, *upon any terms.*"[38]

But Joseph Holt was doing exactly what his brother most feared. During the first two months of 1861, almost certainly the busiest and most pressured interval of Holt's life, he and the reorganized cabinet worked with Buchanan to impede secession. The *Star of the West*, a side-wheeler containing both men and equipment for Anderson, sailed from New York City on January 5. It was repelled by South Carolina gunfire on January 9 as it attempted to enter Charleston harbor. Anderson, using his discretionary authority, withheld return fire and thereby prevented war. He insisted to Washington that he could manage. Holt made plain to Anderson that he should call on the administration were the situation to change. "Whenever, in your judgment, additional supplies or reinforcements are necessary for your safety or for a successful defense of the fort," Holt wrote to Anderson on January 16, "you will at once communicate the fact to this department, and a prompt and vigorous effort will be made to forward them." Anderson, however, offered continued reassurances that he had the capability "to hold this fort against any force which can be brought against me."[39]

So matters stood through February. The standoff at Sumter began to appear less threatening. On February 28, however, Anderson reported to the War Department that South Carolina had ringed the fort with such daunting firepower that it would be almost impossible to defend. He could not sustain himself at Sumter without "twenty or thirty thousand men to capture the batteries that had been erected." Because no such force could possibly have been assembled, Anderson was, in effect, asking to be evacuated. Holt initially reacted with consternation to Anderson's report, which arrived in Washington on the morning of Inauguration Day, March 4. Holt grimly informed the incoming president, Abraham Lincoln, that Anderson's message was an unexpected "surprise," inconsistent with "his previous correspondence." The government was "wholly unprepared," Holt added, to meet the "seemingly extravagant estimates" of force levels that Anderson now considered necessary at Sumter.[40]

The evening of Inauguration Day, Buchanan and the members of his cabinet met for the last time at the home of Robert Ould, the U.S. attorney for the District of Columbia. Anderson's message was so contrary to his previous statements that it raised questions both about his reliability and about his allegiance. Could Anderson have lost his nerve—or even become a secessionist? Should his message be believed? In fact, Anderson found himself terribly conflicted. He was a loyal soldier who stood ready to obey orders, but he hoped that orders to fight never would arrive. Like others from Kentucky and the Upper South, he dreaded war even more than disunion. Because he knew that his beleaguered outpost was the site where war was most likely to begin, he wanted to be ordered to withdraw, not to fight.

Anderson's ambivalence caused anxieties in Washington. Joseph Holt specifically recalled that Lincoln worried about Anderson. One day "very soon" after having received Anderson's troubling message, Lincoln called Holt to the White House and invited him into a private room. "Looking at me earnestly and with a great deal of feeling," Lincoln inquired whether Holt had any "doubt of Major Anderson's loyalty?" Holt said that he did not.[41] The outgoing treasury secretary, John A. Dix, who considered Anderson a friend, likewise recognized that there was "a feeling of doubt" about him. Dix therefore wrote him a letter designed to "encourage him if he was true, or cut him to the heart if he was false." Dix subsequently reported to Buchanan that Anderson's reply had been "perfectly satisfactory." Later that spring, following the fall of Sumter, Holt corroborated Dix's assessment. Holt reported to Buchanan that he had twice seen Anderson after the latter returned to Washington and found him "thoroughly loyal." "If he ever had any sympathy with the revolutionists—which I am now far from believing," Holt continued, then the ferocious cannonade against Sumter in April "crushed it out of him."[42]

Even though initially upset by Anderson's message of February 28, Holt soon decided that it made sense to abandon Sumter. On March 14 and then again on March 20 he shared his new assessment with Buchanan, who had retired to his Lancaster, Pennsylvania, home. Holt predicted that the policies of the new administration would be "decidedly pacific and conciliatory"—and that he approved this apparent course:

> I should not be surprised to learn, any morning, that Fort Sumter had been evacuated. As Fort Pickens can be retained without a collision, it may be differently treated. All is tranquil here, and the tone of feeling prevailing is constantly increasing in hopefulness and confidence. The indications from the border States are very encouraging. The popular mind is rapidly becoming tranquilized. This accomplished, and the revolution will die out. Excitement is the ailment on which it feeds, and without this it could scarcely subsist for sixty days. . . . I have more hope of the result now than I have had for the last three months.[43]

Holt knew that an attack on Sumter potentially offered frustrated Confederates the opportunity to start a war. That desperate act might yet galvanize support for their cause in the eight states of the Upper South that had refused to join the secession movement. But if peace could be preserved, secessionists in the Upper South would be crushed. Holt's thinking substantially paralleled that of young John Marshall Harlan, the future Supreme Court justice and author of the now-famous dissent in the *Plessy* case, who wrote him an eloquent private letter on March 11. The way to undermine support for secession in Kentucky and the Upper South was to withdraw federal troops from Forts Sumter and Pickens, Harlan advised Holt (as we have just seen, however, Holt wanted Pickens held). Harlan, a Union Whig, wanted to prevent any violent hostilities:

> The chief cause of the excitement now in Kentucky, Maryland, Virginia, North Carolina, Tennessee, and Missouri is the constant fear that the Lincoln Administration will attempt coercion, or war commence between "*him*" and the Seceding states. No matter how it may be produced, no matter who may be in the wrong, whenever war commences between the Federal Government under Lincoln, and any of the Seceding states that moment the Union cause in the above states will receive a blow from which it may never recover.[44]

For Harlan and Holt, political considerations dovetailed with military assessments. Harlan predicted that "the cause of secession would sicken and die" in the Upper South if war could be averted. Were the federal government to renounce coercion, Union control of the border slave states would be placed on an "immovable foundation." Even in the seceded states "a formidable party would immediately spring up" to contend for "a return to the National Union."[45] Holt reported to Buchanan that John C. Breckinridge, until recently the vice-president, had destroyed himself by urging his home state to ally with the Confederacy: "Kentucky voted against him [in 1860], on the suspicion merely that he was a disunionist; after this avowal, I doubt not, her condemnation of him will be far more decided." Briefly hopeful that the Union might be peacefully restored, Holt swung around to accepting evacuation of Sumter.[46]

And so did Buchanan. Even though the recently retired president had stood ready to reinforce Anderson whenever he requested it, Buchanan knew that such a step likely meant war. In his annual message in December, he had stated emphatically that even if waged to preserve the Union, war would be far more likely to destroy it and to make impossible any "future reconciliation between the States." While willing to risk war to hold Sumter, he continued to hope that the peace might yet be preserved.

Buchanan therefore was "glad with all my heart," he wrote Holt on March 16, to learn that the policy of the Lincoln administration "seems to be pacific." Buchanan believed that "no other policy" could "preserve and restore the Union." If this happened, Lincoln would "make an enviable name for himself." Buchanan's retrospective view remained the same. He wrote in his memoirs that the "true policy" in March had been to withdraw from Sumter, because that was the only way to maintain "the border States in their allegiance to the Government" and to keep open the possibility that they might yet "bring back the seceded cotton States into the Union."[47]

Two other key Union members of Buchanan's cabinet hardly shared their chief's readiness to see Sumter abandoned. Stanton and Dix, more attuned to Northern sensibilities, were at best ambivalent. Stanton could scarcely conceal his disgust at "relinquishing everything in the seceded states." He saw it as the first step toward acquiescing in Confederate independence and leaving a truncated Union that included only the free states. Stanton recognized, however, in a letter to Buchanan, that Lincoln apparently preferred "a continuation of your policy *to avoid collision*," and that by so doing, the new administration would forfeit any basis for complaining about Buchanan's stewardship. Dix predicted to his former chief that giving up Sumter would cause great "disappointment" in the country and would "go far to turn the current against the new administration." By contrast, Buchanan's record would "brighten in proportion." Any effort to blame Buchanan for the loss of Sumter would prove both "fruitless" and "absurd."[48]

We all know, of course, that the widespread expectation in mid-March about a withdrawal from Sumter proved unfounded. There was smoke but no fire. Lincoln never decided to evacuate, notwithstanding the many newspaper stories. He weighed his options, but ultimately he tried to reprovision the outpost. In so doing he gave the seceded states the opportunity to commence hostilities—the danger that anxious moderates most dreaded. Lincoln concluded that the Union never could be restored peacefully, but that secessionists would have to take responsibility for firing the first shot.[49] Suddenly in mid-April, the situation that Holt had grimly expected since December became reality. The outbreak of war closed off the middle ground and forced all Americans to choose sides.

Holt and Buchanan—Defending the Union War Effort

At this juncture, Holt's unconditional Unionism came to the fore. He had dared to hope in March that there might yet be some peaceful means to resolve the crisis, but once that possibility disappeared he promptly became a full-throated cheerleader for the Union war effort. His stature as a former cabinet member, coupled with his Southern Democratic background, made his contributions especially welcome to the Lincoln administration. Having Southerners on the Union side made it far easier to contend that the war pitted Unionists from across the country against a conspiratorial cabal that had temporarily seized power in the South. And having Democrats on the Union side enabled Republicans to say that the war had nothing to do with party, but rather that it brought together loyalists from both the major parties.

Holt spoke out for the Union cause in late spring and summer—and for the duration of the war. The most widely read and celebrated of his pronouncements was a long public letter written at the end of May. In it he insisted that secession and war were the work of a small group of troublemakers and that their traitorous schemes could only be defeated by military force. His message was aimed especially at his native Kentucky, which dangled precariously during the months after the war began. The Democratic Union Party, a coalition of former Whigs and Democrats, opposed both secession and the war and sought to preserve Kentucky's neutrality.[50]

Holt excoriated the "revolutionists." Faced with evidence in March that the Lincoln administration was seeking "a peaceful solution of our unhappy political troubles" and that its actions were "tranquillizing the Border States," secessionists deliberately precipitated "a collision of arms with the Federal authorities." They hoped the Border States, amid "the panic and exasperation incident to the commencement of civil war," would "array themselves against the Government." Secessionist "conspirators" thus suffocated "the Union sentiment of the South" under "a reign of terrorism which has no parallel but in the worst days of the French Revolution." Even though outnumbered in "every seceded State, except, perhaps, South Carolina," they had established an "insolent and proscriptive tyranny." Any who dared to disagree were treated with "the crack of the overseer's whip." The lash had become the "appropriate emblem" of their authority.[51]

Holt thus embraced the quite misleading idea that a small core of seces-sionists had violently suppressed the Union-loving majority among white Southerners. This was a comforting thought, and one that Lincoln shared, but it was a poor guide for devising wartime strategy. To be sure, signifi-cant concentrations of white Unionists persisted in Kentucky, Missouri, Maryland, Delaware, northwestern Virginia, and east Tennessee, but the polarizing effect of war transformed large majorities of Southern whites into Confederate patriots. Amid hysterical claims that Lincoln intended "to kill all the women and children in the South, and then turn the negroes loose," pro-Union sentiment in much of the South melted like ice cream on a scorching day.[52] Holt received the grim news that many of his kinfolk in Kentucky had become "great secessionists," on grounds that Lincoln was "an abolitionist." His aunt, Mary K. Stephens, confided that "I think what Lincoln is doing is wright but it would cost me my life to say so here."[53]

Holt, by contrast, saluted the new president. Lincoln had appealed to "the loyalty of the country" to repel a deadly threat to national existence. He had been answered by an immense outpouring of volunteer soldiers. They stood ready to protect Southern Unionists from "the cruel domina-tion" by which they had been "oppressed and silenced." Sadly, it appeared that armed force would be needed to overcome secession and that "the ordeal through which we are now passing must involve immense suffering and losses for us all."

Holt insisted that neutrality under such circumstances was a delusion. He would as soon think "of being neutral in a contest between an officer of justice and an incendiary arrested in an attempt to fire the dwelling over my head." The metaphor of a ship in distress was often used in 1861. "We are all," wrote Holt, "embarked in mid ocean on the same common deck. The howl of the storm is in our ears, and . . . while the noble ship pitches and rolls under the lashing of the waves, the cry is heard that she has sprung a leak at many points, and that the rushing waters are mount-ing rapidly in the hold. The man who, in such an hour, will not work at the pumps, is a maniac or a monster."[54]

Buchanan too left no doubts about his support for the war effort, even though his style was not so outspoken as Holt's. The week after Sumter, he wrote Dix that "the present administration had no alternative but to accept the war initiated by South Carolina or the Southern Confederacy. The North will sustain the administration almost to a man; and it ought to be sustained at all hazards."[55] In September Buchanan insisted that "the time has passed for offering compromises and terms of peace to the seceded States." All they would accept is independence, "which it is impossible we should grant." He applauded the men who had enlisted in the Union army and called for "bold, energetic, and united action" on behalf of the war effort.[56] Buchanan's stance as a War Democrat distanced him from many former friends such as his fellow Pennsylvanian and cabinet member, Jeremiah Black, whose partisan instincts soon moved him to the camp of Peace Democrats.

Lincoln appointed Holt judge advocate general of the War Department in September 1862. In this capacity Holt devised military tribunals to prosecute disloyal civilians and, just after the war ended, to try the alleged conspirators behind Lincoln's assassination.[57] Although his position made him a Republican ally, Holt never shared the near-universal disdain for Buchanan among Republicans. Ultimately he stood up to champion his former chief. In retirement Holt made it explicit that he never doubted "the profound earnestness of the President's loyalty"—that Buchanan had been "in all respects and at all times true to the Union."[58]

Holt also defended Buchanan's tactical decisions during the secession winter. He had acted "wisely and judiciously." Had he initiated a war, it could have destroyed the Union. By displaying so much "forbearance" toward the South and by refusing to fire the first shot, Buchanan—and then Lincoln—"gave us great moral strength when war finally came." Because secessionists "first fired upon the flag," loyal Americans were aroused "to a pitch of enthusiasm that carried us through the war": "If we had first fired upon them, the Democrats all over the North would have said: 'See, they are making war upon the South!' and the moral force of having waited to be attacked would have been against us." It may have seemed "queer" at the time that Anderson did not attempt to destroy the "hostile batteries being erected" against him. But viewed in retrospect, "it is easy to see that those conspicuous acts of conciliation on the part of the Government and its officers at that time were wisest and best."[59]

Looking back after almost a quarter century had passed, Holt commended his former chief: "The reproaches heaped upon Mr. Buchanan during the closing months of his administration and afterwards, were due mainly to the conciliatory policy, or as he himself termed it, 'a policy of defense, not aggression,' which he felt it his duty to assume towards the

South. This policy was honorable to him in every way, and its wisdom was fully illustrated by the events that followed." Buchanan's conciliatory policy had been "misunderstood or misrepresented" and his moderation had been stigmatized as "timidity," Holt recognized. Unhappily, "madness ruled the hour" and drowned out Buchanan's "voice of moderation." The secession conspiracy had attained proportions beyond his control. In retrospect, Holt saw that "the treason confronting the nation, with the cancer of slavery, of which it was the accursed progeny, could be extirpated only by the surgery of the sword." But Buchanan deserved respect for having tried in early 1861 to forestall and reverse the nightmare that secession had unleashed.[60]

Conclusion

In March 1861, with the crisis still unresolved, Holt reassured Buchanan that "you need have no fear but that history will do you justice."[61] He echoed that same theme many years later, long after Buchanan's 1868 death. "I never had a doubt but that at some time justice would be done him and his Administration. It could not be done in the heat of the war which followed it. Any man's word in its behalf, no matter how prominent his loyalty, would not have been accepted or his motives understood." The "fierce passions of the war" needed to cool before an honest assessment of Buchanan could take place. "The historian of the future," Holt wrote in 1884, will "pronounce a judgment that must assure to this illustrious statesman and patriot an unsullied fame, and this judgment, I doubt not, coming generations will unhesitatingly accept."[62]

Plainly, Holt's prophecy has not been fulfilled, and probably it never will be. Doris Kearns Goodwin noted that Buchanan "is now considered among the worst of our presidents."[63] This judgment has remained unchanged for almost a century and a half. The slight current revival of interest in Lincoln's predecessor results principally from efforts to tag George W. Bush as the worst president ever. It can be no more than cold comfort to Buchanan's defenders that some commentators would move their man from number one on the list to number two. But the harsh judgment of Buchanan is not one that historians should feel obliged to accept.

What conventional wisdom sees as Buchanan's greatest failing—his handling of the secession crisis—deserves instead the sort of respectful consideration that Holt anticipated. Could any president have preserved the Union and preserved the peace? With hindsight, it appears obvious that one could not do both, and that war was necessary to restore the Union. But first it was essential to try to find a peaceful resolution to the crisis. And if shooting were to start, the Confederates should fire the first shot.

On the whole, Buchanan made as capable an effort to accomplish the impossible as did Lincoln during the latter's first month-plus in office. A few discerning historians have recognized as much. Robert W. Johannsen, who wrote the one full biography of Buchanan's bitter rival, Stephen A. Douglas, and who certainly was not a Buchanan apologist, contended that Lincoln approached secession much as Buchanan had—and that even though Lincoln "gets all the credit," Buchanan should share in it. Kenneth M. Stampp, a scathing critic of Buchanan's ill-fated Kansas policy and someone whose Republican sympathies were unmistakable, likewise judged Buchanan's secession crisis role "altogether honorable." Both Johannsen and Stampp corroborated the judgment of Buchanan's sympathetic biographer, Philip S. Klein.[64]

Let us conclude. Holt's conspicuous pro-Union allegiances during wartime cemented his reputation, but we cannot say that he always had 20–20 foresight. In early 1861 both he and Buchanan were pessimistic that war could restore the Union. Therefore, they were ready to go the extra mile to keep the peace, even to the extent of accepting withdrawal from Sumter. With good reason, they dreaded the impact of war in the Upper South. Buchanan's illustrious successor finally decided that a peaceful reunion policy would lead instead to peaceful separation. And rather than accept that, he decided to risk war. But it was a judgment call, not a test of patriotism or manhood. Nobody knew in advance whether the Union could be restored through war, or how terrible the ordeal would prove to be.

Notes

1. Doris Kearns Goodwin, "Defeat Your Opponents. Then Hire Them," *New York Times*, August 3, 2008, WK11.

2. Variations of these themes may be found in James Ford Rhodes, *History of the United States from the Compromise of 1850 to the Final Restoration of Home Rule at the South in 1877*, 7 vols. (New York: Macmillan, 1893–1906), 3:126–38, 181–92; and Allan Nevins, *The Emergence of Lincoln*, vol. 2, *Prologue to Civil War, 1859–1861* (New York:

Scribner, 1950), 342–51, 356–62; see also David Herbert Donald, Jean Harvey Baker, and Michael F. Holt, *The Civil War and Reconstruction* (New York: Norton, 2001), 132–34, 139.

3. Rhodes, *History of the United States*, 3:224–44; Nevins, *Emergence of Lincoln*, 2:363–84.

4. Roy Franklin Nichols, *The Disruption of American Democracy* (New York: Macmillan, 1948), 319.

5. John Eddins Simpson, *Howell Cobb: The Politics of Ambition* (Chicago: Adams Press, 1973), 131–32.

6. James W. Singleton to Stephen A. Douglas, February 20, 1859, Douglas Papers, University of Chicago, quoted in Robert W. Johannsen, *Stephen A. Douglas* (New York: Oxford University Press, 1973), 698; Nichols, *Disruption of American Democracy*, 317–18.

7. John Bassett Moore, ed., *The Works of James Buchanan, Comprising His Speeches, State Papers, and Private Correspondence*, 12 vols. (Philadelphia: J. B. Lippincott, 1908–11), 10:457–64.

8. Nichols, *Disruption of American Democracy*, 359–62.

9. Simpson, *Howell Cobb*, 141.

10. Ulrich B. Phillips, ed., *The Correspondence of Robert Toombs, Alexander H. Stephens, and Howell Cobb*, Annual Report of the American Historical Association for the Year 1911, 2 vols. (Washington, D.C.: American Historical Association, 1913), 2:505–17, quotations on 508, 514–15. Cobb and other elite Southern Democrats likely did dread the possibility that Lincoln might attempt to attract Southern non-slaveholders into some kind of rival political grouping. But it was irresponsible demagoguery to insinuate that such a development would spawn slave insurrections—or that the Republican Party favored immediate abolition. Cobb knew that he was talking nonsense.

11. Nichols, *Disruption of American Democracy*, 380–81, 385; Buchanan's Fourth Annual Message, December 3, 1860, in Moore, *Works of James Buchanan*, 11:16; James Buchanan, *Mr. Buchanan's Administration on the Eve of the Rebellion* (originally published New York: D. Appleton and Company, 1866), in Moore, *Works of James Buchanan*, 12:80.

12. Nichols, *Disruption of American Democracy*, 70, 79, 91, 375. For a brilliant dissection of the relationship between Buchanan, Mary Ann Cobb, and Kate Thompson, see John Updike's "Afterword" in his *Buchanan Dying: A Play* (1974; reprint, Mechanicsburg, Pa.: Stackpole Books, 2000), 236–41.

13. Moore, *Works of James Buchanan*, 9:7–43, esp. 15–16, 18–20; Nichols, *Disruption of American Democracy*, 385–86.

14. Nichols, *Disruption of American Democracy*, 406; Mrs. Jacob Thompson to Mrs. Howell Cobb, December 15, 1860, in Phillips, *Correspondence of Toombs, Stephens, and Cobb*, 2:522–24; Charles P. Dew, *Apostles of Disunion: Southern Secession*

Commissioners and the Coming of the Civil War (Charlottesville: University Press of Virginia, 2001), 30–32.

15. Moore, *Works of James Buchanan*, 11:100–104, contains the exchanges between Thompson and Buchanan.

16. Buchanan, *Mr. Buchanan's Administration*, in Moore, *Works of James Buchanan*, 12:165; Rhodes, *History of the United States*, 3:236–41; Nichols, *Disruption of American Democracy*, 90–91, 194–95, 327–38, 416–27; James Elliott Walmsley, "John Buchanan Floyd," *Dictionary of American Biography*, 6:482–83; William G. Shade, "John Buchanan Floyd," *American National Biography*, 8:148–50.

17. Daniel W. Crofts, *Reluctant Confederates: Upper South Unionists in the Secession Crisis* (Chapel Hill: University of North Carolina Press, 1989), 154–55, passim.

18. The first modern biography of Holt has just appeared: Elizabeth D. Leonard, *Lincoln's Forgotten Ally: Judge Advocate General Joseph Holt of Kentucky* (Chapel Hill: University of North Carolina Press, 2011). See also Elizabeth D. Leonard, *Lincoln's Avengers: Justice, Revenge, and Reunion after the Civil War* (New York: Norton, 2004), 12–31.

19. Nichols, *Disruption of American Democracy*, 247–48, 322–23, 357; Buchanan, *Mr. Buchanan's Administration*, in Moore, *Works of James Buchanan*, 12:93–94n.

20. Leonard, *Lincoln's Avengers*, 13.

21. Holt to Margaret Wickliffe Holt, November 13, 1858, March 3, 1860, and Margaret Wickliffe Holt to Holt, May 11 (1860?—misfiled as 1861), Joseph Holt Papers, Library of Congress.

22. Holt to M. W. Jacobs, November 30, 1860, Holt scrapbook, Holt Papers. This letter, leaked inadvertently to the press by the recipient, was reprinted in various newspapers. Holt explained the circumstances of its publication in a public letter dated September 13, 1865, that the *New York Times* published on September 16, 1865. At the time he considered the North's personal liberty laws "one of the most powerful levers, by means of which the ignorant and deluded masses of the South had been moved to exasperation and frenzy." Could they be "suddenly swept away," he then hoped, "the wind might be taken out of the sails of the conspirators, and they thus rendered incapable of bringing the people up to the point of armed resistance to the government."

23. Moore, *Works of James Buchanan*, 11:11–12, 22–25.

24. Between 1858 and 1860, after the Kansas controversy subsided, North-South acrimony centered on the question of slavery in other territories. Thomas D. Morris, *Free Men All: The Personal Liberty Laws of the North, 1780–1861* (Baltimore: Johns Hopkins University Press, 1974), contends that the subject of his book "is worth more attention than is usually accorded to it" and that it generated many Southern complaints. But he too agrees that "the crisis of 1860–61 primarily revolved around the territorial problem." Morris, *Free Men All*, 202–18, quotation on 203.

25. Robert S. Holt to Joseph Holt, November 9, 1860, Holt Papers.

26. Robert S. Holt to Joseph Holt, November 20, 1860, Holt Papers.

27. Robert S. Holt to Joseph Holt, December 8, 1860, Holt Papers.

28. Holt to M. W. Jacobs, November 30, 1860, Holt scrapbook, Holt Papers.

29. Ibid.

30. Crofts, *Reluctant Confederates*, 104–29.

31. For a recent expert assessment of developments in South Carolina and the Lower South, see William W. Freehling, *The Road to Disunion*, vol. 2, *Secessionists Triumphant, 1854–1861* (New York: Oxford University Press, 2007), 343–498.

32. James Buchanan to Robert W. Barnwell, James H. Adams, and James L. Orr, December 31, 1860, in Moore, *Works of James Buchanan*, 11:79–84, quotation on 83.

33. Jeremiah Black to Joseph Holt, undated and misfiled at end of March 1861, even though it must have been written on December 30, 1860, Holt Papers.

34. Buchanan to Barnwell, Adams, and Orr, December 31, 1860, in Moore, *Works of James Buchanan*, 11:79–84, quotation on 84. Was Buchanan reluctantly drawn to confront the commissioners because his three pro-Union cabinet members threatened to resign if he did not? This is the conventional view, based on Black's recollections published in the early 1880s. See Jean H. Baker, *James Buchanan* (New York: Times Books, 2004), 135–36. But Holt remembered the situation quite differently. He thought Black's "highly impulsive temperament, and the supreme solicitude under which we were acting" may have prompted him to pose some kind of private ultimatum to Buchanan, but "if so," Holt continued, "no such avowal was made to myself, nor did I make any such to him." Holt also noted that Black had agreed in 1863 that "neither Mr. Stanton nor Mr. Holt ever spoke to the president about resigning." Holt to J. Buchanan Henry, May 26, 1884, in Moore, *Works of James Buchanan*, 11:84–91, quotations on 85–86.

It is also important to recognize that Buchanan was desperately trying to buy time in late December, in the hope that Lincoln would agree either to some compromise formula that might preserve the peace or to the calling of a national constitutional convention. Under the circumstances, Buchanan bent over backwards to prevent hostilities in Charleston harbor. But by December 30 Buchanan learned that Lincoln had rejected his secret overtures. These matters are convincingly argued by Philip Shriver Klein, *President James Buchanan: A Biography* (University Park: Pennsylvania State University Press, 1962), 381–87. See Duff Green to Buchanan, December 28, 1860, January 2, 1861, James Buchanan Papers, Historical Society of Pennsylvania.

35. These momentous developments are detailed in Nichols, *Disruption of American Democracy*, 397–98, 410–32; and Nevins, *Emergence of Lincoln*, 2:357–84, esp. 379–82. Thompson's resignation left a vacancy at the head of the Interior Department that remained unfilled (Nevins, *Emergence of Lincoln*, 2:380).

36. William K. McWhorter to Holt, January 13, 1861, J. G. Dickerson to Holt, February 21, 1861, Francis F. Hoffman to Holt, March 7, 1861, T. S. Bell to Holt, March 11, 1861, Holt Papers.

37. Robert S. Holt to Joseph Holt, January 10, 1861, Holt Papers.

38. Robert S. Holt to Joseph Holt, February 11, 1861, Holt Papers.

39. These matters are conveniently summarized in Holt to Abraham Lincoln, March 5, 1861, copy in George Ticknor Curtis, *Life of James Buchanan*, 2 vols. (New York: Harper & Brothers, 1883), 2:498–99, and Moore, *Works of James Buchanan*, 11:157–58. Having just learned from Anderson that he did not require reinforcements, Buchanan attempted to prevent the *Star of the West* from sailing, but his orders arrived too late. Nichols, *Disruption of American Democracy*, 429; Elbert B. Smith, *The Presidency of James Buchanan* (Lawrence: University Press of Kansas, 1975), 183–84.

40. James Buchanan, memorandum dated March 4–9, 1861, Holt to Lincoln, March 5, 1861, both in Curtis, *Life of James Buchanan*, 2:497–99, and Moore, *Works of James Buchanan*, 11:156–58.

41. F. A. Burr, interview with Joseph Holt, August 31, 1881, in *Philadelphia Weekly Press*, September 8, 1881; see also Michael Burlingame, ed., *An Oral History of Abraham Lincoln: John G. Nicolay's Interviews and Essays* (Carbondale: Southern Illinois University Press, 1996), 72. Holt's interview with Lincoln may have occurred on March 12, when the president sought him out for a private consultation: Abraham Lincoln to Joseph Holt, March 12, 1861, Holt Papers. Until the day before, Holt had remained in charge at the War Department, waiting for his successor to be confirmed, even though "as a Southern man" he was not entrusted with "the fullest confidence of the President or his new advisers." Burr interview with Holt in *Philadelphia Weekly Press*, September 8, 1881.

42. James Buchanan, memorandum dated March 4–9, 1861, John A. Dix to James Buchanan, March 14, 28, 1861, Joseph Holt to James Buchanan, May 24, 1861, in Moore, *Works of James Buchanan*, 11:156, 168–69, 175–76, 195–97. The originals for these and other Buchanan correspondence may be consulted on the microfilm version of the James Buchanan Papers, prepared by the Historical Society of Pennsylvania.

43. Joseph Holt to James Buchanan, March 14, 20, 1861, in Curtis, *Life of James Buchanan*, 2:531–32, 536, and Moore, *Works of James Buchanan*, 11:167–68, 174–75.

44. John M. Harlan to Joseph Holt, March 11, 1861, Holt Papers; see Crofts, *Reluctant Confederates*, 257–83; Loren P. Beth, *John Marshall Harlan: The Last Whig Justice* (Lexington: University Press of Kentucky, 1992), 40–52.

45. Harlan to Holt, March 11, 1861, Holt Papers. Harlan, unlike Holt, thought that the seceding states should ultimately be allowed "to go in peace" if they were "unalterably opposed to reunion."

46. Holt to Buchanan, March 20, 1861, in Curtis, *Life of James Buchanan*, 2:536, and Moore, *Works of James Buchanan*, 11:174–75.

47. Buchanan's Fourth Annual Message, December 3, 1860, and Buchanan to Holt, March 16, 1861, in Moore, *Works of James Buchanan*, 11:20, 171–73; Buchanan, *Mr. Buchanan's Administration*, in Moore, *Works of James Buchanan*, 12:209.

48. Edwin M. Stanton to James Buchanan, March 10, 12, 16, 1861, John A. Dix

to Buchanan, March 14, 28, 1861, in Curtis, *Life of James Buchanan*, 2:528–37, and Moore, *Works of James Buchanan*, 11:163–64, 166, 168–69, 170, 175–76. Stanton also was jealous of Holt. He sourly predicted to Buchanan on March 10 that Holt would be nominated to fill a Supreme Court vacancy, having made himself "the chief favorite of the Republicans." He also gossiped that Holt fed information to James E. Harvey, the widely read correspondent for the *Philadelphia North American* and the *New York Tribune*. Stanton to Buchanan, March 10, 12, 1861, in Curtis, *Life of James Buchanan*, 2:528–31. See also Daniel W. Crofts, "James E. Harvey and the Secession Crisis," *Pennsylvania Magazine of History and Biography* 103 (April 1979): 177–95.

49. The best study of the subject is Russell McClintock, *Lincoln and the Decision for War: The Northern Response to Secession* (Chapel Hill: University of North Carolina Press, 2008), 200–253. Additional discussion of the situation in March may be found in Daniel W. Crofts, *A Secession Crisis Enigma: William Henry Hurlbert and "The Diary of a Public Man"* (Baton Rouge: Louisiana State University Press, 2010), 136, 213–15, 262–69.

50. Joseph Holt to J. F. Speed, May 31, 1861. The letter appeared in many newspapers and as a separate pamphlet. It is conveniently available in Frank Moore, ed., *The Rebellion Record*, vol. 1, *Documents* (New York: Putnam, 1861, reprinted 1977), 283–92.

51. Ibid.

52. Unidentified writer (in Waynesboro, Tennessee) to the editors of the *Louisville Journal*, May 23, 1861, in Mary K. Stephens to Holt, May 28, 1861, Holt Papers.

53. Mary K. Stephens to Holt, April 22, May 1, 12, 1861, Holt Papers.

54. Holt to Speed, May 31, 1861, quotations in Moore, *Rebellion Record*, 1:284–85, 291–92.

55. Buchanan to John A. Dix, April 19, 25, 1861, Dix to Buchanan, April 24, 1861, all in Moore, *Works of James Buchanan*, 11:181–85. Buchanan regretted that he had not authorized Dix to give his letter to the press.

56. Buchanan to Horatio King, September 18, 1861, in Moore, *Works of James Buchanan*, 11:220–22.

57. Leonard, *Lincoln's Avengers*, 26–31.

58. Holt to J. Buchanan Henry, May 26, 1884, in Moore, *Works of James Buchanan*, 11:84–91; Burr interview with Holt in *Philadelphia Weekly Press*, September 8, 1881.

59. Burr interview with Holt in *Philadelphia Weekly Press*, September 8, 1881.

60. Holt to J. Buchanan Henry, May 26, 1884, in Moore, *Works of James Buchanan*, 11:84–91. Buchanan might not have accepted Holt's retrospective strictures against slavery. Buchanan's entire political career reflected confidence that American nationality was strong enough to withstand disagreements regarding slavery.

61. Holt to Buchanan, March 14, 1861, in Moore, *Works of James Buchanan*, 11:167.

62. Burr interview with Holt in *Philadelphia Weekly Press*, September 8, 1881; Holt to J. Buchanan Henry, May 26, 1884, in Moore, *Works of James Buchanan*, 11:90–91.

63. Goodwin, "Defeat Your Opponents"; see Michael J. Birkner, "Introduction: Getting to Know James Buchanan, Again," in *James Buchanan and the Political Crisis of the 1850s*, ed. Birkner (Selinsgrove, Pa.: Susquehanna University Press, 1996), 17–18.

64. Michael J. Birkner, Don Fehrenbacher, Kenneth M. Stampp, Robert Johannsen, and Elbert Smith (discussants), "The Presidency of James Buchanan: A Reassessment," in Birkner, *James Buchanan and the Political Crisis of the 1850s*, 194–97; Klein, *President James Buchanan*, 353–402. Buchanan and Lincoln both denied that a state had a right to secede, both refused to recognize the Confederacy, and both asserted that the federal government could use force to defend itself. In other ways, of course, Buchanan and Lincoln differed. Buchanan eagerly sought compromise, while Lincoln threw cold water on all efforts to soften Republican opposition to slavery in the territories. Don E. Fehrenbacher noted that anything said by Lincoln and Buchanan in early 1861 was bound to be understood differently, because the two had such "totally different backgrounds"—Lincoln was antislavery, whereas Buchanan had been outspokenly "anti-antislavery." Birkner et al., "The Presidency of James Buchanan," 197.

9

A Conversation with William W. Freehling and Michael F. Holt, September 19, 2008

MODERATED BY JOHN W. QUIST

JOHN W. QUIST: Tonight we are pleased to have with us two of the most distinguished and influential historians of the Civil War era: William W. Freehling and Michael F. Holt. After Professors Freehling and Holt make a few introductory remarks, in which they will offer some reflections on the 1850s from the perspective of a lifetime of study, we will discuss the Buchanan years, sectionalism and secession, and then open the floor for your questions.

WILLIAM W. FREEHLING: When I entered this field in the early 1960s, younger and older historians tended to clash over whether the Civil War was repressible. Most of the older scholars urged that blundering politicians caused a needless war, with no fundamental issue—and certainly not slavery—irrevocably dividing two largely similar sections. I joined most of the younger scholars in countering that fundamental differences, especially over slavery, generated an inescapable war.

Forty years later, we have prevailed. I relish our triumph. But we won too total a victory. Erasing everything except slavery's inexorable pressures removes too many provoking supplementary issues, too many accidents that helped stir up controversy—and yes, too many blundering politicians who helped wrench slavery issues into explosive shape. Witness James Buchanan's presidency, where a small dash of presidential bungling and of accidental occurrences must supplement a large dose of remorseless slavery issues, to understand a nation on the brink.

Historians learn from observing the present as well as from studying the past. Contemporary events helped alert me to the impact of accidents and blunders in Buchanan's era. I came to political consciousness during an era of assassinations. Assailants murdered John F. Kennedy, Martin Luther King, and Robert Kennedy. Assassins also wounded George Wallace and Ronald Reagan, but not fatally. Our politics might have been different if the two Kennedys and King had survived and if Wallace and Reagan had perished. And coincidental circumstances, not grand impersonal forces, determined which assassins killed which leaders.

As I interpret my times, blundering statesmen no less than accidents affected events. Some may disagree with me that in the last eight years bungling politicians have harmed our foreign policy. [audience laughter] But no one will disagree that Richard Nixon's Watergate floundering poisoned his presidency.

Blunders and accidents during the years of Buchanan's administration had similar disruptive consequences. To take the indisputable example of an accident's partial impact, in 1859, New England's John Brown seized the federal arsenal in western Virginia's Harpers Ferry, seeking to increase slave resistance. One of white Virginians' U.S. Marine rescuers, Israel Green, came at John Brown with what happened to be a dull dress sword. Green's only potentially killing slash from his dulled blade happened to hit John Brown in the belt buckle. So the captured raider lived.

The accidental survival magnified Brown's impact. The survivor provocatively addressed his judges, bragging about an intervention on the side of the poor and helpless which all right-thinking men should applaud. The brilliant speech, not the inept raid, aroused some Northern intellectuals to broadcast damning indictments of Southern sinners. Southerners responded with furious indictments of Yankee saints. Without those post-address castigations, President James Buchanan would have faced a less convulsed nation. And sectional antagonism had the opportunity to swell into its post-address distended form because a dulled sword happened to hit a belt buckle.

Buchanan's blunders, even more than coincidences beyond his control, escalated sectional warfare. No one will be surprised that yet another historian accuses poor Buchanan of mismanagement. The surprise here will be my argument that the Pennsylvanian usually erred not by passively allowing events to overwhelm him but by counterproductively throwing himself into the breech.

Figure 9.1. James Buchanan's inaugural procession, Washington, D.C., March 4, 1857. *Frank Leslie's Illustrated Newspaper*, March 21, 1857.

True, Buchanan's Kansas disaster sustains the conventional image of this president's unfortunate inertia. At the moment of decision on Kansas's admission into the Union, Buchanan did fall fatally silent about the key issue: whether Kansas's voters had to approve their entire constitution, and especially its legalization or abolition of slavery. Members of his administration attended Kansas's so-called Lecompton convention. They bore no presidential insistence that the convention's entire constitution for the proposed new state must be submitted to Kansas's voters, an ultimatum that Buchanan had previously issued to the Kansas governor. When his uninstructed men on the spot compromised, sanctioning only submission of part of the Lecompton Constitution to the voters, and not the part legalizing slavery, the president had to endorse the partial popular vote. The resulting furor, fatally damaging the Buchanan administration, classically illuminated the consequence of misplaced presidential passiveness.

More often, Buchanan's blunders illustrated the classic folly of misplaced presidential aggressiveness. Buchanan commenced his bull-in-the-china-shop charging before he entered the White House. While the president-elect prepared his inaugural address, the Supreme Court majority privately deliberated between two options about how to decide its infamous *Dred*

Scott case. The majority leaned toward narrow procedural reasons not to free the enslaved Scott family. But the controlling bloc of judges flirted with a broader ruling. The Court could deny the basis of the Scotts' claim for freedom—their temporary residence in congressionally emancipated U.S. territory—because Congress could not constitutionally emancipate U.S. territories.

At this majority's wavering moment, the president-elect secretly intruded. Buchanan wrote friendly judges, urging them to dare the broader decision. He here indulged in harried politicians' decade-old fantasy: if the supposedly nonpartisan Court would decide the issue of slavery in the territories, the controversy would magically disappear, never again to devastate the nation.

The Court majority shifted as the incoming president wished. On March 4, 1857, both Buchanan's inaugural address and his behavior on the inauguration stand raised suspicions that he might be invading the Court's affairs. Two days later, the judges announced that slaveholders' property right to own slaves precluded congressional abolition in the territories. The *Dred Scott* decision divided Southern from Northern Democrats, handed the Republican Party an explosive grievance, and compromised Buchanan's claim to be impartial national steward. I know of no other case where a president or president-elect barged into the Court's deliberations. I can imagine no other occasion when a presidential incursion onto the Court's turf could have been so counterproductive.

That *when* is crucial. Buchanan's aggressive miscalculation came not only when the Court but also when the nation hovered on the threshold of catastrophe. At the moment when a profound social conflict reaches its most potentially dangerous junction, unfortunate accidents and/or erring politicians can most tip the balance.

MICHAEL F. HOLT: I am going to give you a different take on the 1850s than Bill did, not because I disagree with what he says, but we were asked to reflect about the 1850s from our experience in studying it for a number of years. My first reflection really involves what the study of politics of the Civil War era, and not just the 1850s, was like when I entered graduate school in the fall of 1962 and what it is like now. In the fall of 1962 there was a lineup of highly accomplished senior scholars who were training graduate students to write about the politics of the 1850s—at Berkeley with Ken Stampp, at Stanford with Don Fehrenbacher and David Potter, at the University of Wisconsin with Dick Current, at Wayne State with Lee Benson, who would later join Roy Franklin Nichols at the University of Pennsylvania, and my own mentor, David Donald, who had just moved to Johns Hopkins from Princeton, and who was then very much interested in political history. These folks trained a whole generation of people about my age. Some of us have retired already and some of us will retire shortly. I suggest you look at the people who appear on these panels tomorrow and what you are going to see is a lot of white hair, or gray hair, or no hair. The sad thing is, and I think this is the real political crisis of the 1850s, the generation of historians who came after us not only did not opt to do political history, but they were highly scornful of political history. There is going to be a lacuna, I think, of new blood coming out with people studying the politics of the 1850s. That is the real political crisis.

The term "political crisis of the 1850s" comes from a book that I wrote.[1] I discovered that there was a real sense of people in the mid-1850s that government was no longer responsive to the needs of the people, that they lost control of what government did and that something had to be done, to use a phrase from the 1960s and 1970s, to return power to the people. And it was that sense of crisis that shaped the book I wrote, but that book was published in 1978. Let me flash back to 1962, if I could, to say something about the differences in how the politics in the 1850s were studied then and have been studied now. That year, 1962, is a significant date because the preceding year Lee Benson published *The Concept of Jacksonian Democracy: New York as a Test Case*.[2] Benson, who was then at Wayne State, and Sam Hays, who taught at the University of Pittsburgh, were the founding fathers of what was called in the early 1960s "the New Political History." And for a while this was really a go-go field, and it seems to me along with colonial studies of towns, the New Political History was the freshest, the hottest fad in American political history during the 1960s and 1970s.

Well, what was this New Political History? It was an argument that historians really needed to study the aggregate behavior of voters rather than the behavior of elites. In one way this meant doing statistical study of roll-call voting patterns in Congress and in state legislatures. But it also meant the studies of voters. Sam Hays argued that the best way to understand the values of the inarticulate people who have left no documentary record is to trace how they voted and then to speculate on why they may have voted that way. Benson's contribution to the New Political History—the two men did not collaborate, they operated separately—was that most voting was locally oriented, based on membership in local social groups, or what he called reference groups. The New Political History held that people voted either with those who were like them or they voted against people they did not like, and that the major fault line of the nineteenth century was neither along economic lines nor over issues that led to the Civil War. Politics divided over ethno-cultural divisions between Protestants and Catholics, or over issues like prohibition.

In other words, the New Political History maintained that voting was not a referendum on national issues. It was an attack on the existing wisdom that Bill referred to, and this certainly inspired me in my first book. David Donald was then interested in this political history, and he had all of his students learning how to use "coefficients of correlation" with logarithms—there were no computers then—and figuring out who voted for whom. These tools were going to tell us what happened. My first book, a revision of my dissertation, examined politics in antebellum Pittsburgh and concluded that the issues that supposedly caused the Civil War had no impact whatsoever on the city—one that by 1860 was the strongest Republican city in the North. Having grown up in Pittsburgh, it is counterintuitive to think it was once the strongest Republican city in the country.[3]

But I was not the only one doing this kind of work. If you look back at books, and particularly articles, that were coming out on the politics of the 1850s, the focus was on voting behavior, and who voted for whom. The mantra that we were taught when I started graduate school in 1962 was that historians must write about the 1850s on their own terms. You must forget that the Civil War ever happened, because if you point toward the Civil War you are going to get a misunderstanding of what was really driving political behavior in the years when people did not know that there was going to be a war. Bill MacKinnon, who has worked on Buchanan's Utah expedition against Mormons, is a perfect example of somebody who has looked at the 1850s on its own terms. He has taken what happened and not tried to force it into some kind of explanation about the Civil War.

I rapidly grew weary and disenchanted with this approach. First, it took me four months to re-aggregate manuscript census returns for Pittsburgh. It was the most tedious exercise I had ever done, and I did not want to go through it again. But as I did more research it became clear that local politicians and candidates believed that voters paid attention to national issues and questions. It also seemed they knew their constituents much better than I did studying them from afar. I also became convinced, as I was researching my second book, *The Political Crisis of the 1850s*, that not only were Americans disenchanted with the political system as it operated, but that they were expressing themselves in a language that was identical to a language that Bernard Bailyn, a colonial historian at Harvard, had identified in pamphlets leading to the Revolution. Bailyn's student, Gordon Wood, called this language republicanism, and many historians afterwards called it republicanism, too. Republicanism was the notion that power inevitably encroached on individual liberties and that the purpose of political activity was to prevent power from encroaching on liberty. And as I began to look at private letters in particular, but also public statements from the 1850s, it seemed very clear to me that this ideology from the 1760s and 1770s was still alive and well in the 1850s.

My argument in *The Political Crisis of the 1850s* seems counterintuitive. Many people have attacked it, but I still believe it. It seems to me that the Republican Party rose in the North not by pointing out the wrongs that slavery did to blacks, but grew by emphasizing the threat that the so-called Slave Power—white Southern slaveholders and white politicians who represented them—posed to the liberty, the very freedom, of Northern white men. And while Southern slaveholders favored secession because they feared abolition, Southern non-slaveholders acquiesced. Southern non-slaveholders certainly did not lead the secession movement. They acquiesced in secession because they feared that a federal government controlled by Republicans would enslave them. In other words, both Northerners and Southerners were seeking to escape enslavement. This fear of enslavement is what brought on the Civil War.

One of the ways I have been attacked is in books about the motivation behind secession. Some historians argue that the commissioners sent from the Deep South to the Upper South states would say, "We're leaving the Union because we fear abolition." How do you reconcile these two positions? The easiest way to do so is to understand that different appeals were made to different groups in the South to justify secession. This is such an obvious thing that historians should have recognized right away, but we have not. We all weigh some kind of evidence; we make comparisons and declare for the supremacy of our evidence over another person's evidence.

Following a technique initiated by David Donald, I taught a yearlong graduate seminar, a number of years ago, of using different quantitative methods to do political history. One of the students, Bill Link, who is now a chaired professor at the University of Florida and Arthur Link's son, did a content analysis of Georgia newspaper editorials on secession, four papers, all of which supported secession. He had the wit to divide his sample of editorials into two groups: one, from the day of Lincoln's election to the secession delegates' election, and another from the day of the secession delegates' election to the day of the secession ordinance's adoption. He then measured how many column inches were divided into each kind of appeal. That is what you did with content analysis. He found that 85 percent of the arguments prior to the election of the secession delegates stated, in effect, "We've got to get out of the Union to escape the enslavement to the North." A hundred percent of the arguments of the later sample was, "We've got to get out to avoid abolition of slavery."

When you think about these editorials, they make a great deal of sense. The majority of Georgia's voters were non-slaveholders, and so you pitch one appeal to them. One hundred percent of the electors to the secession convention were slaveholders, so you pitch a different kind of appeal to them. This is a way to reconcile one of the arguments among historians of the 1850s.

QUIST: Thanks, Michael and Bill. Your comments raise quite a number of questions. How about one that students often raise: Did slavery cause the Civil War, or did politicians cause the Civil War?

HOLT: I think there would have been no Civil War without slavery, but I think politicians caused it.

QUIST: Bill, do you want to touch that one?

FREEHLING: I have long since learned that you should not try to top a good statement. [audience laughter]

QUIST: Since we are at Wheatland we should probably discuss James Buchanan. Could James Buchanan have run his presidency differently and secured his party's nomination in 1860 and won reelection that year? Or, were the crises he faced ones that would have overwhelmed any president?

FREEHLING: Buchanan's terrible problems probably would have damaged even a mistake-free president. Still, Buchanan's mistakes made the problems worse. So he likely could not have been reelected, but he certainly ensured the impossibility.

HOLT: Had Buchanan made decisions that might have given him a chance at reelection, those decisions would have assured that he would not have been renominated. I am thinking particularly of the Lecompton Constitution issue. If he had joined Douglas in bucking the Southern wing of the Democratic Party, I think the Southern wing of the Democratic Party would have treated him in 1860 exactly the way they treated Douglas, and that two-thirds rule would have prevented his renomination. The more interesting question to me was whether Buchanan ever wanted to be renominated in 1860. I think he was so old and so tired he just wanted to go home; quite unlike Franklin Pierce, who did want renomination and was denied it.

QUIST: David Potter wrote in *The Impending Crisis,* "More than a century of historical writing has stamped the administration of James Buchanan a failure."[4] Potter did very little to challenge this verdict and, with the possible exception of Philip Klein, most historians writing over the last half century have not done so either. Would either of you challenge Potter's assessment of the Buchanan administration's being a failure?

HOLT: I can be even shorter. No. [audience laughter]

FREEHLING: I agree with Michael. But could I talk less briefly about why Buchanan was trouble-prone? The president was a dedicated, frightened Unionist. The dedication and the fright made him a nervous decision maker, whether he jumped into overly passive, or overly activist, directions.
    The circumstances of his election distressed even less-jumpy Unionists. The Pennsylvanian won the presidency in 1856 by an ominously narrow margin, capturing only the South and the most southern rim of the North.

With a change of only thirty-five thousand votes in five states, the new Republican Party would have won the White House. In such an eventuality, Southerners had threatened to secede. Buchanan's campaigners had stressed that only his election could save the Union. And so his victory had. But for how long, after he had won by a whisker?

The question of disunion also troubled Buchanan because of his residence in this lovely area. I have known his neighborhood especially well for decades, because my wife's father has a farm near Christiana. Few American landscapes are more exquisite, especially because of the rolling hills and the rural tranquillity. Yet five years before Buchanan left the serenity for the White House, a terrible race riot over fugitive slaves tore up Christiana. Buchanan considered the horror a trifle compared to the way a civil war would turn his neighborhood into hills of blood. He was not far wrong. Gettysburg is only a few dozen miles away.

His doorstep was even closer to slaveholding Maryland. No other prominent Northerner lived so close to the South. Few Northerners had more good friends from the South. No Yankee more fully felt slaveholders' pain, their anxiety, their terror, and their ferocity. He knew that unless they could be calmed, civil war would savage his environs. His close election and his love for his special area yielded just the edgy man who would treasure the fantasy that a *Dred Scott* decision would spare him, his administration, his neighborhood, and his Union a fright.

QUIST: Let us consider the Buchanan administration from another angle. James Buchanan, as most of us know, may have been the most experienced person ever to take the presidential oath. But in 1856 he ran against a candidate who had more presidential experience, Millard Fillmore, the nominee for the nativist American Party. What would a Millard Fillmore administration have looked like? How might Fillmore have made things different?

FREEHLING: Well, Michael has to answer this one because Michael thinks that Millard Fillmore is the best thing since sliced bread. [audience laughter]

HOLT: I am a great admirer of Millard Fillmore, and I can imagine two differences. First, Fillmore would not have intervened with the Supreme Court about the *Dred Scott* decision. Remember it was a Pennsylvania

THE RIGHT MAN FOR THE RIGHT PLACE.

Figure 9.2. *The Right Man for the Right Place* (New York: Nathaniel Currier, 1856). Lithograph. When former president Millard Fillmore ran for president in 1856 as the American Party's nominee, his advocates depicted him as a moderate-tempered centrist who could transcend sectional divisions. John C. Frémont, depicted holding a gun, snarls, "He's a border ruffian! and I'll shoot the Slave-holding Villain!" Buchanan, wielding the dagger, counters, "Let go! Let me at him! I'll make Mince meat of the rascally abolitionist!" As Fillmore separates the two, he pleads "Stop! Stop! My friends, I cant allow any fighting, there must be peace between you as long as I stand here."

justice, Robert Grier, whom Buchanan pressured, and Fillmore would not have done that. I do not think Fillmore would have been nearly as desperate as Buchanan to bring Kansas in as a state. Had the Lecompton Constitution been written, Fillmore would have opposed it and tried to use the weight of the administration against it. And based on how Fillmore responded to a threat of a shooting civil war in New Mexico in 1850, with federal troops, I think he would have had the army out in Kansas in as much force as it could muster to keep the peace there. Hence the army

would not have been sent to Utah against the Mormons as they were under Buchanan, it would have stayed in Kansas. So, things would have been
different, but it is a "what if" question.

AUDIENCE MEMBER: There is another parallel to Buchanan and Fillmore.
They were both energetic leaders in their communities. Fillmore would
have had the same opportunity to intervene in the *Dred Scott* case as Buchanan did. One of the Supreme Court justices, Samuel Nelson, was from
Cooperstown, New York, and voted with Roger Taney and the Court's
majority. So, Fillmore might have had that opportunity.

HOLT: I do not think Fillmore would have intervened with the Supreme
Court. He had a Whig conception of the presidency, one of passivity.

QUIST: One of the other issues associated with Buchanan is secession,
which began shortly after Lincoln won the 1860 election. Buchanan remains president until March 4, 1861, when Lincoln finally takes the presidential oath. By that time seven states had seceded from the Union. Could
James Buchanan have done anything to slow the secession train that began
following Lincoln's election?

HOLT: Let me say two things about this. First, it seems to me that the
person who could have slowed secession, and failed to do so, was the president-elect, who was bombarded with pleas to do more than he did to reassure Southerners. I think Lincoln was far more culpable than Buchanan in
that regard. Second, most people see secession as James Buchanan's worst
moment. I recollect that in 1991 we had a panel with Ken Stampp and Robert Johannsen. Both of them considered the secession crisis Buchanan's
finest hour as president.[5] If you look at what Lincoln did when he came
in he did the same damn thing; he just waited for something to happen.

FREEHLING: With his secession crisis miscues, as with his *Dred Scott* fiasco, James Buchanan displayed the reverse of his supposed errant waiting.
Historians accuse him of not intervening fast enough to deter or isolate
South Carolina. But only five days after Major Robert Anderson moved
his federal troops in the Charleston area from Fort Moultrie to Fort Sumter, Buchanan made his fateful decision. Before discerning whether Robert

Anderson needed guns or men or food, the president ordered a federal ship, the *Star of the West*, to penetrate inside Charleston harbor, to reinforce Fort Sumter. A note from Anderson, declaring that he did not need immediate help, arrived at the White House just after the *Star* left port. Buchanan then tried, too late, to abort the provoking mission. In contrast, Lincoln would delay over six weeks before making the same decision to reinforce Fort Sumter, and he would decide only after discerning that Anderson needed immediate reinforcement.

Buchanan's rush to decision could not have come at a worse time. When he prematurely dispatched the *Star*, only South Carolina had seceded. Five other Lower South states would vote on secession during the next three weeks. Before Buchanan decided to dispatch the *Star*, the pivotal issue in those elections involved secession's expediency. The debate over expediency especially focused on an uncertain question: Would Lincoln immediately menace slavery? The uncertainty yielded closely fought election campaigns.

Lower South contests over secession rarely remained close after Buchanan decided to send the *Star*. The president's military aggression changed the issue from the *expediency* to the *right* of secession. Few in the Lower South denied a state's *right* to withdraw its citizens' consent to federal governance. That right was sacred because coercive government without consent was an essence of slavery. Lower South citizens would not sit idly by while Buchanan sent guns to enslave neighboring whites.

Worse, enslavement of whites—of *them*—almost instantly seemed to threaten *their* neighborhoods. Thanks to another coincidence, having nothing to do with the slavery issue, the telegraph had newly provided instant communication. Telegraph wires sped Buchanan's decision to send the *Star* down to the Lower South a week before the ship sailed. Then the wires supplied secret coordination for five Lower South governors' plot to seize federal military installations in their states, lest Buchanan reinforce these potential means of white enslavement too. The governors' provocative seizures, almost all successful and occurring before their states embraced secession, inspired headlines that voters literally took to the polls, as they decided the new question that Buchanan had blundered into raising: Should we repudiate our brave boys who had deterred the federal tyrant? The voters' potent answer emphasized the impotency of that one federal ship, sailing into cannon-infested Charleston harbor toward Fort Sumter. The *Star of the West* suffered two shots and then retreated.

AUDIENCE MEMBER: He should have sent ten ships.

FREEHLING: He did not have ten ships. [audience laughter]

AUDIENCE MEMBER: Perhaps Buchanan did not have the real feeling for a situation that we might have today with television and instant communication. You may be quite correct that Buchanan thought he was making a strong, calculated act—one that he hoped would be perceived the right way, and it was simply understood the wrong way. But in thinking about your opening statement, we should always remember the things we cannot count on, as well as coincidences. We cannot always correctly guess how other people will respond to our actions. It would have been easy for Buchanan to misjudge in that very difficult time and place.

FREEHLING: You wisely note that when Buchanan made mistakes, it was always with the right intentions. The counterproductive results were a classic case of unintended consequences. Buchanan, like most human beings, tried to do what he thought was best. But as can happen to us all, the things not understood resulted in the worst outcome.

AUDIENCE MEMBER: My name is Bob King, I am in the history field and work for the National Park Service. I think that Buchanan's approach to the presidency is reflective of how the Southern way of thought dominated the political and social process. When President John Quincy Adams promoted internal improvements and tried to press in another direction, he was rebuked. He tried to act contrary to the Southern political thinking that then pervaded national politics. I think Buchanan was a product of this world. At heart Buchanan was a Southerner like Jackson.

QUIST: Mr. King says that Buchanan reflected contemporary Southern politics. Was there a Northern style of politics and a Southern style of politics during the antebellum years? Or were politics in both sections more similar than different?

HOLT: I will go first because this is one issue on which Bill and I disagree. I think that those who argue that Southern politics were vastly different from the Northern style of politics are wrong. Historians who do so often use South Carolina as their Southern example. There was a South Carolina style of politics and then there was everybody else. If you exclude South Carolina, a state that was really very weird, as they did not have a popular election for president until after the Civil War, I think there were strong parallels between Northern and Southern politics. Bill and I were talking about this as we drove up today, and we agreed that this is one area where we need much more work than we now have. The people who either assert the similarities or assert the differences generally work on only one section or one state in a section, whereas you [Quist] in your book on antebellum reform actually compared Alabama and Michigan.[6] We need many more such direct comparisons. I am not going to bore you with names, but I can think of fairly recent books on Mississippi, South Carolina, and a few other states that stress the differences, which I think are simply false.

FREEHLING: I would like to address Mr. King's other point: that Buchanan was a Northern man with Jackson's Southern principles. I'm not sure whether Andrew Jackson would have favored Northern or Southern principles in that ultimate test of allegiances, the Civil War. But I know how Buchanan chose. The Pennsylvanian's secession crisis presidential messages sharply distinguished between the wrongful coercion of states and the rightful enforcement of the laws against individual rebels. In pursuit of lawless individuals, Buchanan dispatched the *Star*. Lincoln made a parallel choice with the same Northern logic.

The error that Buchanan was still more Southern than Northern feeds on a false dichotomy between North and South. Vast differences distinguished between the farthest North, the farthest South, and the northern and southern borderlands between. Most Americans in the nation's geographic middle wished above all else to save the Union from the extremes. They would go out of their way to appease the South, to preclude secession. But if appeasement failed, they would not permit disunion. That Unionist priority dominated the Border South slave states and that supreme Border North Unionist, James Buchanan. When he acted on the borderlands' truest allegiance, his Southern cabinet members quit. This was a Southern toady?

KING: I am not trying to say that he was a toady of the South. I am sure he was a strong Unionist, but the man did not like the Republican Party, which had its strength in the North. He never went into New England, and he did not like New Englanders. On the Lecompton Constitution he favored a side that was vastly a minority within the boundaries of Kansas. He was out of touch with Northern opinion. Maybe it was because many of his close friends were Southern and his ideas were similar to some of the ideas that influenced Pierce, that influenced Polk and Tyler, and they agreed with the Southern idea of what the country should be like.

HOLT: Could I ask you a question? Why do you think a commitment to states' rights, strict construction principles, which was the Democratic Party line, is Southern? That is certainly the reason that Pierce acted the way he did.

KING: Well, yes. I will argue then that Buchanan was somewhat of a states' rights man even though he was president. You could be a strong states' rights person and still be a strong Unionist, as long as the Union is being run the way the states' rights people want it.

QUIST: Mike and Bill, your thoughts on Northern and Southern politics raise another question. Were the antebellum North and South equally small-d democratic, for white men that is? Did the same kind of small-d democracy operate in both sections? Was one section more democratic for whites than the other?

HOLT: I looked at every congressional election in districts around the country from 1832 to 1856 in a book I wrote about the Whigs.[7] There was an extraordinary difference between Northern and Southern politics. I do not know if it makes it more democratic or not, but if you examine the size of the electoral turnout in congressional elections in the North by district, it will be eleven thousand to thirteen thousand people. In many Southern districts, because of the three-fifths rule, there would be less than a thousand people voting in congressional elections. If participation in the system is an index of how democratic it was, then I would suggest that, yes, the North was more democratic than the South.

QUIST: Bill, you have addressed this question in your most recent book.[8] What differences do you see between the North and South regarding small-d democracy and freedom of expression?

FREEHLING: Michael earlier made the important point that South Carolina differed from every state, North and South, on the question of small-d democracy, for white men only. Voters in South Carolina did not elect the governor, did not elect presidential electors, did not elect sheriffs, did not elect judges, did not elect anybody but their state legislators, who had to have large property holdings and selected everybody else. No other state in the Union selected its leaders so aristocratically. Moreover, every other state relished the small-d democratic national party system, with two partisan organizations battling for popular adulation and office. South Carolinians could not abide that "mobocratic" stuff. The point is crucial because large-A—for Aristocratic—South Carolinians first precipitated the small-d democracy South into disunion, precisely because the peculiar Carolinians feared that everyone else's "mobocracy" would destroy such an aristocratic institution as slavery.

On another corner of the small-d democratic issue, South Carolina joined the rest of the South in damming the Northern gospel that every issue should be openly and freely discussed. Southerners favored a wide-open democracy on every issue *except* slavery. The imperatives of a slavery system, they thought, required that the full-discussion imperative of a small-d democratic system must be partially suspended on that one subject, lest slaves and even non-slaveholders be exposed to "incendiary" ideas. Southerners wanted the slavery topic silenced nationally as well as at home. In contrast, Northern small-d democrats loathed the silencers' undemocratic impact on the national democratic system.

The Gag Rule controversy especially well illustrated how the issue of black slavery often involved the issue of small-d democracy. In 1835 and 1836 the emerging issue was whether abolitionists could petition Congress on slavery-related issues and have their petitions debated. The South said "No! You cannot petition Congress about slavery or have the petitions discussed." Congress then passed the Gag Rule, silencing all congressional discussion of slavery. Buchanan took the Southern side on the gag, realizing how divisive slavery discussion could be. For ten years the Gag Rule controversy served as the big slavery issue in American politics, with the North crying that the South interfered with the political rights of white men by silencing discussion. The cry exemplified Michael's point that the controversy over slavery affected the rights of white men, enraging many Northern whites more than Southern exploitation of slaves.

The gag rule disappeared in 1845. But every subsequent slavery issue centrally involved whether the Northern necessities of small-d democracy for white citizens could be reconciled with the Southern necessities for dictatorial control over black slaves. Controversies over the undemocratic return of fugitive slaves, over undemocratic territorial governance in Kansas, and over cracking open the South for the Republican Party's democratic agitation against slavery—all this travail spun from collisions between slavery and democracy as ruling systems. The grinding impact of this partial North/South division over small-d democracy, together with the impact of South Carolina's more sweeping war with white men's "mobocracy," ultimately tore the national fabric so extensively as to leave James Buchanan little room for error.

QUIST: Let's turn to the audience.

AUDIENCE MEMBER: As a history junkie since elementary school, and as someone who has visited Wheatland twice and read James Buchanan's autobiography,[9] I agree that he really faced a huge crisis before the Civil War. Buchanan thought that both the abolitionists and the secessionists were a threat to the stability of the Union, but I also believe that he did what he thought was best to keep the country together. I believe that while he made some mistakes, we are all human beings and human beings make mistakes. Buchanan concludes in his book that he did not mean anything but well for his country and his countrymen and he thought that what he was doing was best. Buchanan's account views the country's problems differently than how historians have described them.

QUIST: It sounds as though you believe that historians have not been fair to James Buchanan. He did his best, and historians have not appreciated that he did his best.

AUDIENCE MEMBER: I am saying that.

HOLT: Could I comment on that question? Jean Baker, who has written a brief biography of Buchanan, may comment.[10] The nooses are coming out, Jean! [audience laughter] But there is something else shaping Buchanan's thinking during the secession crisis, and that was the hope that Congress could work out some kind of compromise. After all, Congress had worked out a compromise in 1820, they had worked out a compromise in 1832–33, and they had worked out a compromise in 1850. I do not think it was unreasonable on his part to hope that compromise would happen again; stalling for time should not rock the boat and may have been the best strategy. Don Fehrenbacher has pointed out, however, that all those other compromises that Congress worked out addressed problems that first arose in Congress, and therefore Congress could settle them. The real problem in 1860–61, though, was that the South would not accept the election of a Republican president. It was not a congressional problem, it was something else. But it does seem unlikely that Buchanan thought that way. He may well have been hoping that Congress could work out a compromise, given the success of previous compromises.

WILLIAM P. MACKINNON: You raised the question about whether James Buchanan could have been renominated by his party. In his inaugural address on March 4, 1857, Buchanan announced he would not run for the presidency again. One could raise the question about whether a president taking office makes a terrible mistake in announcing, on the very day of his inauguration, that he will not run for a second term. The other thing on which I would like to comment regards Bill's use of the word *coincidence*. Not only was the belt buckle incident in John Brown's capture an interesting one, in that Robert E. Lee, the lieutenant colonel of a United States Army Cavalry Regiment based in San Antonio, Texas, was in Harpers Ferry, Virginia, because of his being on leave in Virginia to settle the estate of his father-in-law, George Washington Park Custis. Lee happened to be sitting outside the door of Secretary of War John Floyd's office when the news of the raid came in. Floyd rushed out, saw Lee sitting outside his office, grabbed a hold of him, and told Lee to get over to the Washington Navy Yard, scoop up all the marines he could find, and go to Harpers Ferry. So, there was another coincidence too.

MAURY KLEIN: Just one small point. I agree with Bill Freehling regarding Buchanan's being strong in making the decision to reinforce Fort Sumter, but you ought to have noted that Buchanan made an even stronger decision, just before that one, in which he decided not to send troops back to Fort Moultrie. And that was the most important decision, because if he had caved on that one the events would have turned out very differently.

FREEHLING: I am reluctant to disagree with Mr. Klein on any aspect of the Fort Sumter story, for he has written a marvelous book on the topic.[11] But no sensible president could have ordered Major Anderson to retreat to Fort Moultrie. That meager fort, unlike massive Fort Sumter, sits in an exposed place, easy to conquer because of a sand hill right above it. Any president who ordered Anderson back would have started the Civil War right there, with rebel sharpshooters slaughtering every Yankee in Fort Moultrie who failed to surrender quickly.

JEAN BAKER: By the time Buchanan had the opportunity to send Anderson back to Fort Moultrie the South Carolinian militias had already taken it over. And surely, as our distinguished commentators have already said, that would have started the war.

AUDIENCE MEMBER: I am quite sure that slavery was an issue in the Civil War, but I would be interested in hearing a little background on the economic issues of that decade, and how economic issues might have influenced the policies of that time, and have perhaps led to Civil War.

HOLT: Historians once argued that anger at protective tariffs motivated secession, or that fewer federal subsidies for internal improvements fueled Southern anger and pushed Southerners toward secession. Historians no longer accept these arguments. I might rephrase what you said a little bit differently, though. Economic issues and their influence on policy did not have that much to do with the war. But as we know, the absolute indispensable trigger for Deep South secession was Abraham Lincoln's election as president. So, then we ask, to what extent did economic policy issues in the Republican platform help account for Lincoln's election in 1860? Historian James Huston argues that the tariff issue was quite significant in Pennsylvania and New Jersey, both of which the Republicans had failed to carry in 1856 but carried in 1860. The Republicans also endorsed a Homestead bill, which Buchanan vetoed. So, Republicans expressed a clear difference from the Democratic Party on an issue that was important to many western farmers, or those who were thinking of moving further west to get cheaper land.

I hardly think that economic issues were the most important explanation for why people voted for Lincoln, but they were important. They were probably less important than something else, which we have not mentioned at all. People favorable toward the Buchanan administration may not wish to hear it, but congressional committees exposed the Buchanan administration as the most corrupt one since the Constitution. Republicans ran against corruption. Michael Burlingame, the author of a new two-volume biography of Lincoln,[12] is absolutely convinced that the corruption issue, and nothing else, elected Lincoln—which was why Republicans were so appalled when Lincoln appointed Simon Cameron to his cabinet.

FREEHLING: When we talk about economic issues OR slavery issues, we broadcast another false dichotomy. The continuation of slavery was, among other things, the nation's most important economic issue, involving the country's largest capital investment and greatest source of exports. Not just slaveholders but also everybody who traded with a slaveholder, everybody who served as a physician for a slaveholder, everybody who served as an overseer for a slaveholder had a profound economic stake in the regime. Economics also helps explain why South Carolina became the capital of Southern extremism. South Carolina had the South's largest concentrations of investments in slave labor and in the internal improvements necessary to make slavery profitable.

Still, the state had not matched the rest of the South's recovery from the depression of the 1840s. South Carolinians thought they were smarter than anybody else, more aristocratic than anybody else, more patriotic than anybody else, and yet their economy was weaker than everybody else's. Theirs was a provoked position—to feel yourself growing poorer than all your supposed inferiors, when they are growing powerful enough to make all the wrong decisions for the South. From that fury—fueled, in part, by economic declension—emerged South Carolina's 1860 explosion.

QUIST: So far we have discussed economics, politics, and slavery. Does religion have anything to do with the coming of the Civil War?

HOLT: Here I have to revert to my first book,[13] when I was in the throes of all that ethno-cultural analysis. Again, if we go back to the events that led to the outbreak of war, the election of a Republican president is a key. In certain parts of the North, where it paid off, Republicans attacked Democrats as being a pro-Catholic party and posed as defenders of Protestantism. The leading Republican newspaper in Pittsburgh (which was really one of the leading Republican newspapers west of the Allegheny Mountains), the *Pittsburgh Gazette*, ran editorials continuously in 1860 reminding readers that Douglas had a Catholic wife, and predicted that if Stephen Douglas were elected, then another Catholic inquisition would ensue. So, Protestantism, or fear and hatred of Catholics, was a reason, in some places, why people voted for Lincoln and the Republicans. Other historians agree with this reasoning, but many historians do not. But that is how I would put religion into it.

FREEHLING: Buchanan believed that too much religious fanaticism, and especially a resulting abolitionist fanaticism, infested the country. We say that without slavery, there would have been no civil war. He said that without abolitionist extremism, there would have been no secessionist extremism. That may sounds like the religious side of a Northern man with Southern principles. Remember, however, that a good half of Northerners, including many moderate Republicans, were deeply affected by the new Protestant imperatives and yet had no use for antislavery extremists.

AUDIENCE MEMBER: My name is Brian Forbes, and this question is for Dr. Holt. I am very glad that you raised the issue about corruption in the Buchanan administration. Why this corruption happened has always puzzled me. I do not think anybody doubts that Buchanan was a man of integrity, and I assume he was not involved in any of this corruption, but certainly men in his administration were. And I believe that you have written about the evidence discovered by Republicans in Congress that the administration bribed some members of Congress to vote for the Lecompton Constitution, among other things. A congressional investigation documented this very sorry record of graft and bribery. So why did he let that happen? Did he know what was occurring, or was he just asleep at the helm?

HOLT: That is an interesting question. I am not sure. Let me give you a counterintuitive answer. I have taken on the job of writing a short biography of Franklin Pierce in the same series as Jean Baker's biography of Buchanan.[14] Pierce had many faults, but he ran a squeaky clean administration, and there were no charges of peculation. I think many co-riders with the Democratic Party, once Buchanan came in, saw a chance to raid the Treasury and submitted inflated bills to the federal government. Whether it was real corruption or not, we do not know. But corruption was, as Bill MacKinnon well knows, involved with the expenditures on that army expedition out to Utah, thanks to Secretary of War John Floyd. Cornelius Wendell, the printer of the *Washington Union* and the printer for Congress, ran up egregious cost overruns and then kicked the money back to local Democratic machines. So, my best guess is that Buchanan did not exercise the kind of oversight that Pierce did. Achieving honesty in government was one of the things that Pierce most wanted to do. There had been scandals under both Zachary Taylor and Millard Fillmore, and Pierce probably provided more oversight than did Buchanan. But of course it has been proven that Buchanan tried to buy votes for the Lecompton Constitution with federal cash.

FORBES: Just to follow up on your response. Does that raise questions about Buchanan's administrative ability? This was the man, whose nickname was "Old Public Functionary" because of his long experience in government, and yet he gets to the office of the presidency and he does not seem to manage his administration very well.

HOLT: Your question raises ones that I will defer to my friend, Jean Baker.

JEAN BAKER: Part of the explanation lies with this interesting relationship that James Buchanan has with his cabinet. We all know that four of those seven cabinet members were slaveholders from the South, and he was greatly influenced by what they told him, and some of things that they told him led to this terrible corruption that took place during his administration.

DANIEL CROFTS: I find the Buchanan administration's corruption to be something of a puzzle. Here is, in many ways, the most qualified person who had ever become president and, as Bill Freehling and Jean Baker have pointed out, he was an activist president. The knock on him as a passive, hands-off leader who never took control does not seem to fit. And yet, on this issue of corruption, the guy seems to have been flat-out blind. Many people knew that [Secretary of War] John Floyd was fully incompetent, but somehow Buchanan could not bring himself to fire the guy until the very end—and then he would not even do it himself. He tries to get [Attorney General] Jeremiah Black to send the word to Floyd that he better take an exit at this point, and Floyd, damn it, would not even do it. So, he was still sitting there in the middle of the Sumter crisis, and then he uses that crisis as a kind of fig leaf to try to escape, saying that he was resigning on principle instead of resigning in disgrace.

FREEHLING: Dan Crofts here provides fine perspective on Buchanan's activism and passivism. I have urged that the image of Buchanan's overriding inertia requires reconsideration. Witness the president's handling of the *Dred Scott* and *Star of the West* affairs. Yet Buchanan did allow his subordinates a free hand to blunder at the Lecompton convention. As Dan now points out, members of his cabinet had an equally free hand to bungle corrupt patronage affairs. So a rounded portrait must show that this president erratically swayed between excessive aggressiveness and excessive quiescence, each at inappropriate moments. The immense pressures of the slavery issue caused much of this erratic leadership. The patronage problems, however, had nothing to do with the slavery problems. So why did this richly experienced politician bring impoverished executive skills to the White House?

MACKINNON: The answer, in part, to this puzzling issue of corruption runs to the issue of background and preparation for the presidency. Buchanan was magnificently prepared, well educated, went through the Pennsylvania legislature, both Houses of Congress, secretary of state under Polk, ambassador to Russia, ambassador to the Court of St. James. None of those were managerial or executive positions. He was never responsible for anybody else other than maybe a secretary. He had no executive or managerial experience, so he did a very poor job of controlling John Floyd, who, as Dan Crofts points out, was grossly negligent if not corrupt in his administration of everything. Montgomery C. Meigs, who was the army engineer responsible for the Washington aqueduct and heating system in the Capitol and the Capitol dome's construction, and both Houses of Congress's expansion, was driven to distraction by the corruption that Floyd forced on him, and he went to Buchanan at one point and could not get the president to do anything about it. Buchanan had no experience confronting corruption, and that was dealing with organizations and people who needed to be managed and disciplined.

AUDIENCE MEMBER: Do you know if states had the right to secede?

HOLT: No. And William Tecumseh Sherman proved it to them. [audience laughter]

AUDIENCE MEMBER: I was interested in the topic about compromise discussed earlier. What sorts of options were open for compromise to Buchanan during his administration? In 1848 he advocated just extending the Missouri Compromise line to the Pacific as Lewis Cass, Daniel Dickinson, and George Dallas advocated popular sovereignty. In 1854, of course, the Kansas-Nebraska Act ruins popular sovereignty by negating the Missouri Compromise line. What sectional compromises would have been plausible during the Buchanan administration?

HOLT: This is complicated. Why was the territorial issue the focus of attempts to compromise in the secession crisis when, in a sense, it was a dead issue? There was no chance that slavery was going to expand into any territory that it was not already allowed to enter. It is very long and it would take too long to answer, but I would just tell you something else. If you draw the 36°30' line and extend it to the Pacific Ocean, as Buchanan wanted to do in the 1840s, it would hit the Pacific Ocean at the eighteenth fairway at the Pebble Beach Golf Course. [audience laughter]

FREEHLING: Lincoln and Seward believed that secession crisis statesmen should move from the intractable territorial issue to more easily compromised problems, such as the fugitive slave difficulty and the proposed thirteenth amendment. That amendment declared itself unamendable and decreed that Congress must never interfere with slavery in the states. Congress passed that constitutional amendment on the eve of Lincoln's inauguration. Lincoln endorsed it publicly for the first time in his inaugural address. This version of a thirteenth amendment, if Congress had voted for it and Lincoln had endorsed it months earlier, might have somewhat soothed a South deeply divided over secession, especially if Buchanan had not prematurely ordered the *Star of the West* to sail. But Lincoln's delaying on compromise and Buchanan's precipitancy on the *Star*—a deadly combination—precluded any chance that a national compromise could deter secessionists' victory from spreading beyond South Carolina.

QUIST: Do you agree, Bill, with Michael's position that Lincoln should have done more to reassure the South during the lame-duck phase of the Buchanan administration?

FREEHLING: I agree with Michael. My next book, to be entitled *Lincoln's Growth*, will urge that the Lincoln of the secession crisis had some growing to do, before he could emerge as our greatest president.

HOLT: Could I just add one word? The evidence is fairly clear that Lincoln was behind this proposed thirteenth amendment and that he got Seward, through Thurlow Weed, to introduce it into a Senate committee. Lincoln's biggest mistake was keeping his role, and his sponsorship of that amendment, secret. Had he made his positions public the whole air would have gone out of the territorial issue. Since 1846 Southerners had been complaining and worrying that if the country obtained new territory, and if slavery were to be prohibited from that territory, then there would be seventeen or eighteen new free states. Eventually, the South feared that the North would amend the Constitution to abolish slavery. The proposed thirteenth amendment would have taken all the air out of that threat because, had it passed, it could never have been amended to allow the abolition of slavery.

PAUL FINKELMAN: I just have to say that I think you are both completely wrong, but I will restrict myself to this very last point. Under the Constitution it takes three-quarters of the States to amend the Constitution. If the fifteen slave states remained in the United States, to this day, you could not end slavery with a constitutional amendment because you would need forty-five free states to outvote the fifteen slave states that existed in 1860.

So, to argue, as Michael has just done, that there was a credible real threat, that there could be enough Northern states to ever end slavery, is incorrect.

HOLT: I did not say it was credible.

FINKELMAN: To believe, in 1860, that there was any plausible threat to slavery's being constitutionally abolished would have required a sixty-state Union, and Southerners know this. So, to make the argument that you need an un-amendable amendment is wrong. The idea of an un-amendable amendment is, of course, a non sequitur in constitutional theory, because all you have to do is pass an amendment to amend the un-amendable part. Then you can amend it and it is amendable. There is no such thing as an un-amendable amendment. It is wrong to make the argument that the United States has to guarantee more to the South than the Constitution already does. Lincoln stated in his inaugural address that he had no power to touch slavery where it existed, and anybody who understands legal and constitutional theory understands this point. So, to accept at face value that the Republicans threatened slavery is to buy into the secessionist arguments that had been floating around since the Continental Congress. Congressman John Lynch from South Carolina threatened, in 1777, to leave the Union if Northerners threatened Southerners' slave property. And they had been making that threat over and over and over again.

Buchanan could have headed off secession if he had the resolute backbone to stand up to the secessionists and say, "Not on my watch does the United States become smaller as a nation." Remember, he is the only president who leaves office with the nation's being smaller than when he entered office. It is not the problem of compromising. Instead, it is the problem that for once the president stares down the secessionists and says, "No, we are not giving in to your treasonous notions that you can destroy the Union because you lost an election and you do not like the outcome." I really think that there is strong evidence for all of this, and so that is where I think you are wrong, Bill.

FREEHLING: The notion that the secessionists would have been terrified because James Buchanan said "Not on my watch" strikes me as preposterous. [audience laughter]

FINKELMAN: That may be true.

HOLT: Paul, I think your count is right, that it would take forty-five States—although, of course, Southerners believed that slavery was gravely endangered in Delaware and Maryland, and increasingly in Kentucky, and the count might have been different. All I can say is that if you read the debates in Congress about the territory that is acquired from Mexico, Southerner after Southerner after Southerner makes that argument: that unless we win the right to take slavery into the territories, they will all become free states [and] then they will amend the Constitution to abolish slavery.

FINKELMAN: I understand they make those arguments, but what politicians say on the floor of Congress—ah, need I say more? [audience laughter]

HOLT: No!

QUIST: And with that we should probably end it this evening. Thank you very much for coming. Thank you also to Michael Holt and Bill Freehling. [audience applause]

Notes

1. Michael F. Holt, *The Political Crisis of the 1850s* (New York: Wiley, 1978).

2. Lee Benson, *The Concept of Jacksonian Democracy: New York as a Test Case* (Princeton: Princeton University Press, 1961).

3. Michael Fitzgibbon Holt, *Forging a Majority: The Formation of the Republican Party in Pittsburgh, 1848–1860* (New Haven: Yale University Press, 1969).

4. David M. Potter, *The Impending Crisis, 1848–1861* (New York: Harper and Row, 1976), 297.

5. Michael J. Birkner, moderator, "James Buchanan and the Political Crisis of the 1850s: A Panel Discussion," *Pennsylvania History* 60 (July 1993): 281–83.

6. John W. Quist, *Restless Visionaries: The Social Roots of Antebellum Reform in Alabama and Michigan* (Baton Rouge: Louisiana State University Press, 1998).

7. Michael F. Holt, *The Rise and Fall of the American Whig Party* (New York: Oxford University Press, 1999).

8. William W. Freehling, *The Road to Disunion*, vol. 2, *Secessionists Triumphant, 1854–1861* (New York: Oxford University Press, 2007).

9. James Buchanan, *Mr. Buchanan's Administration on the Eve of the Rebellion* (New York: D. Appleton and Company, 1866).

10. Jean H. Baker, *James Buchanan* (New York: Times Books, 2004).

11. Maury Klein, *Days of Defiance: Sumter, Secession, and the Coming of the Civil War* (New York: Knopf, 1997).

12. Michael Burlingame, *Abraham Lincoln: A Life*, 2 vols. (Baltimore: Johns Hopkins University Press, 2008).

13. Holt, *Forging a Majority*.

14. Michael F. Holt, *Franklin Pierce* (New York: Times Books, 2010).

Epilogue

Buchanan's Civil War

MICHAEL J. BIRKNER

If James Buchanan uttered any memorable line during the Civil War era, it was doubtless the one he purportedly expressed to Abraham Lincoln on Inauguration Day, March 4, 1861. "My dear sir, if you are as happy in entering the White House as I shall feel on returning to Wheatland, you are a happy man indeed."[1] Like other retired presidents, Buchanan had an opportunity to focus on pursuits unrelated to politics. Community members welcomed him, and local institutions, including Franklin and Marshall College, periodically sought his counsel or beneficence. Buchanan's estate, along with his finances, needed the attention that he was at last prepared to give. The stresses of daily decision making in the White House were behind him. Although the ex-president could not look forward to a lucrative book contract, seats on corporate boards, or large speaking fees, his situation in 1861 was comfortable. A small staff, dominated by Buchanan's housekeeper, "Miss Hetty," kept things running smoothly for a sociable bachelor who loved nothing more than to entertain.[2]

Unlike James K. Polk, the president he served during the 1840s as secretary of state, Buchanan actually left the White House in better physical condition than he entered it. This development is unsurprising, given Buchanan's affliction in March 1857 with what Roy F. Nichols has called "National Hotel Disease," so denominated because of the dysentery the president-elect contracted during the weeks leading up to his inauguration.[3] Departing Washington after Lincoln's inauguration, Buchanan was escorted by a Lancaster citizens' committee. He made a well-received speech in Baltimore; then, as he arrived home, he briefly addressed a

Figure E.1. James Buchanan in retirement. Courtesy of LancasterHistory.org.

military company that escorted him into his domicile. According to one contemporary account, Buchanan "regretted that having just reached his home, he was not prepared to entertain them. The doors of his house had been always open, the latch-string was out. At any other time" when his visitors felt disposed to call, they "should receive a very cordial welcome." Later in the evening, Buchanan was serenaded by local musical groups.[4]

Subsequently Buchanan settled into a regular and generally pleasant regimen. He took quiet walks, examined the conditions of his estate, and kept in touch as best he could with former cabinet officers, both about what had been done during the secession crisis under his watch, and beyond, into the Lincoln presidency. Before Sumter fell to Confederate fire in April, he enjoyed spending time at the Grapes Tavern or conversing with friends at Lancaster's Lawyers' Row. Once federal forces had been forced to capitulate at Sumter, however, Buchanan became the target of what one of his biographers has called "ugly mutterings" and nasty correspondence. There is no question that Republicans in the North viewed Buchanan in the darkest terms.[5]

For much of the next four years, the war—"Buchanan's War," some called it—would dominate the news and ultimately reshape the meaning of American nationhood. While on the sidelines as the great conflict played out, the ex-president kept abreast of everything. In quiet ways, behind the scenes, he also attempted to influence the affairs of his beloved Democratic Party in Pennsylvania. Much of his intellectual energy, however, was devoted to self-justification. Firmly convinced that his handling of the secession crisis was judicious—neither too aggressive nor supine in sustaining federal authority at Sumter—Buchanan spent many hours in his book-lined study at Wheatland organizing documents to sustain his self-image as a "steady," wise, and patriotic chief executive. As he told James G. Bennett, "I feel conscious that I have done my duty . . . & that I shall at last receive justice."[6] According to George Ticknor Curtis, Buchanan began collecting material for his defense "soon after his retirement to Wheatland." By 1862 he vowed to publish a full-bore defense of his presidency, a project he held in abeyance during the war because, he said, he did not want to engage in partisan politics. *Mr. Buchanan's Administration on the Eve of the Rebellion* saw print through the auspices of a New York publisher in early 1866 and in Buchanan's estimation enjoyed robust sales.[7] Not surprisingly, the Republican press did not think much of the elderly ex-president's apologia.[8]

About his successor Buchanan was of two minds. One the one hand, Abraham Lincoln was a "black Republican," emphatically hostile to slavery and committed to putting the peculiar institution on the road to ultimate extinction. Yet at the same time Lincoln faced challenges that Buchanan could empathize with. Buchanan found Lincoln's "plain, sincere and frank" persona appealing. The sixteenth president's efforts to restore the Union he heartily endorsed.

Buchanan expressed none of the vitriol toward Lincoln that former president Franklin Pierce uttered privately and, by 1863, publicly.[9] Buchanan spoke of Lincoln as "a man of honest heart & true manly feelings" and "an honest and patriotic man."[10] He added that Lincoln's policies before the firing on Sumter were appropriately "pacific" and expressed on several occasions his hopes that Lincoln would succeed in putting down the rebellion. Prior to the firing on Sumter, Buchanan told Joseph Holt that he hoped Lincoln would "make an enviable name for himself & perhaps restore the union."[11] Convinced that secession was illegal, Buchanan endorsed Lincoln's decision to reinforce Sumter as well as his call for troops to suppress the rebellion once the South Carolinians attacked and took the fort. As he wrote to former treasury secretary John A. Dix, "the present [Lincoln] administration had no alternative but to accept the war initiated by South Carolina or the Southern Confederacy. The North will sustain the administration almost to a man; and it ought to be sustained at all hazards."[12]

Buchanan expressed his patriotic sentiments in a moment of heightened alarm and emergency for the nation. But his were not the words of a sunshine patriot. An examination of the former president's correspondence during the Civil War demonstrates Buchanan's consistent support of the war effort. On April 26, 1861, in a letter to a friend, he called the firing on Sumter "an outrageous act" that would have provoked from him the same action that Lincoln had taken.[13] In July he observed to his friendly associate, former assistant postmaster general Horatio King, that "The assault upon Fort Sumter was the commencement of war by the Confederate states, and no alternative was left but to prosecute it with vigor on our part."[14] To accept Southern secession, he told Charles Manley, would be a "disgrace." He avowed to this pro-Southern friend that the Union was in a "deadly struggle" with a "formidable assailant."[15] And in September, after the Union's embarrassing defeat at Bull Run, he told former Pennsylvania congressman George Leiper, "Every person who has conversed with me knows that I am in favor of sustaining the government in the vigorous prosecution of the war for the restoration of the Union."[16] A defender of the Union he remained.

The phrase "every person who has conversed with me" is noteworthy. Buchanan made no public speeches and sent few public communications through the press expressing these views. One significant exception was a letter he wrote to a committee of citizens of Chester and Lancaster Counties, in September 1861, appealing to them to support the war effort "& join the many thousands of brave & patriotic volunteers who are already in the field." He added that it was their duty to "support the president with all the men & means at the command of the country."[17] As a rule, insofar as

Buchanan engaged in further public discourse, it was not to express opinions about the conduct of the war or the merits of political candidates, but rather to correct what he perceived as errors, distortions, and untruths that regularly cropped up in the press regarding his behavior during the secession crisis. On that subject he could be relentless, bent on vindicating his every decision as president, sometimes in collision with the recollections of key members of his own cabinet.[18]

Why did not Buchanan speak out more frequently and forcefully on the range of political issues facing the Republic? There is no one answer to that question. Surely he worried about pushback from people who found his arguments deficient or who were disposed to dislike him because of past political differences. Part of an answer doubtless lies in Buchanan's belief that the main job of ex-presidents was to tend to their own gardens and avoid engaging in public debate. Or as he put it in a somewhat melancholic letter to a close friend, he was living on the rock at St. Helena—a reference to Napoleon after Waterloo—and it was not seemly for him to be engaged in public controversies.[19] Buchanan, moreover, believed that anything he said would be misconstrued—for example, as an effort to make up for errors of judgment and dereliction of duty that were widely ascribed to him by the Northern press, but which he believed were partisan slanders when they were not simply foolish falsehoods.

When visitors to Wheatland raised the issue of the war, Buchanan did his best to refute misconceptions and what he characterized as lies about his outlook, past and present. J. Ridenour Jr., a staunch Union man, stopped at Wheatland in September 1862 en route to Kentucky to see his son, who had recently lost an arm in a battle. In light of the controversy surrounding Buchanan's presidency, Ridenour pressed his host to outline his position on the key issues of the day. From their extended conversation he concluded that Buchanan believed "this war was brought on by the Southern Rebels" and that once the war was "forced" on President Lincoln, "it was his bounden duty to prosecute the war to a speedy and honorable peace." Ridenour left Wheatland convinced that had Buchanan still occupied the White House "you would have your right arm severed from your body before you would sign a compromise or acknowledge one inch of their infernal Southern Confederacy."[20]

Despite his disclaimer that he was fully retired and not engaged in political activity as ex-president, Buchanan retained his decided loyalty to the

Democratic Party and its creed of strict construction. His correspondence throughout the war years, unsurprisingly, reflects the conviction that if only the country would embrace his notion of constitutionalism, all would be well. At one point deep into the war Buchanan even suggested that if the South would return to the Union on the "old constitutional basis," meaning with slavery intact and protected, all would be forgiven.[21] He never explicitly took note of Lincoln's evolution in thinking about the war's meaning, much less accepted the possibility that a "new birth of freedom" could justify the sacrifice of men and treasure entailed in defending the Union.

Buchanan consequently opposed Lincoln's re-election and offered occasional advice to Democratic office-seekers in Pennsylvania during the war years. For example, he counseled party stalwarts against opposing the draft as unconstitutional. He was satisfied with General George B. McClellan's nomination for president on the Democratic ticket and McClellan's refusal to embrace a peace platform. He hoped for a McClellan victory even as he told friends he did not expect it once Atlanta fell to the Union forces.[22] Yet there is scant documentary evidence that Buchanan ever said or wrote a cross word about his successor. Periodically he recalled his positive feelings about Lincoln in their brief encounter on Inauguration Day 1861. And he was deeply disturbed by Lincoln's assassination. Shortly after Lincoln was assassinated, Buchanan suggested that the South had harmed itself through this awful act, as Lincoln was probably the best hope for quick and meaningful reconciliation between the sections. He did not extend this charitable view to congressional Republicans like Ben Wade, Charles Sumner, or Thaddeus Stevens, all of whom he viewed as seriously misguided in their priorities and lusting for power in Washington.[23]

* * *

Any account of Buchanan's Civil War must take cognizance of his age. Having lived seven decades at the time of his retirement from politics, Buchanan had well earned a season of repose and the chance to enjoy a pleasant daily routine at Wheatland. He took full advantage of his new status, spending hours each day perusing newspapers and public documents, while devoting further hours to correspondence, of which there was no end. His business interests occupied him for many hours most weeks.

But it was not all business. There were also guests to entertain, both relatives and friendly acquaintances, in a near-steady stream at Wheatland. By every account Buchanan welcomed these guests, some of whom (like former attorney general Jeremiah Black and former Pennsylvania governor David R. Porter) were old political associates. Most of his company, however, consisted of an extensive coterie of grandnieces, children of friends, and friends of those nieces and friends' children, who brightened meal times and enlivened his household. Buchanan called them his "young ones" and did his best to model good manners, deportment, and sprightly conversation.[24] He relished opportunities to spend time both at Wheatland and at the Baltimore home of his beloved niece, Harriet Lane Johnston, with whom he maintained a voluminous, chatty correspondence.[25]

Many of Buchanan's letters either begin or close by imploring former political associates and others he cared about to spend time at Wheatland or regretting that his correspondents' ill health or other circumstances prevented such visits. At Christmastime in particular Buchanan craved company. As he told his friend John Blake, a physician, in December 1863, Wheatland had been more "gay" than in previous months, thanks to the "good deal" of company he had enjoyed. A year later he begged Blake to "spend the Christmas holidays with us," while on another Christmas he told Blake that two nieces in the house "have made the house gay and agreeable."[26]

Although Buchanan suffered from intense bouts of what he called "gouty rheumatism," his health through the war was more or less robust, and so were his spirits. Throughout the Civil War years and beyond, Buchanan journeyed most summers to partake of the restorative waters at Bedford Springs in western Pennsylvania for at least two weeks. His letters often mentioned how good he felt for a man of his age, while at the same time expressing awareness that his time on earth was limited and that he was preparing for meeting his maker.[27] Buchanan well understood that a man in his seventies not only had outlived most contemporaries but was also living on borrowed time. His approach was to appreciate each day, hail the arrival of spring and major holidays, and support worthy causes to the greatest extent possible. Good food, wine, cigars, and conversation were equally important to his enjoyment of life.[28]

To be sure, Buchanan could not completely ignore political attacks, or avoid cold stares, when he attended church services, from Lancaster

County Republicans. Because of his wealth and standing, he was importuned for financial assistance from a variety of individuals and institutions. Generous to relatives and other persons he knew well, Buchanan nonetheless had to draw some lines. When a trustee of Dickinson College, Buchanan's alma mater, sought $25,000 to endow a professorship, Buchanan replied that he lacked that kind of money. Besides, he added, he had not enjoyed the kind of experience at Dickinson that would make him feel warmly about the school. Dickinson needed to find another donor.[29] Still, he did make modest financial contributions to Dickinson, as well as to Gettysburg and Franklin and Marshall Colleges.[30] He was generous to his many nieces and nephews. At his own expense, moreover, Buchanan entertained hundreds of guests during his retirement years, some for weeks at a time, without the hint of complaint that accommodating so many visitors created a financial burden. A common refrain in his correspondence was regret that his visitors could not stay longer with him.

*　*　*

While Buchanan, like his predecessor in the White House, remained a devoted Democrat, it must also be said that his partisanship during this turbulent era took on a different complexion than Franklin Pierce's. To be sure, there were points of convergence. Both men spoke and corresponded with fellow Democrats, offering counsel on election tactics and issues to pursue. Both prayed their party could regain control of the Congress and clip the Republicans' wings. Both disliked the idea of emancipation and any restriction on freedom of dissent during the war years. Both were convinced that the country would have been better off with the constitutional arrangement of 1787 still in place.[31]

There were noteworthy divergences as well. If one examines how Pierce lived his Civil War—his activism against the Republicans, his choleric attacks on Lincoln, specifically for the Emancipation Proclamation and the recruitment of black troops—one notices a difference of style and substance from Buchanan. Pierce penned bitter diatribes against Lincoln and the Republicans in 1862 and 1863. Where Buchanan made his peace with emancipation (if not Radical Republicanism), Pierce emphasized that blacks could never benefit from freedom. Where Buchanan saw Lincoln as kind and intelligent, if on certain issues misguided, Pierce viewed Lincoln as a man of "narrow intelligence" and dangerous views.[32]

A war fought to "abolish slavery by arms," Pierce wrote to a political friend after Lincoln issued the Emancipation Proclamation, was "truly treason, flagrant treason to this Constitution." Lincoln, he said, was determined to eliminate states' rights entirely and to "destroy" the rights of eight million Southern whites on behalf of a degraded, inferior race. "Is it too late," he asked, "to stay the reckless march to barbarism to save the remnants of our honor as may warrant as to claim & deserve a place among the civilized people of the earth?"[33]

Pierce viewed the Emancipation Proclamation as unconstitutional, and by one account he was "infuriated" by Lincoln's suspension of habeas corpus and the extension of military law in the North.[34] Further appalled by the arrest and prosecution in the spring of 1863 of Ohio Copperhead Clement L. Vallandigham for calling the war a failure, Pierce determined to say his piece. Invited to address a large Democratic rally in Concord, New Hampshire, in early July 1863, he attacked Lincoln and the war, calling the war "fearful, fruitless [and] fatal." "How futile are all our efforts to maintain the Union by force of arms," he proclaimed—uttering these words just as the telegraph was relaying news of the Union's triumph at Gettysburg. Needless to say, Pierce's speech elicited a hostile response even among many Democrats, and he was for all intents and purposes a pariah even in his own community thereafter.[35]

Buchanan had the good sense to keep his opinions more private, and to make clear to friends that he supported the war effort even as he disagreed with Lincoln's extension of war aims to include freeing slaves and giving a portion of them citizenship rights. As he told one friend early in 1864, Lincoln's main "error" was turning a war for the Union into a campaign for "the subjugation of the Southern States and the destruction of slavery."[36] At dinner parties during travels to Baltimore and Philadelphia, and doubtless in Bedford Springs as well, Buchanan avoided what he called "violent Republicans." He had no difficulty, however, breaking bread with "principal men" across a political spectrum, as well as leading Union generals such as George Gordon Meade.[37] In comparison to Pierce's war, Buchanan's Civil War exemplified discretion and restraint. It thereby better served his reputation. Rather than making mischief by criticizing his successor's actions and the Republicans' policies generally, Buchanan stayed one step removed from contemporary political discussions.

If one is to credit Buchanan with a discretion that Pierce lacked, it must be added that he was not commenting about politics from the vantage of a dispassionate observer. The perspective through which he viewed the coming of the Civil War and his role in the events leading to Fort Sumter was astigmatic. Buchanan was so convinced of his own righteousness that he accepted no responsibility for the bad feelings that contributed to the breakdown of the Union. Nor would he acknowledge that the cost of the great civil war required some broader meaning than simply keeping the old Union intact, with continued and perhaps enhanced protections for slavery.[38] He felt at times like St. Sebastian in bearing up under the arrows directed at him by partisan editors who blamed him for the war and called his actions during the secession crisis borderline treason. Referring to Republican editors' assaults on his stewardship, Buchanan noted, "It required much Christian patience to bear with tranquility the falsehoods now current."[39] Buchanan's favorite phrase in describing his work during the war years—particularly writing, publishing, and promoting his memoir of the secession crisis—was that he was "triumphantly vindicated" by all facts. Only the most narrow-minded doughface could ever accept that he had been "triumphantly vindicated" on his policies and style of presidential leadership.

Convinced that history would treat him better than his contemporaries, Buchanan gave history an assist by telling his side of the story, accompanied by pertinent documents, in *Mr. Buchanan's Administration on the Eve of the Rebellion*. As he put it in a letter to Harriet Lane, the documents he had collected will "justify me in all I did and all I did not do since the election of Mr. Lincoln."[40]

Buchanan did not submit his presidential memoir to his publisher until 1865 because he feared a political backlash and wanted, he said, to avoid any suggestion that he was trying to "embarrass Mr. Lincoln's administration."[41] Written in the third person, the book attempted to justify virtually every act of a tempestuous and, at the time, largely discredited presidency. He portrayed himself as a moderate among extremists. With the major exception of the disappointing close to his tenure in the White House, Buchanan called both his domestic and foreign policy "eminently successful."[42] A reader will need to look hard to find any instance in the book, or in Buchanan's private correspondence, where he felt he had erred.

Buchanan was not blessed by what the great jurist Learned Hand once described as the "spirit of democracy," a spirit that is "not too sure that it is right."[43] He would meet his maker confident, as he told his former navy secretary, Isaac Toucey, that he had nothing to regret and nothing of which to "repent."[44] And, perhaps, nothing more to learn.

Notes

1. Portions of this epilogue are adapted from a lecture delivered at Wheatland on September 5, 2005. Buchanan's quote derives from a transcription of his speech in John Bassett Moore, ed., *The Works of James Buchanan, Comprising His Speeches, State Papers, and Private Correspondence*, 12 vols. (Philadelphia: J. B. Lippincott, 1910), 11:161–62.

2. On the return home see George Ticknor Curtis, *Life of James Buchanan* (New York: Harper & Brothers, 1883), 2:507–10. Buchanan spent considerable time getting his private affairs in order at Wheatland, since they had been "sadly neglected during the last four years." See, for example, his draft letter to Samuel W. Black, April 6, 1861, Buchanan Papers, Reel 51, Historical Society of Pennsylvania. The former chief executive had a diversified portfolio of investments, including real estate, and during the remainder of his life he actively managed them.

3. Roy F. Nichols, *The Disruption of American Democracy* (New York: Collier Books Edition, 1962), 75–76.

4. Moore, *Works of James Buchanan*, 11:162.

5. See Curtis, *Life of James Buchanan*, 511–12 and passim; Philip S. Klein, *President James Buchanan* (University Park: Pennsylvania State University Press, 1962), 408. Klein suggests that attacks on Buchanan grew in number and deeply affected his sense of well-being. For Buchanan's mordant view of "Black" Republicans, see his letter to Gen. George W. Bowman, September 21, 1861, a transcript of which appears in *Profiles in History: Autograph Catalog 48* (Calabasas Hills, Calif., 2011), 14.

6. The original letter is in the Buchanan Papers, Dickinson College. See also Moore, *Works of James Buchanan*, 11:165–66. On his "steady" approach to secession see James Buchanan to Joseph Holt, March 16, 1981, ibid., 171–73.

7. Quote is from Curtis, *Life of James Buchanan*, 2:575. On the origins of the book project see Klein, *President James Buchanan*, 417–18. For Buchanan's upbeat view of the book's appeal, see Buchanan to Dr. John B. Blake, January 19, 1866, in Moore, *Works of James Buchanan*, 11:412–13. Curtis says the book sold five thousand copies.

8. See, for example, "Mr. Buchanan and His Book," *New York Times*, December 1, 1865. For Buchanan's conviction that many of the assaults on his character and policies were a "deliberate policy of the Republican Party," see Klein, *President James Buchanan*, 415.

9. The most informative, if partisan, account of Pierce's Civil War is Peter A. Wallner, *Franklin Pierce: Martyr for the Union* (Concord, N.H.: Plaidswede, 2007), chapter 14. See also Roy Franklin Nichols, *Franklin Pierce: Young Hickory of the Granite Hills*,

rev. ed. (Philadelphia: University of Pennsylvania Press, 1969), 519–23; and Michael F. Holt, *Franklin Pierce* (New York: Henry Holt, 2010), 123–25. For Buchanan's positive assessment of Lincoln's character see his letter to Horatio King, April 27, 1865, in Moore, *Works of James Buchanan*, 11:384–85.

10. Buchanan to Charles V. Pene, December 21, 1861, and Buchanan to John A. Parker, February 3, 1862, quoted in Klein, *President James Buchanan*, 420.

11. Buchanan to Holt, March 16, 1861, in Moore, *Works of James Buchanan*, 11:173.

12. Buchanan to Dix, April 15, 1861, ibid., 183.

13. Buchanan to Joseph Baker, April 26, 1861, ibid., 186.

14. Buchanan to King, July 13, 1861, ibid., 209. When Charleston fell to Union forces in March 1865, Buchanan expressed great satisfaction, along with his disgust for the state's "disunionists" whom in retrospect he viewed as a pox on the body politic during his years in public life. See Buchanan to George Leiper, February 24, 1865, ibid., 379–80.

15. Buchanan to Manley, September 14, 1861, in Buchanan Papers, Microfilm Reel 51, Historical Society of Pennsylvania.

16. Buchanan to Leiper, September 4, 1861, in Moore, *Works of James Buchanan*, 11:217; for similar views see also Buchanan to Leiper, August 31, 1861, ibid., 216, and Buchanan to Jeremiah Black, March 4, 1862, which emphasized that once South Carolina launched its "wicked bombardment" of Fort Sumter, Lincoln had "no alternative" but to defend the country "against dismemberment." Curtis, *Life of James Buchanan*, 2:585–86. For his relief in July 1862 that Gen. George B. McClellan's army had "escaped destruction" near Richmond, and another letter wishing McClellan success in his efforts against Robert E. Lee, see Buchanan to William Flinn, July 12, 1862, and Buchanan to Dr. John Blake, July 12, 1862, ibid., 591–92.

17. Buchanan to a Committee of Citizens, September 28, 1861, in Moore, *Works of James Buchanan*, 11:222–23. His close associate from Pennsylvania, former attorney general Jeremiah Black, cautioned Buchanan that such statements would compromise any effort to defend the previous administration by contrasting it with the actions of the present one. That advice does not seem to have deterred Buchanan from saying his piece. On this point see Klein, *President James Buchanan*, 416–17.

18. In a letter to C. J. Faulkner, October 21, 1865, Buchanan observed that "I pursued a settled consistent line of policy from the beginning to the end, and on reviewing my past conduct, I do not recollect a single important measure which I should desire to recall, even if this were in my power." Curtis, *Life of James Buchanan*, 2:643. Philip S. Klein points out that five of Buchanan's cabinet officers joined the Lincoln administration in one capacity or another and therefore had different agendas than he did in reflecting back on the secession crisis. Klein, *President James Buchanan*, 413–14. An earlier biographer, George Ticknor Curtis, thought Buchanan had been "insulted" by four of these officers (Toucey, Holt, Dix, and Stanton) but does not make clear the reasons for the alleged insults.

19. Buchanan to George Leiper, January 11, 1862, in Moore, *Works of James Buchanan*, 11:246.

20. Ridenour to Buchanan, October 1, 1861. A recent gift to LancasterHistory.org (formerly known as the Lancaster County Historical Society), this letter has been placed in the James Buchanan Collection, MG-96, Box 1. It should be noted that Ridenour left Wheatland equally convinced that Buchanan believed Lincoln's Emancipation Proclamation was "proper and right" under the circumstances, namely, "military necessity." Other evidence suggests that Buchanan remained ambivalent about the virtues of emancipation and the extirpation of chattel slavery.

21. See, on this point, Buchanan to Dr. John B. Blake, November 21, 1864, in Moore, *Works of James Buchanan*, 11:377.

22. Buchanan to James Buchanan Henry, September 22, 1864, and Buchanan to Dr. John B. Blake, November 21, 1864, ibid., 371–72, 377–78.

23. Klein, *President James Buchanan*, 421–22.

24. Buchanan to Harriet Lane Johnston, July 7, 1866, Buchanan's "Wheatland" correspondence, Box 3, Lancasterhistory.org. The letters in boxes 2 and 3 of this correspondence provide a richly textured understanding of Buchanan's domestic life during the retirement years at Wheatland.

25. Buchanan's former associate John W. Forney, who fell out with him during his presidency, likened the fifteenth president to a "masculine Miss Fribble." The nature of Buchanan's correspondence during his retirement years, weighted as it was to domestic details and interactions with children and lady friends, underscores the relevance of Forney's sardonic remark. Consider, for example, his August 3, 1863, letter to Harriet Lane, written from Bedford, where his "principal amusement" was spending time with "naughty secession girls" from Baltimore. He enjoyed their company and that of various women friends and their consorts. "I am treated by all with kindness and respect," he noted. Curtis, *Life of James Buchanan*, 2:612–13. For Forney's observation see *Anecdotes of Public Men* (New York: Harper & Brothers, 1877), 65.

26. Buchanan to Blake, December 5, 1863, November 21, 1864, December 25, 1867, in Moore, *Works of James Buchanan*, 11:351, 378, 459.

27. See, for example, Buchanan to Jeremiah Black, March 4, 1862, to Isaac Toucey, March 19, 1862, to Nahum Capen, November 7, 1862, to John B. Blake, March 21, 1863, to Nahum Capen, August 25, 1864, and to George Leiper, August 23 and October 26, 1864, ibid., 260–63, 308–9, 333–34, 369–70, 374.

28. Buchanan to Dr. John B. Blake, July 23, 1863, refers to a rheumatism attack, as does Buchanan to Mr. Schell, February 12, 1864, and Buchanan to Isaac Toucey, May 13, 1864. Curtis, *Life of James Buchanan*, 2:610, 618, 620. See also Buchanan to Harriet Lane Johnston, May 19, 1867, in which he refers to renewal of his "rheumatic gout." "I was able to hobble downstairs yesterday," he notes, "but it will be some days before I can walk about." Pertinent letters include Buchanan to James Buchanan Henry, March 1, 1864, Buchanan to Clementine Pleasanton, June 11, 1867, and Buchanan to Harriet

Lane Johnston, November 5, 1867, all in Buchanan's Wheatland Papers, Box 3, LancasterHistory.org.

29. Buchanan to Rev. Pennell Coombe, May 2, 1865, in Moore, *Works of James Buchanan*, 11:387. I am indebted to Dickinson College Special Collections librarian James Gerencser for confirming that Coombe served on the Dickinson Board of Trustees at this time.

30. In 1850 Buchanan donated fifty dollars to the Pennsylvania College (now Gettysburg College) Library. Charles H. Glatfelter, *A Salutary Influence: Gettysburg College, 1832–1985* (Gettysburg: Gettysburg College, 1987), 136. On the Dickinson gift to one of the college's literary societies, see Philip S. Klein, "James Buchanan at Dickinson," in *John and Mary's College: The Boyd Lee Spahr Lectures in Americana, 1951–1956* (Westwood, N.J.: Fleming H. Revell, 1956), 173. In 1851 Buchanan subscribed one thousand dollars toward the formation of Franklin and Marshall College; the money was used to support the erection of buildings on the new campus in Lancaster. See Subscription Booklet for F&M College, January 5, 1851, Special Collections, Franklin & Marshall College. Buchanan also served for several years as titular head of the college's board of trustees and maintained a close friendship with Rev. John W. Nevin, its former and future president. For more on the Franklin and Marshall connection see Sally F. Griffith, *Liberalizing the Mind: Two Centuries of Liberal Education at Franklin & Marshall College* (University Park: Pennsylvania State University Press, 2010), 57–58, and Klein, *President James Buchanan*, 210, 262, 415, 424.

31. Buchanan's discreet cheerleading from the sidelines for Democrat nominees for statewide office in Pennsylvania is reflected in the published versions of his correspondence in Curtis, *Life of James Buchanan*, and Moore, *Works of James Buchanan*, respectively. At the same time, he consistently supported the war effort and in 1862 applauded Lincoln's decision to replace Simon Cameron in the War Department with Edwin Stanton. Buchanan to Horatio King, January 28, 1862, in Curtis, *Life of James Buchanan*, 2:579. For a discussion of Buchanan and Pierce see Michael J. Birkner, "Looking Up from the Basement: New Biographies of Franklin Pierce and James Buchanan," *Pennsylvania History* 72 (Fall 2005): 535–43.

32. Pierce to Col. H. George Jan 2, 1863, Pierce Papers, Box 4 New Hampshire Historical Society; see also Nichols, *Franklin Pierce*, 520–21, and Birkner, "Looking Up from the Basement."

33. Pierce to F. O. Smith, October 3, 1862, Pierce Papers, Box 4 New Hampshire Historical Society; see also Pierce to John H. George, January 2, 1863.

34. Holt, *Franklin Pierce*, 124. Peter Wallner describes Pierce as "incensed" at the jailing of Vallandigham. *Franklin Pierce*, 350.

35. Quoted in Wallner, *Franklin Pierce*, 351. On negative reaction to the speech, see ibid., 351–52. Holt, *Franklin Pierce*, 125, suggests that Pierce's antiwar views were popular with a significant segment of the Democratic Party, leading to calls for his candidacy to oppose Lincoln's 1864 reelection bid. Nichols, *Franklin Pierce*, 525–26,

observes that only "a very few of his friends" supported a Pierce candidacy in 1864 and that "Pierce himself knew the fallacy of this idea and refused to consider it."

36. Buchanan to Mr. Schell, February 12, 1864, in Curtis, *Life of James Buchanan*, 2:618.

37. Buchanan to his son-in-law Henry Johnston, December 12, 1866, Buchanan's Wheatland Papers, Box 3, LancasterHistory.org.

38. Weeks after Lincoln's reelection Buchanan told one confidant, John B. Blake, that he believed the time was right for Lincoln to make a generous offer to the Confederate leadership, "leaving the slavery question to settle itself." Buchanan to Blake, November 21, 1864, in Curtis, *Life of James Buchanan*, 2:629.

39. Buchanan to the Rev. Dr. Philip Schaff, October 17, 1861, Buchanan Papers, Library of Congress, Series IV, Box 5. For good background on Schaff, a noted theologian who taught at both Marshall College and the Lancaster Reformed Seminary, see Griffith, *Liberalizing the Mind*, 33–34.

40. Buchanan to Harriet Lane, January 16, 1862, in Moore, *Works of James Buchanan*, 11:246–47.

41. James Buchanan, *Mr. Buchanan's Administration on the Eve of the Rebellion* (New York: D. Appleton, 1866), iii.

42. Ibid., 231.

43. As quoted in Gerald Gunther, *Learned Hand: The Man and the Judge* (New York: Knopf, 1994), 549.

44. Buchanan to Toucey, March 19, 1862, in Moore, *Works of James Buchanan*, 11:262–63.

Contributors

Jean H. Baker is the Bennett-Harwood Professor of History at Goucher College in Baltimore, Maryland. She is the author of eight books, including *Margaret Sanger: A Life of Passion* as well as a biography of James Buchanan.

John M. Belohlavek is professor of history at the University of South Florida, where he teaches nineteenth-century U.S. history.

Michael J. Birkner is professor of history and the Benjamin Franklin Professor of Liberal Arts at Gettysburg College. He is the author or editor of twelve books, including *James Buchanan and the Political Crisis of the 1850s*.

Daniel W. Crofts, professor of history at The College of New Jersey, studies the Old South and the North-South sectional conflict that led to civil war. His books include *Reluctant Confederates: Upper South Unionists in the Secession Crisis; Old Southampton: Politics and Society in a Virginia County, 1834–1869;* and *A Secession Crisis Enigma: William Henry Hurlbert and "The Diary of a Public Man."*

Nicole Etcheson is the Alexander M. Bracken Professor of History at Ball State University. She is the author of *The Emerging Midwest: Upland Southerners and the Political Culture of the Old Northwest, 1787–1861; Bleeding Kansas: Contested Liberty in the Civil War Era;* and *A Generation at War: The Civil War Era in a Northern Community.*

Paul Finkelman is the President William McKinley Distinguished Professor of Law and Public Policy at Albany Law School. He is the author or editor of more than 30 books and 175 scholarly articles. His most recent book was a presidential biography, *Millard Fillmore*.

William W. Freehling, the Singletary Professor of American History Emeritus at the University of Kentucky, is currently senior fellow at the Virginia Foundation for the Humanities, Charlottesville. The author of several prize-winning histories of the Civil War era, most notably the two-volume *Road to Disunion*, he is now writing a biography of Abraham Lincoln.

Michael Holt, the author of eight books on nineteenth-century American politics, has taught at Yale, Stanford, and since 1974 at the University of Virginia, where he is the Langbourne M. Williams Professor of American History. In 1993–94 he was the Pitt Professor of American History and Institutions at the University of Cambridge.

William P. MacKinnon is an independent historian living in Montecito, California. For half a century, he has published articles, essays, and books about Utah's long, violent territorial period while serving as a fellow of the Utah State Historical Society, president of the Mormon History Association, and chairman of the Yale Library Associates. He holds degrees in history and business administration from Yale and Harvard and was vice president of General Motors Corporation.

Michael A. Morrison is associate professor of history at Purdue University and former coeditor of the *Journal of the Early Republic*. He is the author of *Slavery and the American West: The Eclipse of Manifest Destiny and the Coming of the Civil War*.

John W. Quist is professor of history at Shippensburg University and the author of *Restless Visionaries: The Social Roots of Antebellum Reform in Alabama and Michigan*.

William G. Shade is professor emeritus of history at Lehigh University. He has authored or edited seventeen books and over fifty scholarly articles.

Index

Page numbers in *italics* refer to illustrations.

CPSIA information can be obtained
at www.ICGtesting.com
Printed in the USA
BVHW040318070622
639030BV00004B/199

9 780813 060996